MORAL COMBAT:

Black Atheists, Gender Politics, and the Values Wars

Sikivu Hutchinson

INFIDEL BOOKS
Los Angeles, California

Publisher's Cataloging-in-Publication

(Provided by Quality Books, Inc.)

Published 2011 by Infidel Books

Hutchinson, Sikivu.

Moral combat : Black atheists, gender politics, and the values wars / by Sikivu Hutchinson.

p. cm.

Includes bibliographical references and index.

ISBN-13: 978-0-578-07186-2

ISBN-10: 0-578-07186-X

1. African Americans--Religion. 2. African Americans --Politics and government. 3. Christianity and atheism. 4. Feminism. I. Title.

BR563.N4H88 2011 277'.3'008996073

QBI11-600019

Acknowledgments

A book is never possible without a community of friends, co-conspirators, and constructive critics. Thanks to all the generous interview respondents in the African American atheist and free thought communities who took the time to provide their rich insights for this work. My deep appreciation to my husband Stephen Kelley and friend Kamela Heyward-Rotimi for their support as well as patient, thoughtful critiques of early drafts of this book. Thanks are also due to Diane Arellano, Heather Aubry, and Naima Cabelle for their unswerving encouragement of this work. Moorhead State University professor Shondrah Nash also provided early reinforcement and advocacy for the publication of this book. And finally thanks to my parents Yvonne Divans Hutchinson and Earl Ofari Hutchinson for providing the intellectual spark, and the secular context, that set me on my way.

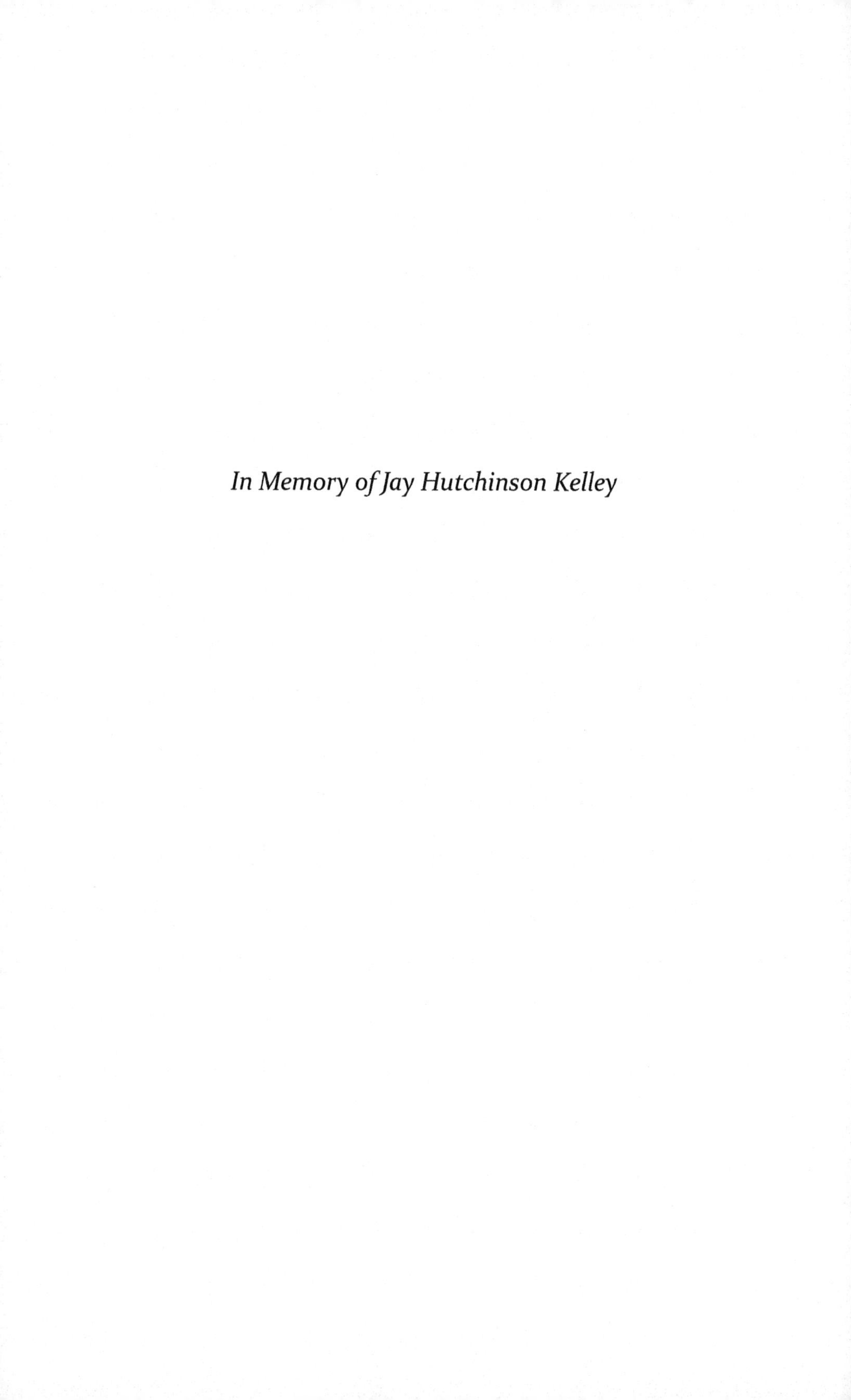

In Memory of Jay Hutchinson Kelley

Contents

Chapter 1

"Out of the Closet": Black Atheists in Moral Combat

Anyone living in a community with 400 churches who hasn't found 'god' in any of them hopefully has figured out that there is no god.

—Naima Cabelle, black atheist feminist

Faith's smorgasboard beckons irresistibly from America's city streets. A cross-country drive tells the story of its market value and allure, its unshakeable hold on the schizoid psyche of sex and Jesus-obsessed Americana. There is a church for every family, every true believer, every providence haggler, and every fence sitter; a supernatural crack fix for every creed, taste, and predilection. In the one mile radius from my house in South Los Angeles to the corner of Florence and Normandie, there are fourteen churches. Most of these structures are storefronts, austere and unobtrusive, denominations flowing from Latino Pentecostal to black Baptist to multiracial Catholic. Woven seamlessly into the workaday facades of other businesses, they offer quiet testimony to the area's shift from a predominantly African American enclave to a mixed Latino and black community. In the aftermath of the 1992 Rodney King beating verdict, Florence and Normandie gained national notoriety as a bellwether for black rage. There is an auto parts store on the northwest corner where white truck driver Reginald Denny was pulled from his vehicle and beaten by four African American young men after news of the verdict exploded across the city. On the other side of the street two gas stations bustle, fronted by a strip mall to the northeast. Emblems of the Southern California trinity of cars, faith, and quick cheap retail, these spaces each tap into different yet similar reservoirs of urban yearning.

In the seventeen years since the verdict and ensuing civil unrest, these streets have not dramatically changed. Whereas development in predominantly white communities to the west has flourished, the grand photo-op promises of federal redevelopment made about South L.A. by then President George H.W. Bush have gone largely unfulfilled. Time lapse photography might reveal the dedication and construction of the strip mall, new oil companies taking over the gas stations, the opening of a Mexican panaderia, and a Salvadoran pupuseria. Time lapse photography would also reveal the resilience of the storefront church, an indelible fixture of segregated communities of color.

While the storefront church is a bit player in my narrative, it has a premier role in the spiritual geography of contemporary African American communities. In an era in which African American communities nationwide are in socioeconomic crisis, the cultural dominance of organized religion merits critical evaluation. In a political climate in which the social justice compass of the Black Church has been broken by consumerism, institutional sexism, and faith-based witch hunts of gays and lesbians, its moral capital is increasingly dubious. Yet, as the late evening audiences at the fourteen storefront church services demonstrate, the narcotic of faith still seduces, captivates, and inspires.

A balm for suffering, a source of atonement, and a nexus for kinship and community, organized religion serves multiple functions in African American communities. However, alternative secular belief systems can challenge its hierarchy of moral principle and offer a basis for meaning and social justice. In this book I will contextualize this 21st century struggle through the feminist lens of black humanist atheist belief, examining such themes as "moral combat" in contemporary American politics, the gender complexities of free thought and atheism, and secular humanist social justice possibilities in African American communities.

According to the *New York Times*, a small but growing segment of the American population, galvanized in part by the political extremism of the Religious Right, has begun organizing nationwide and becoming more vocal about its atheism.[1] Over the past several years, atheism has emerged as a dynamic social and political force. Championed by such popular white author-activists as Richard Dawkins, Christopher Hitchens, Sam Harris, and Daniel Dennett, the so-called "New Atheist" movement has inspired a broad cross-section of atheists who have grown increasingly vocal about the incursions of organized religion into American politics. Although these writers approach atheism and the politics of religion from varying ideological and disciplinary perspectives, their "militancy" has inspired worldwide atheist advocacy. In dramatic departure from the marginalization of atheism during the era of notorious twentieth century atheist activist Madalyn Murray O'Hair, the New Atheists have commandeered a space in popular discourse.

While African Americans are not prominent in the New Atheist movement, the 2008 American Religious Identification Survey concluded that more people of color are "moving away" from religion.[2] Despite longstanding traditions of secular humanism, skepticism, and "freethought" in African American intellectual discourse, atheism remains a largely taboo belief system in black communities.[3] In most African American communities, atheism is akin to donning a white sheet and a Confederate Flag. In others it's ostensibly tolerated yet whispered about, branded culturally incorrect and bad form if not outright sacrilege.

According to the Pew Forum's 2009 "Religious Portrait of African-Americans," blacks "are more likely to report a formal religious affiliation (than other groups) with fully 87% of African Americans describing themselves as...religious."[4] In addition,

> 79% say religion is very important in their lives, compared with 56% among all U.S. adults...Even a large majority (72%) of African Americans who are unaffiliated with any particular faith say religion plays at least a somewhat important role in their lives...More than half of African Americans report attending religious services at least once a week, more than three in four (76%) say they pray on at least a daily basis and nearly nine-in-ten (88%) indicate they are absolutely certain God exists...*On each of these measures African-Americans stand out as the most religiously committed racial or ethnic group in the nation* (emphasis added).[5]

In a 2009 Barna study, 92% of African Americans identified themselves as Christians and were more likely than whites to identify as "born-again."[6] The study also revealed that the religiosity of African Americans had actually increased over a fifteen year period. A whopping 84% believed that "God is the all-powerful, all-knowing Creator of the universe who rules the world today."[7] As a result, Barna concluded that the "faith of African Americans is...generally moving in a direction that is more aligned with conservative biblical teachings."

Given the pitched roar of hellfire and damnation, for many black atheists actively breaking with religious tradition is an even graver rejection than that of white intellectuals electrified by the "pew-storming" rhetoric of Hitchens and Dawkins. According to Donald Barbera, "Probably the most controversial stance in the majority black community is the disbelief or disregard for a personal God…non-believers and freethinkers in the black community tend not to shout it out. They are invisible in a sea of Christianity."[8] This invisibility is partly due to the fact that the history of African American civil and human rights resistance is heavily steeped in Judeo-Christian religious dogma, which informed the development of the Black Church. Despite the White Anglo Saxon Protestant religious justification for slavery and domestic terrorism, African Americans converted to Christianity and utilized it as a source of succor, community and spiritual redemption. No matter one's actual deeds, life path or personal mores, to be unquestioningly religious in some quarters is to be inoculated from moral criticism. Noting this historical irony in his blog "The Black Atheist," Wrath James White states, "In these (black) communities you find more tolerance towards gangbangers, drug addicts, and prostitutes, who pray to God for forgiveness than for honest productive citizens who deny the existence of God." For White, this "is one of the most embarrassing elements of Black culture, our zealous embrace of the God of our kidnappers, murderers, slave masters and oppressors."[9]

While there have been critical appraisals of African American adoption of Christianity within the context of European conquest and racial slavery, few propose humanism and/or atheism as a corrective. Indeed, atheism seemingly flies in the face of a cultural ethos that frames earthly pain and suffering as a crucible for achieving rewards in the afterlife.

In the midst of extreme brutality, religious faith can be seen either as a means to mental health, or, as Karl Marx bluntly stated, an opiate.

The historical context of black Christian adherence yields important clues to the enduring power of African American religiosity. For example, in the moral order of the 17th century America only Christians of European descent were considered fully human. Only Anglo American male propertied Christians were granted full civil and legal rights.[10] Indeed,

> Historically, the English only enslaved non-Christians, and not, in particular, Africans. And the status of slave (Europeans had African slaves prior to the colonization of the Americas) was not one that was life-long. A slave could become free by converting to Christianity. The first Virginia colonists did not even think of themselves as "white" or use that word to describe themselves. They saw themselves as Christians or Englishmen, or in terms of their social class. They were nobility, gentry, artisans, or servants.[11]

The complex status of Europeans during this period sheds light on how African others were perceived. The fact that whiteness was not a fixed or coherent racial category meant that religion played a critical role in regulating and shaping "difference." If religion and class status superseded racial categorization then the terms of who or what was considered human were ostensibly mutable:

> In the early years of the colony, many Africans and poor whites—most of the laborers came from the English working class—stood on the same ground. Black and white women worked side-by-side in the fields. Black and white men who broke their servant contract were equally punished. All were indentured servants. During their time as servants, they were fed and housed. Afterwards, they would be given what were known as "freedom dues," which usually included a piece of

> land and supplies, including a gun. Black-skinned or white-skinned, they became free.[12]

The advent of racial slavery was an arduous process, neither coherent nor linear. For example, in the 17th century Dutch controlled colony of New Amsterdam (i.e., New York) slavery was an indelible fact of life for many Africans but it also co-existed with "a variety of forms of servitude" for Europeans and Native Americans as well.[13] Indeed, "Although weighed down by the burden of slavery...(Africans)... integrate(d) themselves into New Amsterdam society, forming families, trading with residents, and communing in the Dutch Reformed Church, where they registered their marriages and baptized their children."[14] Seeking to bolster their militias during conflicts with Native Americans, the Dutch granted enslaved Africans freedom in exchange for their military service.[15] After 1664, when New Amsterdam was seized by the British and renamed New York, black people enjoyed fewer opportunities to gain freedom. Stricter slave codes were imposed under British rule and "white servitude was restricted."[16]

Hence, the British regime was especially invested in the slave trade. Under British rule the numbers of African slaves in New York increased dramatically. By the 1730s New York had one of the largest urban slave populations in the U.S. Nonetheless, the relationship between Christian identity and enslavement continued to be a source of ambiguity and anxiety for the colonists. Due to English laws "stipulating" that Christians should not be enslaved, many slave owners resisted Christian evangelical efforts to convert Africans to Christianity. Subsequent revisions to these laws held that freedom not be granted to Africans or Native Americans who converted after their bondage. These nuances gave white slave owners the "moral" clarity and reassurance they needed.

According to Winthrop Jordan, "From the initially common term *Christian*, at mid-century there was a marked shift toward the terms *English* and *free*. After about 1680...a new term of self-identification appeared—*white*."[17] This transition would have important implications for how race and Christian morality were intertwined in American history. For example, right wing propaganda about the U.S.' status as a "Christian nation" has as much to do with racial purity and white supremacy as with the desire to establish an ironclad connection between American democracy and Christianity. Being an authentic American, an authentic *white* American, is deeply connected to being Christian. And anti-Obama zealots in the Tea Party, "birther," and resurgent militia movements have masterfully exploited this relationship. Thus, in the 17th century, there was intense debate about whether or not blacks could be redeemed from heathenry even if they did convert to Christianity. Both Southern and New England slave owners routinely invoked biblical scripture (with references to Africans as the accursed descendants of Ham) to justify the brutalization and exploitation of African slaves.[18] African docility and white supremacy was part of the "natural" order ordained by God. Nonetheless, Christianity became an integral part of the lives of slaves because it was such a big part of colonial culture. The native religions that African Americans brought over from Africa had been largely destroyed due to the physical and cultural dispossession of the middle passage and racial slavery. Judeo-Christian tenets emphasizing forgiveness and redemption of earthly suffering in heaven appealed to African slaves struggling to define their own sense of personhood within holocaust conditions.

Christianity provided African Americans with a theological lens for exposing the brutal contradictions of a new democratic republic based on Enlightenment values of individual liberty, inalienable rights, and equality. Hence, African slaves' adoption of Christian spiritual traditions became a source of community, spirituality, and cohesion. It gave African Americans yet another vehicle to resist and critique a "righteous" empire based on the appropriation of black productive and reproductive labor (via rape and forced breeding). If whites invoked the Almighty while pillaging black bodies and black labor, *they* were the true savages. If the colonists could preach the gospel against British tyrants—tyrants who promised to grant blacks their freedom for fighting on their side during the Revolutionary War—then the Bible was truly a malleable living document. Hence, African American resistance was both religious and secular humanist in orientation. Petitioning colonial courts for freedom, enslaved blacks used the very language of the Declaration of Independence to indict the slavocracy. While anti-British rhetoric fueled the American Revolution, patriots like George Washington sought to enforce the Treaty of Paris, which ensured that colonists could reclaim their slaves at war's end.[19]

In this sense, contemporary black religiosity emerges from a culturally specific survival strategy. It is in many ways a form of dialogue with the unique paradoxes of American national identity. Urban churches are reminders that racial segregation is still very much the defining factor of contemporary American life. They remind us that the bromides of post-racialism and colorblindness are toxically false. They sit in silent witness to the race/class metamorphosis of "inner city" neighborhoods, memorializing the ritual turn from white to black and brown. They flatter the rich and damn the poor to dependence, testifying to the lie of American exceptionalism and the American dream. They provide a window onto how faith-based social welfare buttresses capitalism. For, in below poverty level communities with a church on every corner, commerce and "the sacred" are wedded as the antidote to ghetto "depravity."

Recent surveys indicate that young people are less religious than previous generations.[20] Secularists point hopefully to this so-called "millennial" generation as a sign that a fundamental shift in religious affiliation is on the horizon. Yet, in communities of color, the business of saving souls continues apace. The moral authority of religious *culture* (if not churches themselves) remains largely unchallenged, and the absence of flesh and blood black secular humanist institutions underscores faith's racial divide. Given this climate, who will nurture the budding non-believer of color? Provide her with context, cause, and a sense of legacy? Ensure her that there is moral reinforcement, practical resources and, most importantly, a living breathing community for a life free of religious faith?

In my research on and conversations with African American atheists, freethinkers, and humanists across the country, several themes emerge. Few have been overtly victimized by religious persecution, yet all have felt the sting of marginalization and otherness. Some remain closeted due to convention and fear of social stigma. A small minority have come out in their real time networks and communities. Black secularists on the East Coast are far more visible than those in any other region of the country. Those in the Southern Bible Belt and the Midwest are less so. Black atheists are distinct from white atheists in that they tend to emphasize social justice and human rights rather than just fixating on science and the separation of church and state. Black women who identify as atheist and humanist exhibit strong feminist and anti-heterosexist world views on gender roles, the family, sexuality, cultural identity, and education. Black men who identify as atheist and humanist generally support gender equity principles and hold liberal political views. Virtually all hunger for greater political visibility and sustained *real time* community.

In an era of Facebook, email, instant messaging, and other demolitions of classic time/space divides, community remains elusive. It ultimately requires struggle, sacrifice, and *presence*. It demands a level of sweat equity that the most impassioned online community simply can't capture. There is also the matter of the ecstatic otherness and bonding in "purposeful unreason" that religious communality elicits. For what secular experience can match the familiar rhythms of ritual performance, the soothing cadence of call and response, the deep contemplation of individual purpose, the seductive sense and shared vision of being Chosen, the bittersweet masochism of self-denial? How can secular society, to paraphrase an old rap cliché, "touch" this?

A major barrier to building sustainable humanist organizations of color is the urban Jesus train. Social service, care giving, and cultural identity are intertwined in black faith networks. These deeply embedded traditions of black religiosity require black secular community-based organizations to look to the Black Church as an important coalition partner and resource. Hence, despite high profile sex abuse and financial scandals, the Church is still uncritically perceived as the "backbone" of the black community.[21] However, as the firestorm over California's Proposition 8 anti-same-sex marriage initiative demonstrated, the notion that there is a monolithic "marching in lockstep" black religious community is outdated. The overwhelming opposition of many prominent black churches to civil rights for partnered African American gays and lesbians is morally indefensible.

The intersection between the black civil rights movement legacy and religiosity has produced a curious schism. While the African American electorate remains politically liberal, it is socially conservative on so-called values issues like same-sex marriage, government vouchers for religious schools, and (to a lesser extent) abortion.[22] The 2008 debate over same-sex marriage in California underscored this tension. After the passage of Proposition 8, some same-sex marriage advocates scapegoated African Americans.[23] Initial news reports from the Los Angeles Times and CNN touted up to 70 percent African American support for Prop 8. Branded moral hypocrites, blacks who supported the measure were accused of betraying their commitment to civil rights. After the dust settled from the election season, the 70 percent statistic was refuted in a study by Fernando Guerra from Loyola Marymount University.[24]

Despite this timely corrective, opposition to same-sex marriage among African Americans remains solid. The religiosity of African Americans and long-standing black hostility towards designating gay rights as a civil right has made same-sex marriage a third rail issue among many straight Christian and Muslim African Americans.[25] During the campaign, progressive political analysts of color often drew parallels between prohibitions of interracial marriage prior to the 1967 *Loving vs. the State of Virginia* anti-miscegenation ruling and prohibitions of same-sex marriage.[26] For the most part, these analogies were rejected because of the argument that discrimination against gays and lesbians is not comparable to racial discrimination. Supporters of this view dubiously point to the absence of Jim Crow laws expressly barring gays and lesbians from housing, education, employment, and other major elements of public life. Some go even further, arguing that homosexuality is a European "aberration," imposed upon people of African descent post-

Diaspora. Rampant homophobia within African American communities, coupled with biblical literalism, make Lesbian Gay Bisexual and Transgendered (LGBT) African Americans largely invisible as a cultural or political force. Moreover, the perception among some African Americans that white LGBT activists have opportunistically appropriated the civil rights mantle exacerbates black suspicion of LGBT communities. In this charged climate, it is often difficult to assess the legitimacy of grievances about conflating anti-gay discrimination with racial discrimination.

Yet the fact remains that every Sunday, scores of LGBT worshippers and closeted church officials pack black churches and worship elbow to elbow with straight brethren. These same congregants see their families, relationships, and right to love marginalized and demeaned in scripture.[27] They see themselves routinely dehumanized in the homophobic rhetoric of "fellowship" that some congregations promote.[28] During and after the election season, a few progressive black ministers and church figures—most notably the Reverend Eric Lee, the Southern California head of the Southern Christian Leadership Conference—spoke out in opposition to Proposition 8.[29] But their viewpoints were not widely aired, and the general impression of black hostility to same-sex marriage solidified in the public mind.

The failure of black religious progressives to challenge the destructive role that fundamentalist religiosity plays in contemporary skirmishes around civil rights reveals a moral crisis. When it comes to "values" issues in the U.S. the most visible and vocal constituency is the attack dog army of the Religious Right. The Religious Right emerged in part as a white conservative backlash against the gains of the civil rights, women's rights, and gay rights movements. According to writer Frederick Clarkson, the Religious Right has been so successful because it has mobilized a broad white conservative Christian constituency around electoral politics.[30] Pro-big business, pro-imperialist, and xenophobic, the Religious Right has been both architect and beneficiary of the reactionary political climate of the past three decades. With a formidable network of Christian broadcasting outlets, political action committees, lobbyists, advocacy groups, mega churches, and motivational speakers, the Religious Right is an especially powerful special interest. Unfortunately, national politics has not yet produced a vigorous counterpart to the Religious Right on the Left. And since there is no comparable organized coalition on the "Religious Left" the Religious Right has singlehandedly defined, framed, and distorted the debate about the role of religion and morality in the so-called "public common." This leadership vacuum has allowed the Religious Right to hijack public discourse around "values" issues and fetishize morality from an ultra-conservative stance. The absence of counter-voices has eclipsed secular-religious coalitions such as Americans United for Separation of Church and State.

Perhaps the most pernicious Religious Right strategy has been its appropriation of the language of civil rights in its campaigns against choice, church-state separation, and gay rights.[31] Black religious and secular progressives could play a vital role in shifting the terms of debate from the shrill fascist agenda of the Religious Right to a more social justice-oriented compass. For the right wing, the lessons of Proposition 8 were fairly clear. Put simply, Prop 8 backers such as the Mormon Church exploited the absence of moral leadership on the Religious Left by appealing to the most conservative elements of both the black and Latino communities.[32]

In this regard, the absence of high profile mobilization amongst the left-leaning faith community is not insignificant because it allows the Religious Right to assume the moral high ground on public policy. Perhaps the only figure with national stature on the "religious left" who has been consistently vocal in his opposition to fundamentalist Christian orthodoxy is Jimmy Carter. Other prominent "religious left" ambassadors like Jesse Jackson, Cornel West, and Michael Eric Dyson are more closely identified as activists or rock star "public" intellectuals who transcend any particular social movement. Clearly, if a coalition existed on the Left that was comparable to the Religious Right, the latter's ability to leverage such issues as abortion, same-sex marriage, stem cell research, and intelligent design would be minimized.

In his book *God's Politics* Jim Wallis, editor of the progressive religious journal *Sojourners*, advocates a "prophetic politics" in which faith could be "a positive force in society—for progressive social change."[33] In sharp contrast to the Religious Right's "traditional family values" playbook, Wallis' organization has staked out leftist pro-peace positions on economic justice, the death penalty, health care, and the Iraq War. Wallis argues that America is suffering from a crisis of values. Progressive religious belief is the antidote to this crisis because "history is most changed by social movements with a spiritual foundation."[34] This view fails to consider the extent to which American social movements—from the white supremacist imperialist spiritual foundations of the Revolutionary War to the patriarchal and heterosexist spiritual foundations of the modern civil rights movement—have been hindered by their "spiritual" foundations. By romanticizing the spiritual foundations of social movements, Wallis demonstrates that he is unwilling to interrogate how Judeo-Christian dogma undermines women's rights and gay rights. Hence Wallis' prophetic politics is based on cherry picking scripture to articulate a social justice agenda fundamentally incompatible with the patriarchal, imperialist, sexist, homophobic, inhumane thrust of the Bible.

Ultimately, the concept of a religious left is problematic at its core because the Bible (or for that matter the Koran, Torah, etc.) cannot be used to unequivocally defend and advance human rights. Using Fox News, Christian radio, and the Internet as bully pulpits, Christian fundamentalists have capitalized on this simple unimpeachable fact and built a political empire. They have hidden behind scripture to justify and advance a fascist agenda that has set the struggle for democracy in the U.S. back decades.

In his book *Away with All Gods* Bob Avakian elaborates on the real insidiousness of the Religious Right:

> It is important to come to grips—to confront—what is the real nature of the Religious Right: its character as a Christian Fascist movement, aiming for a theocratic fascist form of capitalist-imperialist rule within the U.S. and domination on this basis throughout the world...this Christian Fascist movement...has as a major engine, the forceful reassertion of an absolutist kind of patriarchy, but also white supremacy, with a potentially genocidal dimension. And this movement is an ardent advocate of militarism and military marauding of U.S. imperialism around the world.[35]

The politicization of the Christian fundamentalist establishment and its insertion into virtually every aspect of electoral politics has transformed the American political landscape. In his book *Head and Heart: American Christianities*, historian Gary Wills chronicles the trajectory of the Religious Right's galvanic influence on George W. Bush.[36] Bush's faith-based initiative policy infused the fundamentalist movement with even greater political capital than it had enjoyed during the Reagan and George H.W. Bush administrations.[37] President Obama's pledge to continue much of Bush's faith-based approach has bolstered the Religious Right's assault on secular public policy under the guise of a moral mandate.

The repeal of the military's "Don't Ask Don't Tell" policy and the move to repeal the federal government's Defense of Marriage Act has put gay equality into the national forefront. That said, the Black Church's inflexibility on same-sex marriage and homophobia continues to imperil the moral health and social capital of communities of color. It is for this reason that the Black Church has become largely irrelevant as a social justice organizer in the post-Jim Crow era. Consequently, secular humanists of color have an opportunity to enter the breach. Although the depth of black religiosity is a significant obstacle to broadening the appeal of secular humanism, the numbers of African Americans willing to publicly call themselves freethinkers, humanists, agnostics, and atheists has increased within the past several years.[38] And as more Americans question and ultimately reject the encroachment of organized religion on everyday life, secular humanist alternatives to the straightjacket of religiosity will have greater appeal.

Despite the historic election of President Barack Obama in 2008, African American communities are worse off now in many key "equality index" areas than during the Jim Crow era.[39] This is due in large part to the legacy of residential segregation, which has had far-reaching implications for black social mobility. Nationwide African Americans remain among the most segregated racial "sub-groups" in the U.S. Residential segregation limits access to jobs, education, health care, transportation, and park and recreational space. Plagued by double digit unemployment, sub-standard segregated schools, and over-incarceration, poor urban African American communities have not reaped the benefits of the so-called post-affirmative action era. Indeed, the divide between the African American middle class and the white middle class is still egregiously deep. According to the 2004 U.S. Census, white Americans command over 85% of the top income "quintiles" for median family income, while African Americans are "overrepresented" in the bottom quintiles. Further, because African Americans have historically been segregated into poorer urban and suburban neighborhoods they generally have less home equity than do whites. Due to the high incidence of predatory lending practices and other inequitable mortgage schemes in low income black and Latino neighborhoods, the home mortgage crisis has disproportionately impacted the equity of homeowners of color.

The domino effect of socioeconomic instability and diminishing job and education returns has apparently bolstered the influence of organized religion on African American communities. Certainly the experience of surviving racism and racial terrorism has greatly affirmed the role of religious observance in the lives of many African Americans. For example, in the absence of equitable government programs, the Black Church has traditionally been prominent vital social welfare resource in African American communities. Social welfare programs such as funding assistance to poor families, food supplies, housing services, and day care provision are among the many resources that community-based churches offer. Yet the question remains as to what impact the challenges and shifts of the twenty first century have had—not only on the Black Church as a community and cultural institution, but on the consciousness of African Americans doubtful of its relevance. Over the past two decades, the Black Church has increasingly come under fire from black progressives for its anti-gay prejudice, failure to act on the African American HIV/AIDS epidemic, retrograde treatment of women, and financial improprieties. Many progressive worshippers have criticized these disparities and sought to change the church from within. However, they are distinguished from those who have made a definitive break from religious faith for *secular* moral and ethical reasons.

In addressing the emergence of 21st century black atheist world views, I will amplify the influence of social justice politics and ideology. As aforementioned, a significant number of black atheist women subscribe to feminist or womanist views of gender roles, the family, sexuality, cultural identity, and education. The challenges of achieving baseline skepticism in a traditionally religious, racially and economically disenfranchised community are especially onerous for women. Therefore, I will examine the dynamics and implications of religious observance, skepticism, humanism, and atheism from an African American feminist perspective. Constructions of mainstream African American female gender roles and social responsibilities are unquestionably linked to religious observance. Because it was one of the few solid African American institutions in a white supremacist nation, the Black Church has historically been a vehicle for black ambition, enterprise, and upward mobility. A cornerstone of black patriarchy, the Black Church has often been depicted as a bulwark against the "emasculating" effect of white racism. Of course, as "keepers of home and hearth," black women are vital to the maintenance of patriarchal roles and responsibilities. And if the Black Church--as an institution in flux--has had a "redeemer", it has been the perseverance of black women, who comprise the majority of its members. Thus, for many black women, skepticism, humanism, and atheism are dangerous frontiers that threaten their sense of gendered identity and social mooring.

Consequently, when it comes to attitudes about traditional gender roles, gender-based assumptions about black female religiosity are double-edged. While black male non-believers are given more leeway to be heretics, black women who openly profess non-theist views are deemed especially traitorous, having abandoned their primary role as purveyors of cultural and religious tradition. Images of black women faithfully shuttling their children to church and socializing them into Christianity are prominent in mainstream black culture. If being black and being Christian are synonymous, then being black, female, and religious or "spiritual" (whatever the denomination or belief system) is practically compulsory. Insofar as atheism is an implicit rejection of both black patriarchy and "authentic" blackness, those who dare to come out of the closet as atheists are potential race traitors.

On the national level, the contradictions between American secularism and religion have produced a schizoid tension in the U.S. As President Obama proves his American bona fides by wrapping himself in scripture, mainstream hostility toward secular thought has become the norm. When it's practiced in the non-Western world, Americans routinely brand this kind of propaganda backward and extremist. Much of right wing Islamophobia thrives on the caricature of the theocratic Middle East and the secular democratic West. Yet, *American* values wars over women's bodies, gay rights, racial justice, and economic justice, are a battle for fundamental human rights. It is a battle against the tide of Christian fascism and historical revisionism. And it is a call for radical remembrance. The politics of race and gender have always defined American notions of public morality. That old time religion gave African slaves purchase on being human, on being American, and on being moral. For non-theist African Americans, embracing a belief system that challenges "the price of the ticket"[40] may be one of the final ideological frontiers.

Endnotes

1. Laurie Goodstein, "More Atheists Shout it From the Rooftops," *New York Times*, April 27, 2009.
2. Barry A. Kosmin and Ariela Keyser, *American Religious Identification Survey*, Hartford: Trinity College, March 2009, p. 17.
3. See Norm Allen, *African American Humanism: An Anthology* (New York: Prometheus Books, 1991) and *The Black Humanist Experience: An Alternative to Religion*, (New York: Prometheus Books, 2003).
4. "A Religious Portrait of African Americans," The Pew Forum on Religion and Public Life, January 30, 2009, 1.
5. Ibid.
6. "How the Faith of African Americans Has Changed," The Barna Group, July 2009 (http://www.barna.org/barna-update/article/13-culture/286-how-the-faith-of-african-americans-has-changed?q=blacks).
7. Ibid.
8. Donald Barbera, *Black and Not-Baptist: Nonbelief and Freethought in the African American Community*, (Illinois: iUniverse, 2003) 22.
9. Wrath James White, "The Invisibility of the Black Atheist," *Words of Wrath,* May 2008, (http://wordsofwrath.blogspot.com).
10. Winthrop Jordan, *White Over Black: American Attitudes Toward the Negro, 1550-1812 (Chapel Hill: University of North Carolina Press, 1968)* 179-212.
11. "From Indentured Servitude to Racial Slavery," *Africans in America*, WGBH Educational Fund, 1988 (http://www.pbs.org/wgbh/aia/part1/1narr3.html).
12. Ibid.
13. Ira Berlin and Leslie M. Harris, *Slavery in New York* (New York: New Press, 2005), 7-9.
14. Ibid., 8.
15. Ibid.
16. Ibid., 60.
17. Jordan, 179.

18. Ibid.
19. Berlin and Harris, 15.
20. Robert D. Putnam and David E. Campbell, "Walking Away From the Church," *L.A. Times*, October 17, 2010 (http://articles.latimes.com/2010/oct/17/opinion/la-oe-1017-putnam-religion-20101017).
21. These include such cases as the sex abuse allegations against Atlanta Bishop Eddie Long, financial impropriety charges against Reverend Creflo Dollar of College Park, Georgia and sex abuse and financial impropriety allegations against Reverend John Hunter of Los Angeles First AME church.
22. While polls indicate that the majority of African Americans are pro-choice, anti-abortion anti-choice forces are far more visible in black communities.
23. Alex Koppelman, "Don't Blame Proposition 8 on African Americans," *Salon Magazine*, January 9, 2009 (http://www.salon.com/politics/war_room/2009/01/09/race_prop8); John Wildermuth, "Black Support for Proposition 8 Called Exaggeration," *San Francisco Chronicle*, January 7, 2009. Black support for Prop 8 was closer to 57%,
24. Robert Cruikshank, "Mythbusting the African American Vote and Prop 8," *California Progress Report*, November 20, 2008. (http://www.californiaprogressreport.com/2008/11/mythbusting_the.html.
25. Keith Boykin, "Why the Black Church Opposes Same-sex marriage," *Village Voice*, May 18, 2004.
26. Sikivu Hutchinson, "The Moral Choice: Blacks, Homophobia and Proposition 8," *Our Weekly*, October 29, 2008, 6.
27. Leviticus 18:22: "Thou shalt not lie with mankind, as with womankind: it is abomination; Deuteronomy 23:17: "There shall be no whore of the daughters of Israel nor a sodomite of the sons of Israel.
28. Ibid.
29. Ibid.
30. Frederick Clarkson, Becoming a Christian Citizen: Electoral Lessons from the Religious Right for the Religious Left, *Public Eye Magazine*, May 2008, Volume 23:3. (http://www.publiceye.org/magazine/v23n3/guest_commentary.html).
31. Robin Abcarian, "A New Push to Define a Person, and to Outlaw Abortion in the Process," *Los Angeles Times*, September 28, 2009.
32. White fundamentalists like the Family Research Council have also vigorously reached out to black evangelicals. See for example, Sarah Posner, "The Future of Anti-Gay Activism," *The American Prospect,* June

18, 2007 (http://www.prospect.org/cs/articles?article=the_future_of_antigay_activism).

33. Jim Wallis, *God's Politics: Why the Right Gets it Wrong and the Left Doesn't Get it* (San Francisco: Harper Collins, 2005), 81.

34. Ibid., 24.

35. Bob Avakian, *Away With All Gods: Unchaining the Mind and Radically Changing the World* (Chicago, Insight Press, 2008), 170.

36. Gary Wills, *Head and Heart: American Christianities* (New York: Penguin Press, 2003), 414-495.

37. Ibid.

38. According to the 2009 Pew Report a scant 1% of African Americans identify as atheists.

39. Obama's election has prompted some overzealous pundits to proclaim this the post-racial era, yet objective indicators like health, unemployment, income and education indicate that African Americans have in fact fallen further behind white Americans. See for example the Urban League's 2009 *State of Black America Report* and the California Black Legislative Caucus' 2008 *State of Black California Report.*

40. This is a reference to James Baldwin's metaphor about blacks' fatal dream of becoming white ("the price of the black ticket is involved—fatally—with the dream of becoming white. This is not possible because white people are not white"). Part of European Americans' process of becoming white and becoming American was establishing Christian identity as a line of demarcation between the civilized self and the savage immoral other. See Baldwin, *The Price of the Ticket* (New York: St Martin's Press, 1985), xiv.

Chapter 2

This Far By Faith? Race Traitors and Gender Apostates

A woman should learn in quietness and full submission. I do not permit a woman to teach or have authority over a man; she must be silent. For Adam was formed first, then Eve. And Adam was not the one deceived; it was the woman who was deceived and became a sinner.

—1 Timothy 2:11-14

Martin Luther King, Jr. famously dubbed Sunday at 11:00 a.m. the most segregated hour in America, a microcosm of the titanic divide that separates black and white America. Yet racial divisions are not the only prominent schism in the Sunday churchgoing ritual of one of the most God-obsessed nations on the planet. Despite all the "liberal" revisions to biblical language and claims to progressivism among some Christian denominations, mainstream Protestantism is still, of course, a Jim Crow throwback and a "man's man's world." As Mark Galli, editor of the evangelical magazine *Christianity Today* glibly remarked, "It's a cliché now to call institutional religion 'oppressive, patriarchal, out of date and out of touch.' So what else is new? I feel sorry for those people who don't think there's anything greater than themselves…It leaves out the communal dimension of faith."[1]

According to the Pew Research Forum on Religion and Public Life:

> African-American women... stand out for their high level of religious commitment. More than eight-in-ten black women (84%) say religion is very important to them, and roughly six-in-ten (59%) say they attend religious services at least once a week. No group of men or women from any other racial or ethnic background exhibits comparably high levels of religious observance.[2]

From the Deep South to South Los Angeles, the "communal dimension of faith" has deep resonance for women of color. It is the glue of hope and perseverance, despair and concession; it is the subject of historical inspiration and ribald pop culture caricature. It quietly shapes the tenor of many urban neighborhoods, interrupting and complementing the unseemly glut of fast food franchises, liquor stores, check cashing services, and Laundromats that have become America's de facto "inner city" landscape. One of the many dream sequences in the 2009 film *Precious* speaks to the tragedy and romance of communal faith. After escaping a brutal attack by her mother, the lead character wanders through her snowy Harlem neighborhood, distraught and emotionally adrift. She happens upon a storefront church where the congregation warmly embraces her and her child. The sequence concludes with Precious integrated into the congregation, launching into a gospel song with her baby in her arms.

This dream is juxtaposed with the reality of her waking life as a 16-year old mis-educated incest survivor with two children and a monstrously abusive mother. It is implied that this magical church is a port in the storm—and a figment of her romanticized notion of community and togetherness. Here, the Black Church is a familiar space, a safe haven of harmony and wellbeing.

But of course, familiar spaces are not always safe. In her landmark 1928 novel *Quicksand,* writer Nella Larsen paints an insidious picture of a young black woman's first encounter with a storefront church congregation also set in Harlem. In a key scene, Larsen protagonist Helga wanders into a church and is literally swept up into the congregation's hungry vortex. Her affiliation with this church and its predator pastor trigger her emotional downfall and retreat from personal ambition. As one of the first explicitly skeptic fictions of organized religion by a black woman, Larsen's work broke new ground for black feminist humanist social thought.[3]

According to a 2007 survey, 70% of American atheists are male.[4] Given the social and cultural gender norms that organized religion reinforces, the disproportionate male-to-female ratio for self-identified atheists is not difficult to explain. Yet there has been much crackpot speculation about the supposed emotionalism of women versus the rationality of men. Bloggers muse about women's intuitive sensitivity to the warm and fuzzy "verities" of religious dogma. Women are monolithically stereotyped as naturally timorous and thus less inclined to question or challenge organized religion. There has been scant serious evaluation of the perceived gendered social benefits of religious observance versus the social costs of being an atheist. In addition, there is virtually no critical literature assessing the implications of this issue for American women of color. Reflecting on this quandary Black Atheists of America founder Ayanna Watson notes:

> Many women of color do not want to deal with societal pressures associated with identifying as either an atheist or humanist. For many of us, it's a form of social suicide. Hence,

> many women of color who are atheists or humanists choose not to be visible in the movement. Additionally, I know that, until recently, I had not met any black females who identified as an atheist or humanist. It was difficult coming out knowing (or at least believing) that I was the only one who had to deal with the type of societal pressure imposed upon a triple minority (black, atheist, female).[5]

Out atheist women of color are few and far between because of these stigmas. In many communities of color, relationships, professional connections, and social welfare resources often revolve around church ties.

So the character Precious' church time fantasies were not unusual. Religious devotion has come to be a kind of shorthand for black female selfhood. Her desire to be embraced by the church congregation was just as visceral as her tragic wish to have light skin. In a culture that privileges European standards of beauty, having light skin translates into being perceived as physically desirable and hence worthy of love. The closer one is to the European beauty ideal, the more "authentically" feminine one is. The lighter one's skin, the more virtuous one is. And, according to biblical iconography and Western cultural norms, the more virtuous one is, the closer to God.

In African American communities, there is a profound connection between Christian religiosity and the quest for authentic femininity. Organized religion provides context for the articulation of female gendered identity in resistance to white supremacy. Responding to the stress of Holocaust conditions, African Americans revised white supremacist Christian traditions to suit their needs. As a space for women-centered social and community networks, the Black Church has been a source of female agency and oppression. For example, the late 19th century black women's club movement emerged from both secular groups and church organizations. African American female civil rights activists such as Ida B. Wells and Fannie Lou Hamer drew much of their oratory and inspiration from Christian themes of redemption and were active in the Black Church. Forerunning African American female abolitionists like Maria Stewart and Sojourner Truth heavily influenced these movement leaders. Yet traditional Christian values requiring female submission to male authority were also critical to the emergence of the Black Church. As historian Paula Giddings notes, the Black Church played a key role in enforcing black patriarchy because it "attempted to do this in much the same way that Whites had used religion, by putting a new emphasis on the biblical 'sanction for male ascendancy."[6]

The 19th century feminist abolitionist Maria Stewart was deeply influenced by the contradictions of religious doctrine, patriarchy, and black dehumanization under slavery. As the first black woman to publish a political tract, Stewart consistently challenged white supremacy and patriarchy.[7] She preached women's equality in an era in which female religious leaders were routinely vilified for not knowing their place. She frequently drew on biblical references to support the position that women could be leaders in the struggle for racial and moral uplift. She also "wrestled with the perennial conundrum of a supposedly just and merciful God's ostensible willingness to tolerate the…undeserved suffering of the innocent."[8] Like many African American religious thinkers during this period, Stewart utilized the rhetorical "Black Jeremiad" tradition, warning her audiences that blacks would ultimately be redeemed for their suffering while God would punish whites for the evils of slavery.[9]

Stewart embodied many of the contradictions that would come to characterize black feminist/womanist Christian ideology and practice. She deconstructed biblical literalism, refuting "the most frequently cited injunction against female activism by placing Paul's admonitions to women to remain silent in religious affairs...against the demands of the black woman's social and historical context."[10] Thus, when articulating a politically radical religious vision for women's equality, the misogyny of scripture was "irrelevant."[11] Yet Stewart was also bound by gender conventions. She counseled black women that it was their unique duty as mothers and caregivers to instill black children with love of knowledge and virtue.[12] She also argued that women should develop themselves intellectually and seek to have men "fall in love with their virtues."[13] At the beginning of her career as a public figure she advocated that black liberation struggle was best served by allowing young black men to thrive and assume positions of authority.[14] Although she abandoned this position in later years, her initial ambivalence reflected a recurring theme in black social thought and civil rights resistance—the tension between black women's liberation from patriarchy and institutional sexism versus black male domination as the linchpin of black empowerment.

While Stewart's activism set the stage for a black feminist *human rights* discourse, black female subservience still hinders black liberation struggle. Two centuries after Stewart and Truth, women's work is still the uncompensated work of child care, "cultural" care giving, cooking, cleaning, and elder care. Of course, one of the most important ways patriarchy is perpetuated is through the delineation of asymmetrical gender roles. As the primary caregivers in the family, women have been trained to transmit cultural and moral values to children; the burden of educating and socializing children on ways of being and behaving has traditionally fallen on women. This is especially true in African American communities where single parent female-headed households predominate. While there is a broad spectrum of belief within African American communities, there is a tacit assumption of Christian adherence amongst African Americans. These assumptions are informed by equally powerful assumptions about the relationship between Christian values and proper moral values. In her book *Salvation,* bell hooks frequently waxes nostalgic about how Christian scripture used to be a moral compass to guide and center black people:

> Religious teachings about love form the foundation of most black people's understanding of love's meaning. Even though we have diverse religious experiences, a vast majority of us still identify as Christians...From the book of Corinthians I learned to be loving and kind, forgiving and full of compassion...Yet the full vision of love evoked in the Scriptures was not realized in most of our homes...Growing up in the fifties, I was raised in a world where women endeavored to please their husbands, to be the angel in the house for the man.[15]

Hooks' vision of unconditional Christian love is contradicted by the actual language of Corinthians, which lays the foundation for the "1950s style" female subservience that she deplores:

> But I want you to understand that the head of every man is Christ, the head of a woman is her husband, and the head of Christ is God. Any man who prays or prophesies with his head covered dishonors his head, but any woman who prays or prophesies with her head unveiled dishonors her head--it is the same as if her head were shaven. For if a woman will not veil herself, then she should cut off her hair; but if it is disgraceful for a woman to be shorn or shaven, let her wear a veil. For a man ought not to cover his head, since he is the image and glory of God; but woman is the glory of man. (For man was

> not made from woman, but woman from man. Neither was man created for woman, but woman for man.) That is why a woman ought to have a veil on her head, because of the angels. (1 Corinthians 11)

Similar language is found in other verses of Corinthians, as well as in Genesis, Timothy, Ephesians, and on and on. The fascist language of the bible is inconsistent with the vision of "secular" moral degradation versus "sacred" moral purity that hooks attempts to project. There is no shelter for women in the bible's fascist universe—merely license for the misogyny of morally upright 1950s Ozzie and Harriet households.

As a child in segregated Arkansas during the late 1940s, my mother recalls being taken to church by community members when her non-practicing mother was at work. Like many black women during this era, my grandmother had to work outside of the household. While most low to middle income white women had the privilege not to work outside of the home due to race-based wage disparities, black women were critical to their family's incomes. Because of sexist racist notions about black women's "questionable" mores and work ethic, popular imagery rarely celebrated the contributions of breadwinning black women (as opposed to white men). Yet there was ample promotion of black female devoutness and religious responsibility. Hence, taking "un-churched" black children to church was an accepted ritual especially prevalent in tight knit black communities during the Jim Crow era.

Community involvement in the religious socialization of children is a recurring theme in black life. Female relatives and neighbors often volunteer to escort children of non-practicing parents to church. Had my grandmother refused to allow her children to be taken to church, social scrutiny about her "morals" as a mother would have followed. This illustrates the strong gender dimension underlying the indoctrination of black children into Christianity, as well as the collective and communal nature of belief amongst African Americans.

For example, "Patricia," an atheist African American woman in her sixties, recalls being taken to church occasionally by her mother, who read the Bible to her.[16] Her father, on the other hand, "never attended church and never talked religion." Before she embraced atheism, Patricia continued her mother's tradition, taking her own daughter to church. Patriarchy entitles men to reject organized religion with few implications for their gender-defined roles.[17] Men are more likely to be unaffiliated with any religion; and black men are also more likely to be unaffiliated than black women.[18] This is not to say that men in a Judeo Christian context face no social risk in being openly agnostic or non-theist. I maintain that men do not run the risk of compromising their *masculinity* if they question, don't participate in and/or actively reject organized religion. Because traditional masculine identity and subjectivity is based on conquest, dominance, control, and personal agency, men who do not subscribe to the dictates of organized religion have other social institutions to rely on for gender reinforcement and moral worth. Masculinity is simply not governed by the same religious and cultural prohibitions on sexuality and the body as femininity. In both Judeo Christian doctrine and American cultural ideology, female sexuality and the female body are objectified territories. From the mainstreaming of pornography, to the normalization of sexualized media violence against women, female sexuality (and by implication feminine purity) is a heavily policed commodity. "Good" women establish feminine moral worth—sexual purity, modesty and virtue—via proper traditional relationships with men, in service to home and family. Conversely, masculine moral worth is defined by the exercise of power and control over women, children, and other men.

Therefore, the Judeo Christian regime of organized religion is far more prescriptive for women. The construction of women as "the body" has its counterpart in the construction of men as "intellect" or "knowledge." Racial difference further complicates this binary of masculine and feminine. Because of the history of Western colonialism, people of color have been constructed as racial "others."[19] In the cultural propaganda of the African slave trade, the dark primitive savage African was the polar opposite of the civilized rational European. Enlightenment values such as rationalism and empiricism were informed by white supremacy.[20] Here, the black body provided the basis for validation of empirical methods of categorizing race and defining racial difference. The intersection of white supremacy, Judeo Christian ideology, and Enlightenment epistemology established hierarchies of masculine/feminine, black/white, civilized/savage that legitimized racist and sexist views of white women and people of color.

Thus, because of the legacy that ascribes rationalism, individualism, intellectualism, and secular or scientific inquiry to masculinity, men have greater cultural license to reject organized religion. However, women in traditionally religious communities don't have the cultural and authorial privilege to express skepticism, much less publicly voice their opposition to organized religion. In African American communities where devoutness is the default position, the presumption of female religiosity, reinforced by cultural representation, is a binding influence that makes public skepticism taboo.

Mainstream representations of African American women provide a vivid case in point. Imagery such as filmmaker

Tyler Perry's bible thumping malapropism spewing Madea, stereotypically heavyset black women in brightly colored choir robes belting out gospel music, and sweat-drenched revelers cataleptic from getting the Holy Ghost are very common mainstream representations of black femininity. In the 1997 film *The Apostle* Robert Duvall plays a white Southern Christian fundamentalist preacher and murderer on the lam seeking redemption. The film is cluttered with images of devout blacks, from black women swaying in the breeze at a big tent church revival to a particularly indelible church scene of dozens of black men chanting "Jesus" in rapturous response to Duvall's pulpit-pounding call. I found *The Apostle* perversely fascinating because it trotted out this totally revisionist romanticized narrative of black obeisance to yet another charismatic but flawed white renegade savior figure in Louisiana (where, contrary to Hollywood flim-flammery, most of the congregations are racially segregated). These popular fantasies of black religiosity typically revolve around images of good, matronly black women eternally quivering with a strategic "Amen" or "can I get a witness", subject to break out into a Blues Brothers back flip down the church aisle at any moment.

These caricatures are buttressed by the unwavering financial and social support the Black Church gets from African American communities of all income brackets. Tithing is the practice of giving 10 percent of one's income to church as prescribed in the Book of Malachi. According to Stephen Rasor of the Interdenominational Theological Center in Atlanta, "Within the black churches, there is an emphasis on tithing because of the pastors...their main reason is to call on church members to keep their covenant with God by supporting the church."[21] Often, the most impoverished members of the community tithe their hard-earned money to churches that support the middle class to lavish lifestyles of church officials. In a timely article entitled "Why Megachurches don't Deserve Your Tithe," writer Brandale Randoph examines this ritual. He argues, "For centuries, many impoverished African Americans have been tithing to...churches but their communities, church and even they themselves have received very little benefit...many African American churches have robbed, misappropriated and even embezzled money from poor African Americans under the guise of tithing and this must stop."[22]

Biblical injunctions, coupled with cultural/community obligations to tithe, keep poor blacks indebted to their churches. Yet even on a casual level, religiosity is never far from day-to-day African American life. In both working and middle class African American communities it is typical to be addressed by friends, relatives, and colleagues with religious language and aphorisms as a matter of cultural code. Everyday sayings like "Have a blessed day," "God is good," and "I'll pray for you" or "You're in my prayers" are commonplace among African Americans of all class backgrounds. They have become shorthand for being and belonging in the black community, essentially transcending class status.

The legacy of Jim Crow and de facto segregation has limited black residential mobility, creating socioeconomic conditions in which blacks of all classes, incomes, and education levels live in close proximity to each other. Hence, African Americans remain the single most segregated racial group in the U.S. When such factors as residential patterns, income levels, health outcomes, educational outcomes, incarceration rates, and transportation access are evaluated collectively, African Americans experience the greatest disparities of any racial "subgroup" in the U.S. This is significant because it perpetuates African American insularity and social isolation. This in turn reinforces the inculcation of traditional belief systems and limits broader African American exposure to secular belief systems.

Sunday in and Sunday out, between the hours of 8 a.m. and 5 p.m., a familiar scene plays out in working and middle class black communities across the nation. Black women shuttle dutifully to church in their sartorial best, backbone of a dubious institution that still accords them second class citizenship. In many black churches, power, access, and control are still largely determined by gender. For example, while more black women have been allowed to assume leadership roles in black churches in recent years, they remain a minority among deacons, pastors, and senior pastors. So although black women are far more likely than men to attend church more than once a week, the officialdom of black religious establishments, and certainly the political face of the Black Church, is steadfastly male.[23]

What is the relationship between these gendered religious hierarchies and cultural politics in African American communities? Christian religiosity pervades the slang of misogynist black hip hop artists and sports figures and worms its way into their Jesus touting boilerplate award acceptance speeches. Christian religiosity engorges multi-million dollar faith-based empires in poor urban black communities where prime real estate is often a triad of storefront churches, liquor stores, and check cashing services. Sex scandals and financial improprieties fester amongst the leadership of the Black Church yet sexist and homophobic rhetoric remain a mainstay. In a "controversial" article published on her blog "Surviving Dating," feminist dating advice columnist Deborrah Cooper challenges the Black Church's centrality in black women's lives. She says, "It is my belief that the Black church, structured around traditional gender roles which make women submissive to and inferior to men, greatly limits females. Single Black women sitting in church every Sunday are being subtly brainwashed, soothed and placated into waiting without demand for what they magically want to come to them. Who is doing this to Black women? The male standing at the front of the Church in the role of spiritual leader, that's who!"[24]

Cooper argues that many single black women give their all to the Church in the mistaken belief that it will help them find a husband. Rather than flail through the rituals of an oppressive institution where marriageable black men are largely MIA, Cooper advises black women to get out of the Church and focus on themselves and their children. She rightly warns that black women's lives shouldn't revolve around "a religion which Black men use to castigate and control an entire race of women."[25] Yet her focus on "hooking up", coupled with her broad heterosexist caricatures of black men who do frequent church (those who do are either gay, aging "players" or terminally dysfunctional because "no man of strength or purpose is going to church and have another man tell him what to do"), are problematic. Cooper condemns the Black Church's relentless marriage, home, hearth, and help mate propaganda. Yet she reinscribes this reductive onus by advising women to leave the church to find greener pastures for partnership. Certainly many black women frequent church to find eligible partners, but many also do not. Many argue that they derive genuine spiritual, cultural, and communal fulfillment from their involvement with the Church, separate and apart from the now all too hackneyed media-hyped quest to find a "good black man." In order to fundamentally challenge black women's allegiance to a belief system that socializes them to accept misogyny, patriarchy, and sexism as a way of life and identity it is important to understand why this is so. While critics of the Black Church abound, few with an avowedly atheist or humanist sensibility, who question the basic relevance of all regimes of organized religion to black identity, black socioeconomic sustainability and social justice, have achieved mainstream visibility.

Black people control virtually no wealth in the U.S. No corporations, no major industries, no hedge funds. Yet church empires ripple unbroken across the urban horizon. Since Malachi exhorts even the most destitute worshippers to give God his due until it bleeds, churches are the community's biggest parasites. Here, blind faith continues to speak through bulging collection plates and special tithes to the latest charity, pastor's pet cause or capital campaign, "blessing" donors with another chit to heaven and certitude that black apostates are also race traitors. If mainstream African American notions of black identity are defined by a degree of *essentialism*, then religious identity is a key element. Alternative belief systems are viewed with suspicion because they are "inconsistent" with authentic black identity. In her discussion of the tension between essentialism and postmodernist constructs of identity bell hooks notes:

> We have too long had imposed upon us, both from the outside and the inside, a narrow constricting notion of blackness. Postmodern critiques of essentialism which challenge notions of universality and static over-determined identity within mass culture and mass consciousness can open up new possibilities for the construction of the self and the assertion of agency. Employing a critique of essentialism allows African-Americans to acknowledge the way in which class mobility has altered collective black experience so that racism does not necessarily have the same impact on our lives. Such a critique allows us to affirm multiple black identities, varied black experience. It also

> challenges colonial imperialist paradigms of black identity which represent blackness one- dimensionally in ways that reinforce and sustain white supremacy. This discourse created the idea of the "primitive" and promoted the notion of an "authentic" experience, seeing as "natural" those expressions of black life which conformed to a pre-existing pattern or stereotype. Abandoning essentialist notions would be a serious challenge to racism. Contemporary African-American resistance struggle must be rooted in a process of decolonization that continually opposes reinscribing notions of "authentic" black identity.[26]

As hooks notes, essentialism entails monolithic notions and paradigms of subjectivity, selfhood, and identity that are informed by a myopic view of what constitutes "authentic" blackness. The idea of "multiple black identities" contradicts the notion that a universally shared set of racialized experiences and beliefs is the single most important index of blackness or being black. In the moral universe of mainstream African American communities, essentialism dictates that those who violate the tacit contract of religious observance are somehow "less" than African American.

Given this context, it is unsurprising that African American comedian and self-appointed dating guru Steve Harvey's widely circulated TV talk show diatribe against atheism went unchallenged by African American cultural critics. Harvey is a nationally syndicated radio personality and game show host with a large following in African American communities. He is also a regular columnist for Essence Magazine and the author of the bestseller *Act Like a Lady, Think Like a Man: What Men Really Think About Love, Relationships, Intimacy and Commitment.* Commenting on the dating scene on several popular talk shows, Harvey condescendingly warned women to avoid atheist men at all costs because they simply have no morals. Given his promotion of "black women's issues" his swaggeringly ignorant declaration was not only a repudiation of atheism but a thinly veiled warning to black women that they should toe the religious line. Failure to do so would have serious consequences for racial solidarity and their ability to be good (black) women (the horror of eligible black women hooking up with atheist heathens and contaminating the black race!). In short, it would compromise their heterosexual marketability and legitimacy as marriage partners and mothers. Ivori Patterson, a 28 year old agnostic/atheist who lives in the South, stated that this was one of the reasons why she remained closeted about her beliefs. According to Patterson, "possible suitors will almost undoubtedly ask 'What church do you go to?' on the first date. Not 'Do you go to church?' nor 'Do you believe in God, Gods or goddesses?' but 'What church do you attend?"[27] It is this brand of essentialism that makes stereotypes associating black identity politics with an anti-secularist stance and religious superstition so irritatingly persistent.

While the greater religiosity of women of color in comparison to men is no mystery, why has this peculiarly gendered regime gone largely unquestioned? The gravity of the social and economic issues confronting black communities—and the tremendous cultural capital and social authority that organized religion exercises within them— compels further analysis. Just as women are socialized to identify with and internalize misogynistic and sexist paradigms, religious paradigms that emphasize domestication and obeisance to men are integral to mainstream American notions of femininity. For many observant women, questioning or rejecting religion outright would be as counterintuitive as rejecting their connection to their lived experiences. In this regard religious observance is as much a performance and reproduction of gender identity as it is an exercise of personal "morality." Many of the rituals of black churchgoing forge this sense of gendered identity as community. Whether it be maintaining ties with peers within the context of a church meeting, ensuring impressionable children have some "moral" mooring by sending them to Sunday School or even invoking sage bits of scripture to chasten malcontents, enlighten casual acquaintances or infuse one's quotidian doings with purpose—all carefully delineate enactments of kin and community that have been drilled into women as the proper fulfillment of a gendered social contract. And if this gendered social contract were violated en masse, patriarchy and heterosexism would have less of a firmament.

What, then, are the lessons for promoting secular humanist, agnostic or atheist belief systems? First, there must be more clearly defined alternatives to supernatural belief systems that speak to diverse populations of women and people of color. Second, secular moral values should provide the basis for robust critique of the serious cultural and socioeconomic problems that thrive in communities of color under the regime of organized religion. Finally, in an intellectual universe where rock star white men with publishing contracts are the most prominent atheists, and atheism is perceived in some quarters as a "white" thing, it is critical that humanist belief systems be modeled in communities of color. Only then can secularism defang the seductions of the communal dimension of faith that defines our most segregated hour.

Beyond the Sacrificial Good Woman

As I have argued throughout this chapter, atheism and women of color are widely viewed as fundamentally incompatible. Freethinking African American writers such as Zora Neale Hurston, Alice Walker, and Lorraine Hansberry have expressed secular humanist views in their works. However, few prominent African American women have explicitly expressed atheist views.[28] Although religious skepticism is a major yet traditionally unacknowledged part of African American social thought, atheism is not an intellectual path that is even remotely acknowledged as legitimate. This is partly due to gender hierarchy which is deeply influenced by organized religion and Christian dogma. Yet it is also based on a global intellectual establishment that valorizes and privileges the discourse and scholarship of white male thinkers on religion.

One atheist woman of color writer who has achieved global visibility is Somali feminist Ayaan Hirsi Ali. She is the only internationally recognized Muslim woman of African descent whose personal experience with Islamic fundamentalist repression has motivated her to become an atheist. Ali's work deconstructs the way in which Muslim women in Somali culture subscribe to and perpetuate these conventions. A victim of clitoral mutilation in her youth, she has dedicated her life to challenging institutional sexism and patriarchy in Muslim societies. In her book *Infidel* she writes passionately about her mission as a member of the Dutch Parliament to correct the lack of Amnesty International data on women murdered in honor killings. She has argued that the Koran is inherently misogynistic, fascistic, and anti-human rights, and that "moderate" or liberal Islam is an oxymoron. Her activism against gender-based terrorism and repression of Muslim women has been influential, generating international accolades as well as death threats from Muslim extremists. Rising to global prominence in the post 9/11 anti-Muslim hysteria of the Bush era, Ali has elicited controversy for what some have characterized as Muslim-bashing. After moving to the U.S. she garnered a plum position at the neoconservative

American Enterprise Institute and continues to live under armed guard.

Much of Ali's feminist ideology is based on the contrast between the violent repression of women under Islam and the liberal humanist traditions that supposedly shape women's rights in the West. In her writings and public discourse, she is fond of making sweeping pronouncements deriding the cultures of Muslim societies, while valorizing the West in ways that downplay its cultural hierarchies. In a 2007 interview with *Reason Magazine* she waxed, "Western civilization is a celebration of life...everybody's life, even the life of your enemy." Discussing the plight of Muslim child brides in the *New York Times* she writes:

> The best we can hope for is not for the West to invade other countries in the hope of emancipating their women. That is neither realistic nor desirable (and remains our least plausible war aim in Afghanistan).The best we can hope for is a neo-feminism that reminds women in the West of the initial phases of their liberation movement. Those phases not only highlighted the subjugation of women, they set out to dismantle the foundations of their cages. For the dream of liberation to come true for women in the East it is imperative that we seek to shatter the underpinnings of their subjugation, which are now enshrined in religion and custom.[29]

Of course, in many Muslim societies feminism is still a dangerously radical concept. For many Muslim feminists, the very notion of women's personal freedom is a space of epic struggle. Yet Ali's totalizing assessments set up a false dichotomy between the West and Muslim societies. Clearly the West would never in a million years go to war for Middle Eastern women's rights. The wars in Iraq and Afghanistan have been waged for the U.S.' strategic geopolitical capitalist interests, period. As the numerous drone attacks, rapes, and murders of innocent civilians by U.S. forces attest, such interests undermine gender justice, transforming women and children into occupied territory and "collateral" damage. If Western imperialist leaders cynically invoke women's rights at all, it is to bolster their absurd historically bankrupt claims to "spreading" democracy in the "backward" Muslim world. Anti-imperialist Muslim feminists like Iran's Sussan Gol know all too well that the U.S. is one of the greatest enemies of real gender justice in the Middle East. Scheming to gain control of Iran's oil reserves, the U.S. has consistently opposed secular democratic movements in Iran. In an interview I conducted with her for International Women's Day in 2010, Gol maintained that "Islamic fundamentalism hangs on its 'death to America'" rhetoric as a means of legitimizing and reinforcing nationalism.[30] In some regards, poor people in the region see no other viable alternative to Western imperialism *besides* Islamic fundamentalism.

By portraying feminism as a battle that the West has already won, Ali absolves bourgeois democracies like the United States of their schizoid relationship to women rights and human rights, a relationship in which rape and domestic violence are very much part of the national "democratic" currency. And by ignoring the historical context of the "third world within the first world," she ignores the very real socioeconomic differences that exist between American women of color (both native and immigrant born) and white women.

Western liberal humanism has had a problematic trajectory regarding race, gender, and notions of "personhood." As I argued before, Enlightenment era notions of Western personhood, freedom, and sovereignty were partly based on the oppositional "nature" of blackness and whiteness. As a prominent twentieth century critic of colonialism, Martinican poet Aime Cesaire highlighted the intersection of Western humanism and Christianity in the othering of non-white colonized peoples. As Michael Lackey notes in his book *African American Atheists and Political Liberation,* Cesaire "understands how European humanism presupposes a 'native lack' within uncivilized others...humanism, by establishing a definition of what is properly human, implicitly identifies certain individuals as nonhuman, and thereby necessitates and justifies the ennobling practices of colonizing and ultimately humanizing the savage races."[31]

The construction of this "native lack" also pivoted on gender hierarchy. Femininity and masculinity were racialized based upon European standards of personhood and humanity. Whereas the dark savage other was naturalized as "masculine," the virginal white civilized Western self was naturalized as "feminine."[32]

Despite these constructs, African slaves were still largely bound to traditional male and female roles. For example, delineation of family roles and responsibilities emerged from asymmetrical notions of masculine and feminine identity. These were especially critical under slavery, as work duties and caregiving roles—such as cooking, cleaning, and raising children—were prescribed according to European American gender norms.

In her work on the social construction of African American women under slavery, bell hooks debunks the widespread notion that African American men were emasculated simply because they were enslaved. Much of the rhetoric on the formation of black masculinity under slavery has held that African American men were not "allowed" to assume patriarchal control because of white supremacist rule.[33]

According to this view, black men could not assume their right to manhood because white men exercised terroristic control over the bodies and destinies of black women and children. These perceived disparities were further reinforced by the conclusions of the infamous 1965 Moynihan Report. Authored by then Johnson administration official Daniel Patrick Moynihan, the Moynihan Report notoriously slammed the so-called "matriarchal" structure of black families as an aberration requiring correction. The black matriarchy was a vestige from slavery, amplified by the "pathological" conditions of black urban communities rife with welfare dependence, criminality, teen pregnancy, and joblessness. Moreover, black women were far too dominating and controlling to allow their men to be "real men," thus the high rate of black absentee fathers. Single parent families headed by black women undermined the traditional nuclear family structure with the man as the head of the household. In order for black family stability to be restored, black men should be allowed to be the rightful breadwinners and decision makers in black families. They should be allowed to "strut" like "real men."

Thus, in a postbellum context, African American men would have to compensate for this disparity by assuming conventional patriarchal control over women and children. However, feminist scholars have refuted the notion that slave era African American family structure was radically different from patriarchal norms. Hooks maintains that African American family structure was quite conventional. She takes issue with the common perception that men didn't have any patriarchal rights or responsibilities under slavery. Contrary to the popular belief that black men were emasculated under slavery because they did not have unfettered access to and control over the bodies and destinies of black women and children, black women were still socialized to fulfill gender hierarchical responsibilities like cooking, cleaning and taking care of children. Domestic work, both within black homes and white homes, was the province of black women. Black women were regarded as the primary caregivers of the family, the protectors of home, hearth and the wellbeing of their male partners and children. Black women were the repositories of moral and social values. And it was they who bore the brunt of social expectations to transmit these values to their children, not black men.

Given these complexities, what role did organized religion and socialization into Christian dogma play in solidifying gender differences in slave culture, and what is this dynamic's legacy? Why has Christian religious adherence been so persistent? What weaknesses does this reflect in African American secular institutions and traditions? And are there possible resonances between Ayaan Hirsi Ali's experience and trajectory and that of African American women?

As I discussed earlier, the "good woman" concept is deeply entrenched in most communities of color. Protecting manhood and upholding traditions and customs that maintain masculinist family structures, have been bulwarks against racist oppression. In this regard, adherence to Christianity is a means of redressing the gender asymmetries imposed by what hooks has famously dubbed "white supremacist capitalist patriarchy." African American women's seeming overinvestment in upholding these traditions is a cornerstone of traditional black social cohesion. Female self-image and self-identity are intimately connected to paradigms of masculinity. Men need not be as observant of organized religion because the dominant culture is predicated on a secular-religious blend of patriarchal domination and control over women. Christianity sets up binary paradigms of femininity and masculinity.

Men are expected to be dominant in both the home and the public sphere; women are expected to submit to the will and authority of the man, exercising responsibility for caregiving and domestic work.

Despite the legislative and public policy gains made by the women's movement, cultural representation of modern gender roles remains woefully static. For example, in contemporary American advertising a TV commercial father rarely labors lovingly over a child's fruit punch spill with a "quicker picker upper" or agonizes over the correct solvent to use on a smudged toilet seat. The cleaning product industry's entire marketing strategy is evidently based on reinforcing "outdated" yet naturalized models of submissive domesticated femininity. Similarly, cooking and food preparation are the exclusive realm of women playing doting mothers to eternally fickle eternally famished children in day-glo kitchens. By promoting normative feminine roles, the industry enshrines these gender norms as transparent and timeless. In the ad time universe, "choosy moms" fuss and fixate over the right amount of Splenda to put in Dick and Jane's cookies because it's part of their post-feminist destiny.

Indeed, other than minor stylistic concessions to modernity, many of these commercials would fit right in with 1950's advertisements targeted to Donna Reed, June Cleaver, and Ozzie's Harriet; they are gender propaganda that anchor a media regime dominated by a multi-billion dollar global film industry in which white actresses shuffle through variations on the roles of sex object/wife/mother/help mate. The prevalence of these images belies post-feminist themes of unlimited opportunity and progress trumpeted in mainstream media like *Time* Magazine's 2009 "State of the American Woman" issue.[34] Post-feminism signifies that feminism is passé, unnecessary, a relic of a bygone, unenlightened knuckle-dragging era. As always, white women are the "invisible" standard for post-feminist progress. So although more women may be in the workplace and in higher education, there has been little progress in eliminating the disproportionate representation of women of color in lower paying jobs and professions. When it comes to the "image industries" the numbers of women of color that have behind-the-camera decision making roles are miniscule. Most tellingly, gender disparities in child care, perhaps the single most intractable barrier to women's economic mobility, continue to stunt women's lifetime earning power and professional opportunities.

If there has been so much "post-feminist" progress, where are the alternative models of masculinity in American culture? The paradigm shift whereby male sexuality is just as coveted and valuable a commodity as female sexuality? Why hasn't a culture of male caregiving and anti-violence emerged? Where is this liberated universe where women and girls can walk down the street, walk down the halls at school or go to sleep in their own beds without fear of assault?

Good women accept that violence against women is just a way of life. Male saviors, bent on retribution and divine justice, mandate it. The biblical notion of original sin outlined in Genesis is crucial in the social control of women. The inherent fallibility/evil of women is especially insidious for African American women because of the dominant culture's racist misogynistic representations of women of color. Under slavery, African American women were constructed as hypersexual and promiscuous, the antithesis of virginal white femininity. White femininity signified the pinnacle of European civilization, liberalism, and morality. Because African American women were mired in a backward savage culture, black femininity was perceived as the polar opposite of white womanhood. White womanhood symbolized all of the virtues and cultural/aesthetic achievement of the "new nation." In her book *Playing in the Dark: Whiteness and the Literary Imagination,* Toni Morrison maintains that the "Africanist presence" enabled the new white man of the American republic to construct his subjectivity through the lens of Enlightenment values of liberal humanism. Enslaved Africans were the antithesis of European culture, refinement, and selfhood. They represented a "playground of imagination"[35] whereby:

> The rights of man...an organizing principle on which this nation was founded...was inevitably yoked to Africanism... the concept of freedom did not emerge in a vacuum. Nothing highlighted freedom—if it did not in fact create it—like slavery. Black slavery enriched the country's creative possibilities. For in that construction of blackness and enslavement could be found not only the not-free...but the not-me.[36]

The idea of degraded African American femininity is central to the American national ideal because it affirms the essential moral and cultural superiority of European American democracy. In this regard Judeo-Christian focus on the fallibility and responsibility of the individual correlates well with the American emphasis on individual liberty. Racist myths of black female sexuality justified the commodification of black slave labor and black reproductive labor. Institutionalized rape and forced breeding (by forcibly pairing black women with black men they were not partnered with to produce more slaves) were among the means of controlling and objectifying black female sexuality.

After emancipation, some black women reacted to this regime of control by embracing the "cult of true womanhood."

The "cult of true womanhood" was a socio-cultural movement and ideology spearheaded by European American women in the early nineteenth century. It was designed to elevate the supposed values of American womanhood, i.e., virtue, chastity, humility, domesticity, and moral purity.[37] It coincided with the rise of industrial America and the creation of a new middle class.[38] According to Paula Giddings, free middle class black women in the North "had to overcome notions about the relationship of class—as well as color—to morality."[39] Therefore, middle class black women developed a heightened sense of the delicate relationship between normative, proper femininity, and their tenuous class position. Because of the socially degraded status of African American women, some black women overcompensated by adopting the cult of true womanhood in their own communities. Giddings notes that many black ladies' "moral improvement" societies sprung up during this period. In this regard, black women were socialized into the cultural structures of the mainstream European American dominant culture. However, African American feminists were conflicted about the relevance of this model in a context of institutional sexism, misogyny, and racial terrorism. There was much debate about whether or not African American women should emulate the Anglo-American example or challenge the hierarchies of conduct and behavior prescribed by the white mainstream.[40] Black women's moral improvement societies combined an emphasis on moral uplift with the pursuit of social justice initiatives, such as establishing schools for black children.

However, on an average day-to-day level the "burden" of transmitting religious belief and religious adherence is uniquely female in tenor. Women are both the biggest enforcers and purveyors of religious tradition. This dynamic is vividly illustrated in Lorraine Hansberry's *Raisin in the Sun* in a pivotal scene between Beneatha Younger and her mother Lena Younger (known as Mama). After slapping Beneatha in the face because she has questioned God's existence, Mama exhorts: "Now—you say after me, in my mother's house there is still God. In my mother's house there is still God." As matriarch of the Younger family, Mama's "policing" of Beneatha's skepticism underscores the pivotal role that black women play in enforcing religious belief.

While the communal foundation of the Black Church was important in this regard, the history and legacy of African American femininity also plays a large role in this brand of policing. In order to be perceived as legitimately "female", black women had to hew to "Christian" ideals of purity and chastity; they had to overcompensate with gestures of piety and obedience to the family and the home sphere. They had to negotiate their sense of feminine duty in an environment in which black masculine authority was "undermined" by a white supremacist pecking order. Institutional racism and discrimination shut black men out of most white collar and many blue collar jobs during the Jim Crow era. As a result, black men earned (and still earn) much less than white men. Unlike middle class and some working class white women, many black women did not have the choice to work outside of the home. Because black women had to be breadwinners for their families, they were even more removed from Anglo-American paradigms of femininity. Here, "the true woman's exclusive role was as homemaker, mother, housewife, and family tutor of the social and moral graces."[41] Black women were required to fulfill these duties *and* work outside of the home. Hence, their degraded racial and economic status prevented them from being considered truly feminine relative to white women.

In this regard, the cult of true womanhood has cast a long shadow on black female religiosity. And it is the nexus between this ideology and Judeo-Christian ideals of femininity that makes black female religious adherence so intractable. Yet the intersection of black female religious belief and civil rights activism is another critical piece. In her book *Witnessing and Testifying,* Rosetta Ross identifies the pursuit of racial uplift and social responsibility as part of black women's obligation to God. After emancipation in 1863, black women utilized their spiritual compass as a basis for advocating for racial and gender justice.[42] In this sense, "religious duty includes responsibility for social structures, since social context significantly influences the meaning and experience of being human. An obvious relationship of social responsibility to racial uplift is the obligation to attend to racial justice, the absence of which hinders or completely obstructs progress to African American freedom."[43]

This obligation to racial and social justice, a linchpin of the Black Church's historical mission, has distinguished African American religiosity from Anglo-American religiosity (the social justice activism of the abolitionist Quakers being a noteworthy exception). According to Anthony Pinn, the emergence of black religious subjectivity can be fully understood only within the terroristic context of antebellum America. Here, "religion manifested in black life is a response to or wrestling against terror, understood in terms of liberation."[44] Black resistance against racial terrorism informed the African American quest for wholeness, dignity, and spiritual redemption through religion. Biblical scripture provided black slaves with a compass for proving their innate worth as human beings and not "things" or "objects."[45] With its emphasis on the redemption of the enslaved Children of Israel and their triumph over a brutal Egyptian Pharaoh, the story of Exodus provided African slaves with an inspiring analogy. In this regard, "recognition of their full citizenship before God...brought into question the validity of the slave system irrespective of the theological justifications of slaveholders and their ministers."[46] The lessons of suffering articulated in the Bible gave enslaved blacks a sense of moral uplift and possibility in the midst of unbearably dehumanizing conditions. And because blacks were linked with one another as racially othered chattel—interchangeable, expendable and ultimately at the mercy of the whims of the slave master—religious belief was not just an affirmation of selfhood but of community.

The bonds forged among African Americans under the Holocaust conditions of slavery were the basis for a revolutionary brand of social justice activism. African American social justice disrupted hierarchical notions of democracy and citizenship espoused by Anglo American society, laying bare its brutal contradictions. Blacks raised fundamental epistemological questions that continue to rock the very firmament of American liberal democracy. For example, how could individual liberty and inalienable rights exist in a "civilized" nation steeped in chattel slavery? How could the U.S. claim to represent the Enlightenment ideal of freedom when its prosperity rested on the theft of black bodies and black labor? And how could this same nation rise as a free world leader and model of tolerance in light of its paternalistic, imperialist stance toward third world nations?

In many respects, Christianity has been central to defining blacks' sense of "American-ness." The crucible of slavery and black adaptation of Christian belief (out of the lived experience of racial terrorism) provided blacks with an "existential" basis to question and resist the dominant culture—a culture based on the image of whiteness as all that was human, good, upright, desirable, and hence moral. Steeped in Christian moral values, black social thought challenged the legitimacy of Anglo-American claims to liberal democracy, citizenship, and morality. For Toni Morrison's "new white man," blackness didn't just signify the "not free" "not me" but a fundamental opposition to liberal democracy. To be black was to be alienated from the very concept of freedom, i.e., "Americanness." And clearly this savage moral claim is one reason why Obama's presidency has elicited the bloodlust of white nationalists and white militias across the country.

In challenging this regime of meaning, African Americans used "white" religion as a moral lightening rod. Religion was a serviceable tool. For some, the pervasiveness of Christian belief amongst African Americans raises the question of whether it's possible to consider black identity and social justice outside of organized religion. Clearly it is important to separate morally just religious practice from the dogma, hierarchy, and bigotry articulated in fascist scripture. Early freethinking traditions in African American social thought focused on the truth claims of organized religion. More specifically, they distinguished the moral vision of Christian charity from white supremacist brutality. From Frederick Douglass' powerful excoriation of the hypocrisy of white Christian slaveholders to Alice Walker's critique of religion as a means of rationalizing Jim Crow era apartheid, black freethinkers have always highlighted religion's reinforcement of white supremacy and social control. These interventions paved the way for progressive Christians to dissect the tyrannies of fundamentalism. Yet few challenged the centrality of organized religion to black life or questioned its impact on socioeconomic conditions in black communities.[47] While black mega church congregations have proliferated over the past few decades, black social mobility has worsened. And while the disparities between black female and black male churchgoing have deepened, social, health, and economic burdens on black women have become more onerous. In fulfilling their traditional roles as caregivers, many black women cite faith as a major motivator and inspiration for just getting through the day. Faced with skyrocketing rates of intimate partner abuse and homicide, HIV/AIDS contraction, single parenthood, over-incarceration, high unemployment, and workplace discrimination, black women turn to faith for succor, affirmation, belonging and community. Thus, part of the legacy of slavery is the deep association between faith and mental health and wellness. Paradoxically, faith has been both a contributor to and a means of surviving the stress of being black and female in white supremacist America. Faith is part of blacks' inheritance of being and becoming American.

There are scores of African American churches that do good works in the name of Christianity. Yet progressive non-believers cannot ignore the essential fascism of scripture. For thousands of years, cherry picking scripture has allowed Christians to claim moral authority, certitude, and ethical superiority over non-believers. Fundamentalism has allowed fascism to stand in the way of and destroy democratic freedoms. When the language of a given creed opposes human rights, no moral high ground can be claimed. In the twenty first century, the historic connection between black social justice traditions and Christianity has been fatally undermined. The explicitly class conscious anti-racist, anti-imperialist "prophetic gospel" of Martin Luther King has been all but abandoned by the Black Church. The Church has become increasingly mired in materialism (represented by the so-called "prosperity gospel"), sex scandals, homophobia, and unrelenting "capital improvement" campaigns for mega church expansion. As Dallas mega church pastor and prosperity gospel practitioner T.D. Jakes commented, "I'm not against marching, but in the '60s the challenge of the black church was to march. And there are times now perhaps that we may need to march, but there's more facing us than social justice. There's personal responsibility, motivating and equipping people to live the best lives that they can really does help them to live the scriptures and to bring them to life."[48] Jakes' sentiments succinctly capture the Black Church's overall retreat from social justice movement organizing in the so-called post-Jim Crow era. Given that the communities traditional African American churches serve are among the most indigent in the United States, this retreat has further undermined the already corrupt moral credibility of many urban faith-based institutions.

Endnotes

1. Mark Galli, *Christianity Today*, 2007 (http://www.religioustolerance.org/chr_prac2.htm).
2. "A Religious Portrait of African Americans," Pew Forum on Religion and Public Life, Pew Research Center 2009.
3. I will focus on Larsen and *Quicksand* in greater detail in Chapter 4.
4. Ariela Keysar, "Who Are America's Atheists?" from *Secularism and Secularity: Contemporary International Perspectives*, eds. Barry Kosmin and Ariela Keysar (Hartford, CT: Institute for the Study of Secularism in Society and Culture, 2007), 34.
5. Ayanna Watson, Interview Questionnaire, November 2010.
6. Paula Giddings, *When and Where I Enter: The Impact of Black Women on Race and Sex in America* (New York: William Morrow, 1984), 64.
7. Marilyn Richardson, "Maria W. Stewart: America's First Black Woman Political Writer," from *Black Women's Intellectual Traditions: Speaking Their Minds*, eds. Carol B. Conaway and Kristin Waters (Burlington: University of Vermont Press, 2007), 13-37.
8. Ibid., 23.
9. Ibid., 23-4.
10. Ibid., 26.
11. Dianne Bartlow, "'No Throw-Away Woman": Maria W. Stewart as Forerunner of Black Feminist Thought," from Conaway and Waters, 84-86.
12. Ibid.
13. Ibid.
14. Richardson, 27.
15. bell hooks, *Salvation: Black People and Love* (New York: William Morrow, 2001), 32-33, 54.
16. Anonymous subject, Interview Questionnaire, December 2010.
17. According to a 2007 Pew Research Forum *Survey on Religious Life* men are far more likely than women to have no religious affiliation

18. "A Religious Portrait of African Americans," 2009.
19. Cornel West, "A Genealogy of Modern Racism," *Knowledge and Postmodernism in Historical Perspective*, (New York: Routledge, 1996), 476-486. West argues that white supremacy was indispensable to the articulation of Enlightenment ideals and values of rationalism, scientism and empiricism.
20. Ibid.
21. Edward Carlson, "Do Worshippers Give God His 10 Percent?" *Philadelphia Inquirer*, April 2001. (http://www.beliefnet.com/Love-Family/Charity-Service/2001/04/Do-Worshipers-Give-God-His-10-Percent.aspx).
22. Brandale Randolph, "Why Megachurches Don't Deserve Your Tithe," *The Loop 21.com*, December 13, 2010 (http://theloop21.com/money/why-mega-churches-dont-deserve-your-tithe?page=2).
23. Barbera, 31, 33. Donald Barbera has reported that black male attendance in the Black Church has declined over the past several years whereas female attendance has increased. This disparity appears to be attributable to the crisis in gender equity that continues to plague African American communities.
24. Deborah Cooper, "The Black Church: How Black Churches Keep Black Women Single and Lonely," *Surviving Dating Blog*, June 10, 2010 (http://survivingdating.com/black-churches-how-black-churches-keep-african-american-women-single-and-alone).
25. Ibid.
26. bell hooks, "Postmodern Blackness," *Yearning* (Boston: South End Press, 1990), 28-9.
27. Ivori Patterson, Interview questionnaire, January 2011.
28. The late actress Butterfly McQueen and comedian Robin Quivers have been identified as atheists.
29. Ayaan Hirsi Ali, "Not the Child My Grandmother Wanted," *New York Times*, December 2, 2010.
30. Sikivu Hutchinson, "Iran and the Global Struggle for Women's Liberation," *Blackfemlens*, March 16, 2010 (http://blackfemlens.blogspot.com/2010/03/international-womens-day-iran-and.html).
31. Michael Lackey, *African American Atheists and Political Liberation: A Study of the Sociocultural Dynamics of Faith* (Gainesville, Florida: University of Florida Press, 2007), 47.
32. This is partly why themes of rape and violent conquest recur in American social thought vis-à-vis the indolent marauding slave or the savage

marauding Indian. Above all else whiteness signifies a purity that is always susceptible to the danger of violent contamination and encroachment. Historically many of the most prominent literary and political symbols of America and the United States have been white females.

33. The work of both E. Franklin Frazier and Daniel Patrick Moynihan have propounded this view. See Frazier, *Black Bourgeoisie* and *Black Bourgeoisie* (Illinois: Glencoe Press, 1957) and Moynihan "The Negro Family: The Case for National Action," United States Department of Labor, 1965.
34. "What Women Want Now: The State of the American Woman," *Time,* October 14, 2009 (http://www.time.com/time/specials).
35. Toni Morrison, *Playing in the Dark: Whiteness and the Literary Imagination* (New York: Vintage, 1992), 38.
36. Ibid.
37. Giddings, 47-8; also Richardson, 27.
38. Ibid., 48.
39. Ibid.
40. Ibid., 49.
41. Ibid., 47.
42. Rosetta Ross, *Witnessing and Testifying: Black Women, Religion and Civil Rights* (Minneapolis: Fortress Press, 2003). Ross writes that "around the turn of the century" the National Baptist Women's National Convention felt it was their duty to "link racial advancement with spiritual and social regeneration." p. 5
43. Ibid.
44. Anthony Pinn, *Terror and Triumph: The Nature of Black Religion* (Minneapolis: Fortress Press, 2003), p. 82.
45. Ibid., 83-86.
46. Ibid., 85.
47. James Baldwin and James Forman are among the notable exceptions.
48. Audrey Barrick, "Black Believers Debate Prosperity Gospel," *Christian Post Reporter*, August 24, 2007 (http://www.christianpost.com/article/20070824/black-believers-debate-prosperity-gospel/page2.html).

Chapter 3

The Politics of Urban Religiosity

Tell that its sculptor well those passions read
Which yet survive, stamped on these lifeless things,
The hand that mocked them and the heart that fed.
And on the pedestal these words appear:
"My name is Ozymandias, king of kings:
Look on my works, ye Mighty, and despair!"
Nothing beside remains. Round the decay
Of that colossal wreck, boundless and bare
The lone and level sands stretch far away

—Ozymandias, Percy Bysshe Shelley

Seventy years ago, the pews of Zion Hill Baptist church in South Los Angeles were all white. The New Deal had altered the national landscape, the nation was a year into World War II, and gaggles of tow-headed children weaved in and out of the neighborhood's sidewalks on their bikes, lapping up the afternoon sun. Zion Hill sprawls over nearly three quarters of a city block. Staring onto an unbroken chain of 1930s Spanish style homes, the church is an elegant curiosity and historical ellipsis in an otherwise mundane residential community. While most of the churches in this neighborhood are of a more recent vintage, Zion Hill has the venerable look and feel of a provincial New England chapel. Surely Reverend Dimmesdale lurks here, anguished, sweaty, listening for the footfalls of pitchfork wielding townsfolk, gunning for Hester Prynne. On Sundays, Zion's block bustles with congregants, jamming the streets with their cars, spilling out post-service onto the church's crisp green lawns in devout Christian finery.

Plucked from the 1940s, Zion Hill would be a perfect Tea Party wet dream, a shining tribute to the halcyon period before civil rights laws perverted the framers' vision of a white City on the Hill. Rooted in the now of recession, foreclosure and political turbulence, the quiet refuge of the church and its clutch of single family homes exemplify the tight melding of black and Latino, working and middle class that is South Los Angeles' future.

Just as the sediment of white flight unsettles inner city communities so the ghosts of "congregations past" haunt old churches. Seth Pickens, pastor of Zion Hill since 2009, recounted to me how two former parishioners had returned to recreate their wedding at the church five decades ago. Dark and labyrinthine with two chapels and a gym, the interior of the church appears largely unchanged from the days when it harbored a white congregation. Revisiting their former neighborhood, the old married couple might have noticed the difference in the commercial makeup of the surrounding neighborhood. Homeward bound, they might have briefly lamented the vanished landmarks of their youth. Pointing out where the drugstore, the movie theatres, the German deli, and the golf course once were, they might have silently contemplated their own mortality, each vanished landmark a paean to death and the enigma of time.

Place and Collective Memory

Standing in the entryway of my house, the older white man wistfully related how he used to hang out at Al's Chili Dogs, a postage stamp sized 1950's style greasy spoon a mile away. Growing up in this neighborhood generations later, I have vivid memories of the dwindling enclave of elderly whites on the block who wore their "last white people standing" status like a military badge of honor. The man has a twinkle in his eye and the perfectly cadenced timing of a barber shop raconteur. The owner of a local carpet cleaning business, he waxed nostalgic about having attended the neighborhood schools, residing in the community until he moved his family to the predominantly white South Bay in the 1960s. Like the fable of the unicorn, the tale of white people living in what are now black strongholds like South L.A. is a source of myth and mystification. Traces of white community presence remain in the artificial boundaries that distinguish "inner city" and "suburb." In the post World War II era, these categories became popular as legal barriers to black and Latino settlement in predominantly white areas fell. A fatal whiff of regret seems to underlie nostalgic reveries into the forgotten landscape of white inner cityhood.

In many regards, the racial identities of white people rest on the now shopworn dichotomy between inner city and suburb. In the final years of World War II, the 1948 Shelley vs. Kramer Supreme Court ruling dismantling racially restrictive covenants was a pivotal moment for the social construction of race in the U.S. The ruling loosened the iron grip of de facto residential segregation in Northern communities. White flight, reinforced by a host of New Deal initiatives that facilitated upward mobility for European Americans (such as the GI Bill, Interstate Highway Act, Federal Housing Administration loans), deepened the physical and social segregation of

African Americans. The social welfare entitlement programs of the 1940s and 1950s enabled working class whites to enter the middle class. Public sector jobs, government subsidized college educations, and easily attainable mortgage loans in segregated white communities helped thousands of working class white families achieve the American Dream. As a result, non-Anglo whites such as Jewish, Irish, and Italian Americans were allowed to assimilate into the Anglo American melting pot.[1] As more working class ethnic white Americans "escaped" to all white enclaves in suburban America, the modern inner city was born.

In postwar Los Angeles, working class suburbs once predominantly white were gradually transformed in into degenerate "ghettos." Decades of racist propaganda against poor black communities, coupled with socioeconomic neglect and rampant police misconduct, culminated in the 1965 Watts Rebellion.[2] Watts was once a predominantly white enclave that even had its own chapter of the Ku Klux Klan during the 1920s. In the 1960s the suburb became the premier symbol of inner city black dysfunction. Isolated from living wage jobs due to sub-standard public transportation, Watts was shut out of white America's social welfare engine of prosperity. Because the Federal Housing Administration (FHA), the government's own mortgage lending institution, would not provide loans to integrated subdivisions, African Americans were confined to inner city communities.[3] In the mind of mainstream America, the fire hose attacks, police dogs, and violent redneck whites of the Jim Crow era are frozen in time as the ultimate symbols of racial segregation. Yet the legacy of de facto segregation practiced by banks, mortgage lending institutions, real estate agents, and average white citizens has been the most insidious barrier to African Americans' pursuit of racial justice.[4]

As Melvin Oliver and Thomas Shapiro note in their book *Black Wealth, White Wealth,* "The equity accumulated in homes represents the most important asset held by blacks."[5] Oliver and Shapiro contend that home equity plays a much larger role in black wealth than in white wealth. Due to the aforementioned patterns of institutional racism in lending and home buying, African Americans have considerably less home equity than whites. The gap between white and black home equity is so pronounced because blacks have historically been concentrated into low income segregated neighborhoods that have lower property values than that of white neighborhoods.

Thus, residential segregation has had a domino effect on every aspect of black social life, including organized religion. In many respects, organized religion has been one of the most effective vehicles of social segregation in the United States. Despite the election of an African American president, Martin Luther King's assertion about segregated Sunday church worship remains virtually axiomatic. For example, while blacks and Latinos coexist in communities like South L.A., interracial congregations are rare. Just as many black and Latino students self-segregate in schools across the nation, so black and Latino parishioners self-segregate in local church denominations. Over the past decade, formerly black-dominated communities like South Los Angeles have become increasingly Latino. According to UCLA's 2008 State of South Los Angeles report, the black population of South L.A. shrank due to out-migration and higher birthrates among Latinos. Despite these trends, 90% of African Americans in Los Angeles live in segregated South L.A. communities. Over half a century after racially restrictive covenants were outlawed, African Americans have the least residential mobility in the city. Even the most affluent black Angelenos, such as those who live in such elite neighborhoods as Baldwin

Hills, Windsor Hills, and View Park, live in closer proximity to poverty conditions relative to Los Angeles County residents as a whole.[6] Despite the fact that greater numbers of African Americans have entered the middle class, Latinos and Asians of lower economic status enjoy greater residential mobility.

The deep segregation of African Americans partly explains why churchgoing patterns remain so intractable. For generations the Black Church provided social services and other opportunities denied black communities due to institutional racism and white supremacy. African Americans of all beliefs (be they secular or religious) utilize the Black Church as a source of social and professional networking. And in many quarters it is simply impolitic for a black woman not to belong to a church, even if she does not attend regularly.[7] In some regards compulsory religiosity is reinforced by the silence of freethinking/skeptic African Americans. Non-believers may see themselves marginalized if not totally ostracized by their family, peers, and community. As one anonymous female poster wrote in response to one of my articles:

> I am very happy that I stumbled upon your site. I am 59 and I have never believed, but as most of you know that wasn't kosher in the black community. So I went through the motions.

Atheist African Americans such as the woman above go to church to affirm their connection to community, even if they find themselves in moral and intellectual conflict. Indeed, associating with a high profile black church is a quick and dirty way for black public figures to gain credibility. Nationwide black politicians such as Barack Obama (who infamously attended the Reverend Jeremiah Wright's Trinity Baptist Church in Chicago) align themselves with prominent black congregations to worship as well as politick with potential donors and supporters.

This is one reason why the secular and the religious remain deeply intertwined in the realm of black politics. Black churches and faith-based organizations such as the SCLC are often active in state and local political campaigns. Black religious leaders like Al Sharpton, Jesse Jackson, T.D. Jakes, Michael Eric Dyson, and Cornel West are routinely called on by the mainstream media to speak as definitive voices for black political and social views. And although fewer black congregations assume a national activist role as they did during the civil rights movement era, some still participate in grassroots organizing around social justice issues such as living wage jobs, affordable housing, universal health care access, education, and prison reform. Consequently, black neighborhoods are ground zero for small multi-denominational churches that have sprung up in the absence of sustainable "inner city" economic development and investment. While black and Latino communities in major cities like Washington DC, New York, and Oakland have been displaced by redevelopment and gentrification projects, horizontal cities like Los Angeles have seen fewer such changes. Much of the redevelopment and gentrification in Los Angeles County have been focused on the downtown area. Downtown redevelopment has further marginalized the area's predominantly of color homeless and indigent population. However, the majority of Southern California's residents of color live in single family and multi-family apartment-based working class suburban communities west and east of downtown. These communities have generally been deemed to be too crime-ridden and too remote from job centers to be profitable enterprise zones for commercial developers.

It could be argued that the geography of Los Angeles makes religiosity and provincialism thrive. The city has a slightly greater percentage of religious affiliation than in the overall U.S. population. Long parodied as a "city with no center" or a "city in search of a city", L.A. boasts a wide array of racial, ethnic, and religious diversity yet lacks a central business district. L.A.'s exurban car-centric model of remote suburbs, anchored by self-contained commercial centers, has become a model for national development. The insular niche-like quality of these localized economies is likely a factor in the proliferation of religious congregations. Indeed, with the growth of Orange County powerhouse mega churches headed by Joel Olsteen and Rick Warren, Southern California has been dubbed the Western Bible Belt. Despite the excess of "faith retail" in Southern California, racially integrated congregations and interfaith collaborations are exceptional.

If organized religion is the social, spiritual, and cultural lifeblood for working class black and Latino communities, the storefront church is one of its most enduring manifestations. Mile after urban mile, from the obscure to the ornate, Jesus facades are never far from view. The flourishing of these churches underscores the failure of post Jim Crow socioeconomic opportunity in black and Latino urban communities nationwide. For example, in North Lawndale, Chicago's "community of 1000 churches", there has been much debate about whether the proliferation of storefront churches is harmful or helpful to the local economy. "In this community, which is believed to have the city's highest concentration of storefront churches, scenes of drug addiction, prostitution and despair unfold, often right outside the church door."[8] A 2009 *Chicago Tribune* article documented community dissatisfaction with the ease with which church congregations utilize tax exempt status to open churches in areas where there is little sustainable commercial development. Thus, "some local business leaders question whether the area's nearly 200 churches, mainly storefronts, are causing more economic harm than spiritual good. Some debate whether having so many non-profit, tax-exempt entities on commercial properties is hurting the tax base and standing in the way of job creation."[9] Indeed, some storefront churches adamantly oppose development that would lead to job creation because it might jeopardize their low rent.[10] As Omar McRoberts, author of *Streets of Glory*, an analysis on storefront churches notes:

> Storefront churches are a transgressive form of religious presence. They are ubiquitous yet out of place. They break tacit societal norms about where and how to worship. They emerge from the depression of the neighborhood and bluntly remind people of that depression by occupying otherwise vacant commercial spaces.[11]

The storefront church is a vestige of the absence of sustainable development in working class communities of color. In Russellville Alabama, the local City Council has considered a ban on storefront churches downtown. The proposal would zone downtown for retail space as "storefront churches are an issue for many cities facing decreasing sales tax revenues."[12] Anticipating backlash, one councilperson repeatedly denied that the measure was "anti-religion."[13] The storefront church debate underscores the power organized religion has upon the imprint of urban communities. In communities where churches represent over fifty per cent of real estate occupants, a moratorium would seem not just logical but necessary. It is difficult to imagine a scenario in which secular tax exempt nonprofits would receive similar deference. However, storefront church officials claim that their presence fulfills a dire need in times of "moral crisis." By capitalizing on the absence of sustainable development in poor urban neighborhoods, these church congregations establish their presence as a kind of "moral" imperative. Whosoever has enough pluck to claim divine right, put a shingle up, call themselves Rev and master the fine art of passing a collection plate can claim this moral imperative.

"Pat Yourself on the Back Today and Reach Into Your Wallets Tomorrow"

Who was it who said that it would be easier for a camel to get through the eye of a needle than a rich man to get into the Kingdom of God? What about the owner of a multimillion dollar church property smack dab in the middle of the "ghetto"? At the time of its dedication in 1999, West Angeles church's $60 million dollar complex on Crenshaw Boulevard in South Los Angeles was revered as a shining example of the black community's resourcefulness and reviled as an Ozymandias-driven vanity project. Often dwarfing other local buildings by a King's ransom and tens of thousands of square feet, mega-church developments in poor urban neighborhoods are even more problematic than their threadbare storefront cousins. When the cathedral opened, West Angeles' pastor Bishop Charles Blake gushed, "The most significant thing about the building is that it's the expression of the persistence of the aspirations of people in the inner city...Inner city people deserve the best, just as anyone would."[14]

Located next to a soon-to-be active light rail right of way, the cathedral glitters from the street like a gilded white elephant. Massive stained glass windows wraparound its coliseum-style girth. At night the church sits dark and sepulchral as people stream in and out of Jack's Chili Factory across the street. The cathedral was constructed after years of dogged fundraising. Celebrity parishioners like Magic Johnson and Denzel Washington donated $5 million apiece. Regular inner city folk donated ten and twenty dollars a pop, presumably because they agree with Blake's view that a budget busting baronial estate is "what God deserves." Yet it's difficult to divine what "God" actually deserves *from* this community, given its glut of deserted businesses, for lease signs, fast food joints, check cashing places, strip malls, and comfy bus benches for homeless street dwellers. Driving past this monument to Blake's ego, thoughts of the social welfare possibilities of the $60 million dollar cathedral's price tag tantalize. According to the *Los Angeles Daily News*, the West Angeles cathedral is Los Angeles' "third largest religious structure." Interestingly, the other two are also located in South Los Angeles, in neighborhoods that have roughly the same racial demographic and economic profile as that of West Angeles' neighborhood. While the good times have apparently been very good for Blake and his empire, the church's magisterial presence has not uplifted the immediate area. The 2009 recession has taken its toll on the corridor, causing widespread closures and evictions among local businesses. Although the church motivated some business owners to open up shop along the corridor, there is little evidence that the cathedral's opening has spurred any major development revitalization in the community at large.[15] The median income for the area is approximately $37,000. According to the *L.A. Times* demographics website, it is low in comparison to the rest of the city. Most residents are transit dependent African American renters and unemployment has soared above 15%.

In the past, Blake and his church officials have been defensive about the mammoth cost of the cathedral. Settling for ten, twenty or thirty million would have been a serious affront to God. Seriously, what would Jesus do? Commenting on the absence of social disapproval for the construction of Sin City casinos, Blake fumed, "when we prepare to invest millions in God's place there are those who would criticize us."[16] Not to be outdone by West Angeles' real estate coup, Bishop Kenneth

Ulmer of Faithful Central Bible Church snapped up the Inglewood Forum for a cool $22 million in 2001. The Forum was itself on hallowed ground, having once been home to the L.A. Lakers and Jimi Hendrix's celestial guitar riffs. Like Blake, Ulmer was partly motivated by the growth of his burgeoning flock and partly motivated by a blazing sense of being called to do God's heavily mortgaged will. Crowing that "naysayers thought we couldn't do it," Ulmer evoked biblical battles to describe the congregation's successful campaign to claim the building. Proving the haters and Pharisees wrong, Ulmer's intrepid Christian soldiers "marched around the Forum seven times like they did the walls of Jericho."[17]

Both Ulmer and Blake's sentiments are common among the moral gatekeepers of faith-based entitlements. According to this view, church officials should be by very definition above worldly criticism and reproach because of their Christian altruism. In his critique of the unimpeachable status of the religious Frederick Douglass noted, "To be an infidel no more proves a man to be selfish mean and wicked, than to be evangelical proves him to be honest, just and humane."[18] This premise is proven time and again by the decidedly non-altruistic, worldly bent of church affairs, where, for example, millions of dollars in prime Catholic archdiocese real estate have been used as collateral in child sex abuse claims.

The age-old association of religiosity with morality is particularly ironclad in African American communities. Because religiosity is evidence of "authentic" blackness, it is difficult for black non-theists to publicly criticize the Black Church's special trifecta of religious dogma, greed, and hubris. As with the Catholic Church, financial and sex scandals in the Black Church fester because of the presumption of religious altruism. Since urban black community and religiosity are almost incestuously intertwined, faith-based leaders are provided with an especially wide political berth and moral license.[19]

In a city where black homelessness is off the charts, the $60 million dollar house that Blake's poor and wealthy parishioners built could have provided affordable housing for hundreds. That the construction of a megachurch in a high poverty area was not considered a contradiction speaks to the cultural desperation of many poor African Americans, who seek not just spiritual validation but a sense of selfhood from the Black Church. As Cecil Murray, former pastor of Los Angeles' influential First African Methodist Episcopal church noted, when it comes to church membership, "you may not have money…houses or land, but you have value."[20]

Yet the precise "value" that urban poor parishioners have is open to question. Physical structures are just as much an expression of culture and identity as literature, visual art, music and media. Even the most obscure places of worship reflect and articulate the identity of a community. Blending seamlessly into the woodwork, the storefront church is a perverse symbol of poverty, community, resilience, underdevelopment, enterprise, and hope. The megachurch is the apotheosis of conspicuous consumption—joyously decadent, swaggeringly obscene, unrepentantly phallic. Defenders of religion argue that these institutions fulfill a vital role and void in an underserved market. However, the ease with which they attach themselves to urban poor neighborhoods underscores the degree to which religious adherence has become a self-fulfilling prophecy among African Americans and Latinos.

Faith-Based Swindle?

The con man real estate investor claimed that he was a devout man of God, the title "visionary" flashing conspicuously from his business card. Traipsing door-to-door with promises of easy mortgage refinance deals, Timothy Barnett used his direct line to the Lord to wheedle his way into the houses of elderly homeowners in South Los Angeles. Scared, vulnerable, and without a safety net, his victims lapped up his God schlock like mother's milk. Isolated in modest homes they'd owned for decades, they welcomed his call to prayer. Fronting like a nattily dressed inner city Elmer Gantry, Barnett's hook was pitch-perfect: Our Christian beliefs unite us in a common value system based on ethics and integrity. The non-belief of non-Christians consigns them to immorality, making them more prone to duplicitous behavior and less worthy of your trust than I. Kneeling in humble service to God as co-pilot he stole the titles to five of his elderly victim's homes—and their "stake" in the American dream—one-by-one.

According to the *L.A. Times,* Barnett, a repeat felon subject to California's Three Strikes Law, could be the "first person in California" to be sentenced to life in prison for a white collar crime.[21] Though his actions were reprehensible, one might ask whether the punishment fits the crime. None of the largely white CEOs of the big Wall Street banks at the center of the mortgage meltdown and its derivatives fraud tsunami are facing jail time or even criminal charges for multibillion dollar malfeasance. Corporate America has suffered no penalty for bilking homeowners of their "secular religion" of the American dream. As is oft noted, President Obama's piecemeal initiatives for "underwater" homeowners have failed to put a dent in the nation's foreclosure crisis, a crisis with an increasingly black and brown face. According to the Center for Responsible Lending, African American and Latino homeowners have been devastated by disproportionate housing debt and foreclosure, their American dream awash in negative equity in segregated communities.[22] Unlike whites who are more likely to have a greater variety of financial assets (e.g., savings, stocks bonds and other investments, retirement and college accounts, inheritances, etc.) besides their homes, the wealth of people of color is disproportionately concentrated in home equity.[23] Thus the collapse of the housing market has exacerbated the racial wealth gap. Nationwide, Blacks and Latinos were targeted by subprime and predatory lenders. These lenders frequently offered higher mortgage interest rates and less flexible terms than they did to white borrowers with similar credit scores and income levels.

While the "small time" faith predator woos with scripture and fake ethnic solidarity, the multinational faith predator seduces with byzantine contractual terms. The small time faith predator's slimy hold over poor black folk exemplifies the historic symptoms of black economic underdevelopment—the ubiquity of religious dogma, the vise of the criminal justice system, and the intractability of residential segregation. In this regard, it is impossible to interrogate African American religiosity without an assessment of blacks' relation to capital, for which Marxist analysis is instructive. In Marx's view, social investment in the God concept is an inevitable stage, a symptom of "alienated" labor and inverted consciousness. Commodity capitalism alienates labor and dispossesses workers of their inner life, such that the more "man puts into God, the less he retains in himself." Institutionalized residential segregation, employment discrimination, over-incarceration, and educational inequities have made African Americans one of the most economically alienated communities in the U.S. This has produced a paradox. African Americans have even less social mobility, less access to the so-called American dream, now than during the Jim Crow era.[24] And in many urban black and Latino communities, capitalism has united the faith industry and foreclosure. While viable retail and commercial businesses languish and die on the vine storefront churches proliferate. While living wage job opportunities in the inner city evaporated during the post Cold War era, property tax exemptions bolstered an urban megachurch development boom right in the middle of some of the poorest communities in black America.

Believers commonly justify organized religion's dominance by pointing to the institutionalization of faith-based charitable giving and resource development in poor communities. In service to the "greater good," churches do what the government cannot or will not do. Operating from that premise, in 2000 the Bush Administration established the faith-based initiative program. Faith based initiatives allowed church denominations and other religious entities to get federal funding to develop "community-based" programming with little government oversight or accountability.

Commenting on the legacy of Bush's faith-based policy, the Reverend Barry Lynn of Americans United for Separation of Church and State said, "I think this is truly one of the most corrupted and useless programs in modern presidential history…It (has) became so totally politicized, utterly nontransparent—nobody to this day knows where most of the money went —and turned out to be kind of the 21st-century equivalent of walking-around money doled out for political purposes to groups which frequently had no record of success at all."[25] A good share of that politicized funding was aimed at African American churches to attract more black voters. Initial jockeying to develop the faith-based program as public policy relied heavily on the advocacy of former African American Republican congressman J.C. Watts of Oklahoma. On his website, Watts describes himself as "the author" of the faith-based initiatives policy. As the nation's only black Republican congressman, Watts was frequently cast in the role of the GOP's go-to guy on "race." He was recruited by George W. Bush to use faith-based initiatives to bring more African Americans into the Republican Party.[26] Initially uncomfortable with his status as the GOP's "black spokesperson," Watts promoted Bush's faith-based agenda with a vengeance.[27] His influence on shaping early faith-based legislation and shepherding it through Congress was critical to its passage.[28] While Bush's faith-based scheme motivated some black pastors to throw their weight behind the GOP, its appeal was undermined by liberal opposition. Suspicious of the administration's motives, and disturbed by the specter of religious discrimination posed by faith-based initiatives, Democratic legislators banded together to block the legislation's passage.

The structure of faith-based initiatives, which encourage charitable giving and community development only within the dictates of a given denomination, is utterly capitalist in effect. They were primarily designed to privatize social welfare programs and legitimize the influence of Christian denominations over public policy. As a result, faith-based initiatives have been widely criticized by civil libertarians and others for undermining the separation of church and state.[29] Undeterred, the Obama administration continued the policy. Obama's failure to discontinue Bush's policy allowing faith-based organizations to discriminate against those who don't share their religious beliefs indicates the Christian right's influence. According to Max Blumenthal, Obama's attempt to court evangelicals in the 2008 presidential campaign was a largely futile gesture intended to make up for lost Democratic political ground among the faithful. His endorsement of the most objectionable aspects of the faith-based initiative policy is undoubtedly a sop to religious communities who fear they'd be shut out from a White House smeared as secular and "socialist" by right wing propagandists. Obama is part of a long line of black politicians who descend on the pulpit for an instant infusion of uncritical black support. For many African Americans seeking political office, the Black Church is the first and last stop, a no-brainer guaranteed to establish "race cred".

The support and visibility provided by the most prominent Black churches can make or break a candidate. Obama's aforementioned alignment with and subsequent denunciation of the Reverend Jeremiah Wright is a notorious example. His political fortunes were greatly enhanced by his association with Wright's church and all of the influential community players Wright provided access to. Without Wright's career endorsement, Obama's inroads into Chicago's Southside community might not have been as deep. Obama's early visibility as a devout Christian was also critical to his appeal among African American voters. Openly secular black politicians are as common as Halley's Comet. Hence, Obama's membership in Wright's church lent him credibility and instant political capital in a climate already biased towards religiously aligned politicians. His subsequent rebuke of Wright over racially controversial comments he'd made years before was a politically expedient move to allay the anxieties of white voters.

Ever sensitive to the Christian Right's influence over the American electorate, Obama has not only openly courted evangelicals but has consistently made reference to his faith in public addresses. Appeals to faith provide politicians with a ginned up connection to a substantial portion of the American electorate. Christian religious faith equals morality, statesmanship, and character. The oft-cited poll noting Americans' aversion to atheists (atheists are believed to be lacking morals by a substantial number of Americans and are therefore unelectable to national office) is a "hidden" advantage conferred on those who "drape" themselves in religion. For African American politicians in urban black communities, this advantage is gold plated. Assessing the unholy alliance of black "prosperity gospel" preachers with centrist black politicians, Black Agenda Report writer Bruce Dixon noted that the lure of government funding through the faith-based initiative pipeline had even motivated some prominent preachers to lend their support to the Republican Party. According to Dixon:

> A new generation of corporate-funded and media-anointed Black leaders, among them a fair number of Republican leaning preachers grown fat on their "faith based" federal subsidies has been raised up. They are decisively uncoupling themselves from the progressive tradition of previous African American leadership, and from the Black Consensus itself. If this new wave of African American leaders have their way, the politics of Black America will soon ape the undemocratic and bigoted worst of white America.[30]

Dixon's article critiques the involvement of black preachers in the race for former Georgia Congresswoman Cynthia McKinney's seat. McKinney was succeeded in 2006 by Hank Johnson, an African American Buddhist. Repelled by Johnson's unorthodox religious affiliation, some black preachers in Georgia lobbied for the candidacy of Vernon Jones, a conservative Democrat who publicly flirted with switching to the Republican Party.[31] Jones received substantial contributions from the now notorious Bishop Eddie Long, the Atlanta-based professional homophobe preacher who has weathered high profile gay sex abuse allegations and a federal financial impropriety investigation through God's grace.[32]

The Jones' case was just one example of political power brokering by powerful black religious interests. The battle over Proposition 8 in California during the 2008 election season exemplified the influence of religiosity on black voting patterns. Similarly, black religiosity has played a role in the political framing of abortion rights. African Americans' long-standing allegiance to the Democratic Party has led to the assumption that blacks are unwaveringly pro-choice. However, there is tension between public support for choice among black voters and deeply held antiabortion sentiments. A 2006 Zogby International poll showed an increase in anti-choice views among African Americans. Black anti-choice factions have gained greater visibility in the national arena in such influential far right media as Fox News. Internet searches for information on abortion and African Americans yield more references to "black genocide" than to pro-choice African American views. For example, a series of antiabortion billboards were placed in Atlanta warning African Americans about a Planned Parenthood engineered "conspiracy" to target black women for abortions.[33] Indeed, until very recently, mainstream black civil rights' leadership has been largely silent on safeguarding legal abortion access and reproductive justice. The emergence of the Religious Coalition for Reproductive Choice (RCRC) has attempted to address that disparity. The group was formed in 1993 as an offshoot of several efforts by progressive faith-based organizations that had been involved in pro-choice advocacy. Although less high profile than the slew of black anti-abortion advocates that has cropped up over the past two decades, the RCRC has actively organized against anti-abortion and anti-choice initiatives on the state and national level. It has also spearheaded a convocation series called Faithful Witnesses for Choice.

The overwhelming religiosity of African Americans, coupled with the political ascent of the Religious Right, has made religious nationalist abortion foes the default "authentic" voice of black America. Some African Americans are particularly susceptible to antiabortion propaganda because of the patriarchal orientation of the Black church. The equation of black liberation with the uplift of black men and the traditional black family strongly influences bias against abortion. The association of abortion with racist classist sterilization policies of the early twentieth century is another key factor. Further, the unfortunate perception that reproductive rights are a "white" female issue is also to blame. Because of these factors, it is virtually impossible to have an honest discussion about the role abortion plays in the crisis of unwanted births in black communities. In California, where African American children are over-represented in the foster care system, unplanned pregnancies and the mounting crisis of parents ill-equipped to provide for their children undermine the sustainability of black communities. This climate fuels black nationalist and religious propaganda equating abortion with genocide.

Religious conservatives' efforts to roll back women's humans rights have led to the creation of more so-called "crisis pregnancy centers" with no medically licensed professionals than reproductive health centers with medically licensed professionals. Christian activism has undoubtedly led to the gradual shift of national sentiment from pro-choice to anti-abortion.[34]

Although pro-choice and generally "rationalist" on church/state separation issues, Obama has demonstrated his susceptibility to Religious Right hysteria. During the campaign, his pandering to the far right was evident in his attempt to retract a statement he made critiquing Middle American provincialism. Explaining these tendencies during a 2008 campaign appearance in San Francisco's affluent Marin County he said:

> You go into some of these small towns in Pennsylvania, and like a lot of small towns in the Midwest, the jobs have been gone now for 25 years and nothing's replaced them and they [working class voters] fell through the Clinton Administration, and the Bush Administration, and each successive administration has said that somehow these communities are gonna regenerate and they have not. And it's not surprising then they get bitter, they cling to guns or religion or antipathy to people who aren't like them or anti-immigrant sentiment or anti-trade sentiment as a way to explain their frustrations.

The comment touched off a firestorm among pundits about Obama's alleged condescension to (white) working class voters. Race was a towering subtext of his comments because of the presumption that working class voters actually denotes "white" voters. Whereas religious working class African Americans and Latinos are not associated with the NRA lobby in the public mind, white Americans are. Hence, Obama's comments were deemed inflammatory because authentically "white" social interests and values were ostensibly under attack.

The "embittered" working class is the very segment of the electorate that Democrats have historically been accused of neglecting in their "disproportionate" emphasis on serving the needs of minorities. Ever since Richard Nixon's Southern Strategy drained blue collar white support from the Democratic Party, every Democratic campaign has tried desperately to devise a magic bullet formula to "win" back this key constituency. Consequently, Obama's cultivation of Rick Warren and other segments of the Religious Right was partly designed to demonstrate that his administration would not abandon this important constituency. Yet, for African Americans, an emphasis upon religious commitment to so-called traditional family values (as promulgated by the right) is also shorthand for affirming one's American-ness. Early in his campaign, Obama demonstrated his willingness to deal in the moralistic code of traditional family values by slamming African American males for their "failure" to accept responsibility for out-of-wedlock pregnancies, criminal behavior, and poor academic performance. Studiously avoiding critique of institutional racism and classism, Obama's "personal responsibility" rhetoric endeared him to disgruntled white voters terrified that he would morph into an Al Sharpton or Jesse Jackson. By trumpeting traditional family values (for blacks), accommodating faith-based special interests, and peppering his speeches with religious references, Obama has frequently used culture war rhetoric to move farther to the right.

When Obama convened a group of secular activists at the White House in the spring of 2010 to discuss a secular agenda, some were hopeful that a new leaf had been turned over. As commentator James Croft wrote in the *New Humanist* blog, "It has taken until 2010 for the White House to officially meet with representatives of the nonreligious in this country. This has *never happened before*. Of course, briefings with representatives of various religious communities have been going on for a very long time. This, in a country that is explicitly secular in its foundation."[35] Coordinated by the Secular Coalition of America, the agenda included making faith-based initiatives conform to secular principles, protecting children from religion related "abuse and neglect," and cracking down on proselytizing in the military. It remains to be seen whether this meeting will engender a tangible shift in the White House's bias toward religious political advocacy and special interests. It also remains to be seen whether the secular coalition will be broadened to encompass communities of color, which have been steeped in decidedly anti-democratic religious partisanship like opposition to same-sex marriage and the growth of prison-ministry proselytizing.

Prison faith-based programs have come under fire from secular lobbyists who charge that they violate the separation of church and state. Yet they serve a more insidious purpose in providing faith-based "entrepreneurs" with a literally captive audience and a breeding ground for religious intolerance. According to Dan Mears of Florida State University, "Despite the call for evidence-based programs and policies instead of belief-and emotion-driven ones, current faith-based prisoner reentry programs don't remotely constitute evidence-based practice."[36] The claim that these programs reduce recidivism is also questionable. One study determined that faith-based prison programs worked primarily with non-violent offenders rather than the more inveterate criminals that such programs would presumably be geared toward rehabilitating.[37] Because these ministries are based on an evangelical Christian model of individual uplift and "rehabilitation through conversion" there is little emphasis on actual prison reform. Exhibit A in the sham of faith-based prison programs is Chuck Colson's Prison Fellowship Ministries. A Watergate ex-convict and Christian evangelical, Colson has established a well-funded network of faith-based prison programs. These programs have been a primary beneficiary of Bush's faith-based legacy. Colson's focus on "biblical education" and "biblical programming" has come under fire from organizations such as Americans United for the Separation of Church and State for constitutional violations.

The popularity of these programs, and their proliferation within the prison industry, can be credited in part to the faith-based climate spawned by George W. Bush. In a 2008 address, Bush famously encapsulated his approach to the faith-based philosophy with a folksy reference to his own struggles with alcohol abuse:

> My philosophy is, find somebody who hurts and do something about it," he said. "Don't wait for government to tell you what to do." He bluntly talked about his own situation. "I was beginning to love alcohol over my wife and kids. It got to a point when Billy Graham came into my life. But I was hardheaded and didn't want to listen for a while. And then I stopped drinking overnight. I am a one-man faith-based initiative. Alcohol was competing for my affections. And it would have ruined me."[38]

To hear Bush tell it, "Government cannot put hope in people's hearts or a sense of purpose in people's lives. That happens when someone puts an arm around a neighbor and says, 'God loves you.'"[39] At nearly half of the prison population, African Americans are disproportionately targeted for rehabilitation by these programs. However, prison ministries appear to do little to deter convicts from re-offending. On its website, the National Baptist Convention Prison Ministry and Criminal Justice Commission describes their mission as "bring(ing) persons into meaningful and right relationship with God by belief and faith in the Lord Jesus Christ through preaching, teaching and healing." As the largest African American Baptist convention and the second largest Baptist organization in the U.S., the National Baptist Convention is an influential player in both the religious and political landscape of Black America. The organization has several prison ministries and mentoring programs for families of prisoners. Over the past several years, it has generated controversy with financial impropriety scandals and conflicts over direction and mission.[40] As of this writing, there have been no longitudinal studies on the outcomes of this particular ministry.[41]

Prison ministries led by conservative church groups also reinforce the prevalence of homophobia and heterosexism in African American communities. Religious bigotry toward gays and lesbians--and Christian emphasis on patriarchal "traditional family values" belief systems-- promote these views. Men who come out of the system steeped in traditional Christian rhetoric are merely primed to cleave to homophobic, heterosexist, and misogynist views endorsing female submission and rigid masculine roles. Moreover, there is a divide between prison ministries that promote actual prison reform and those that emphasize the more conservative theme of personal redemption and uplift. Certainly the fundamentalist evangelical bent of most ministries ensures that the status quo of revolving door black and Latino incarceration is not seriously challenged. At the end of the day, racist sentencing guidelines, biased courts, and non-existent reentry programs are not the concern of multi-million dollar empires like Colson's.

Like faith-based initiatives, these "rehabilitative" enterprises exemplify a capitalist labor regime. Faith-based institutions receive government welfare subsidies as profit making private enterprises. Because African American communities have such an egregious pattern of mass incarceration, the lack of evidence-based research supporting the effectiveness of these programs has far-reaching implications. As the Obama administration sorts through the thicket of faith-based policy, there must be a reassessment of the government's stance on these initiatives. Clearly, Bush's reliance upon faith-based initiatives as a proxy for public social welfare programs is a recipe for unethical conduct and religious discrimination. To address these improprieties, some have suggested that faith-based organizations adhere to the same requirements as nonprofits by applying for 501c3 status. Although this would be a worthy change, the dominance of faith-based strategies in socioeconomically depressed communities of color in particular is still in question.

Prayer Cult Nation

Perhaps nowhere has Marx's adage that religion is the "opiate" of the people been more apt than in the United States, where prayer is a national pastime and obsession. African Americans in particular use prayer as their primary means of healing and emotional therapy.[42] On a popular Black Entertainment Television talk show, R&B singer Monica pitched her new reality show and extolled the virtues of prayer. Suited up in hip-high boots like an emissary from God's army, she credited God with guiding her through life and imbuing her with purpose. His word was her marching order, she proclaimed, as the rapt studio audience nodded in approval, giving credence to Pew Research Center surveys that indicate African Americans are more likely to subscribe to Creationism and more apt to consult the Bible for guidance and counsel than any other group in the U.S.

Yet not since the Great Awakening of the 18th Century has "God" so unequivocally spoken through so many American public figures. The medievalist Sarah Palin has risen to cult status touting her personal speed dial to the Lord. The Old Testament God has become the kamikaze co-pilot of the Republican Party. And President Obama, in his role as faith "bipartisan-in-chief," frequently invokes both God as an adjudicating figure and prayer as an antidote to tragedies like war casualties, natural disasters and the deaths of prominent national figures.

Prayer has become the national bromide for suffering. If it can't be sanitized, domesticated and defanged by prayer, then it isn't worth experiencing. Prayer has increasingly wormed its way into the most mundane of American moments. Prayer or "moments of silence" have become more commonplace during local government meetings and at schools, social functions and games. African American community gatherings (religious or secular) are often punctuated with a prayer. An AOL poll surveying site users about a Southern school's decision to post a message to God at a football game received overwhelming support. In December 2010, Los Angeles gang prevention organizers kicked off a month-long citywide "prayer-a-thon" with local churches as a "strategy" to reduce homicides.

As more and more Americans shrug in apathy at the leaky wall separating church and state, those who abstain from or question mass spiritual entreaties are viewed as curmudgeon naysayers at best and un-American public enemies at worst. The explosion of public prayer—exemplified by the near manic drive to enshrine the most simple of pursuits with Godly sanction—bespeaks some deep-seated crisis of American selfhood that afflicts all classes and ethnicities. In his book *American Fascists*, Chris Hedges details Trinity Broadcasting Network's (TBN) "prayer warrior" phenomenon.[43] TBN is the global media outlet created by superstar televangelists Paul and Jan Crouch. TBN telethons are staffed by prayer warriors who provide spiritual guidance and, of course, financial stewardship for troubled souls ready to part with their credit cards. Beleaguered Americans can tap into prayer networks, avail themselves of prayer rooms, and even decamp to a World

Prayer Center (developed by disgraced Colorado evangelical Pastor Ted Haggard) if they are so inclined.[44]

The prayer cult phenomenon was further exemplified by the insertion of a prayer healing provision into the 2009 health care reform overhaul bill. In the midst of the healthcare deliberations, prayer healing "therapy" was proposed as a legitimate form of government subsidized medical treatment. In the early stages of the deliberations, this obscure provision authorized coverage for Christian Science prayer as a medical expense. The provision was sponsored by Senator Orrin Hatch, ultra-conservative lawmaker from Utah and Senator John Kerry, former Democratic presidential candidate of Massachusetts. This strange bedfellow pairing was part ideology and part political expedience. Hatch is a notorious Mormon ideologue and the Christian Science Church is based in Kerry's state.[45] The decision to include prayer healing in the Senate healthcare bill was naturally attacked by separation of church and state advocates such as the Freedom from Religion Foundation.[46] Currently, the IRS does allow itemized deductions for faith healing treatments.[47] However, managed care insurers reject faith healing and other "alternative" therapies such as acupuncture that are not supported by research-based evidence.

According to the Christian Science Church, a faith healing internship takes the form of an "'intensive' two-week class instruction in Christian Science healing" after which practitioners "may take patients." Treatment "may rely on passages of the Bible…or may simply be a period of silent communion. There is no formula and 'treatment' can be given in absentia by telephone or email." Since Christian Science practitioners can hang up their virtual shingles after a two-week crash course, why can't apostles of Frodo or oracles of Pan be similarly credentialed? Ethnocentric bias has apparently banished Pentecostal snakes, Santeria chants, Wiccan spells, and animist rituals from consideration as insurable faith treatments. The Senate provision would have opened the gate to all manner of medically dangerous, clinically unproven treatments. Due to opposition from then House Speaker Nancy Pelosi and others contesting the provision's constitutionality, it was omitted from the final Senate and House health reform bills.

Public embrace of prayer as transcendent antidote to social problems is perhaps symptomatic of a general decline in civic and community engagement, a thesis that has been posited by several scholars over the past decade.[48] The Bush administration's elevation of faith-based approaches, coupled with the rightward drift of mainstream America, has privileged more insular approaches to collective engagement. Indeed, the overall conservatism of the American political climate has hindered left-progressive organizing among churches and faith-based institutions. In its place, American first world "democracy" has nourished a criminal Religious Right insurgency against abortion, same sex marriage, and evolution.

As I have argued in previous chapters, individual social responsibility and uplift have largely replaced mass movement organizing and coalition building for many high profile black churches. In his article "The Black Church is Dead," Eddie Glaude, Professor of Religion and director of Princeton's Center for African American Studies contends, "We have witnessed the routinization of black prophetic witness... in each instance, a backward glance defines the content of the church's stance in the present—justifying its continued relevance and authorizing its voice...because it has become alienated from the moment in which it lives."[49] In response to Glaude's article, Ronald Neal writes:

> The common ground that black Christians share with conservative Protestants outside of black America can be seen in the eye opening and mind boggling cross-racial alliances that have been forged over the last decade or so, between theologically conservative black and white Christians. One only has to follow the trails of highly popular and conservative clergy such as T.D. Jakes, Creflo A. Dollar, Eddie L. Long, and a whole host of other men and women, and they will lead to the churches, offices, and homes of the most theologically conservative white men in America: Dr. James Dobson, Pat Robertson, Ted Haggard, John Ashcroft, Billy Graham, George W. Bush, et al. These alliances between black and white Christians, wedded by shared Christian orientations, confound the prophetic and progressive view of the Black Church. And they speak volumes about why prophetic religion and progressive politics do not characterize the language and ethos of the Black Church today.[50]

Neal's comment highlights the degree to which the Religious Right has influenced the politics of religion in African American communities. Indeed, Glaude stresses that conventional wisdom about the progressiveness of the Black Church belies the "complicated" reality of conservative traditions within black Christian denominations.[51] As aforementioned, ideological differences between the National Baptist Convention and progressive black pastors aligned with Martin Luther King Jr. led to the formation of the Progressive Baptist Convention. Hugely popular early twentieth century pastors such as Detroit's Prophet Jones (who lived in a mansion, preached from a throne in his movie palace church, and owned several tricked out Cadillacs) and Chicago's Reverend Ike were foppish predecessors to today's black prosperity gospel practitioners. For Jonathan Walton, "nostalgic" preoccupation with the progressive orientation of the Black Church is destructive. The Black Church will cease to be relevant, he says, "Unless Afro-Protestants become less consumed with building institutions characterized by tribal racial insularity, autocratic cult of personalities [sic] and/or idolatrous inward-oriented, henotheistic theologies."[52]

Twenty first century shifts in the political and cultural complexion of African American communities will continue to test the relevance of the Black Church. The increase of non-believing African Americans, unaffiliated with and in some instances strongly critical of the Black Church (and organized religion in general), is a small but growing trend. Building on a robust history of secular humanist belief amongst black activist-intellectuals, atheist, agnostic, and skeptical African Americans pose an emergent challenge to the received wisdom of the Black Church and its teetering empires.

Endnotes

1. Karen Brodkin Sacks, "How Jews Became White," from Steven Gregory and Roger Sanjek, eds. *Race* (New Brunswick, NJ: Rutgers University Press, 1994), 78-102.
2. Like the Los Angeles civil unrest of 1991, the Watts rebellion has been dubbed a riot, an uprising, and a disturbance, depending upon political outlook and affinity.
3. I will discuss the racial dynamics of the FHA in greater detail in Chapter Six.
4. For example, white landlords and homeowners' associations routinely discriminated against black homebuyers and renters through and engaged in blockbusting to dislocate new black residents.
5. Melvin Oliver and Thomas Shapiro, *Black Wealth, White Wealth: A New Perspective on Racial Equality* (New York: Routledge, 2006), 17.
6. African Americans in Los Angeles are disproportionately concentrated in South Los Angeles. Although the region as a whole is predominantly Latino, African Americans are the most highly segregated racial group in Los Angeles County. "Three times more blacks live in L.A. than in the County overall." See, *State of South Los Angeles* (UCLA, School of Public Affairs, 2008), 5.
7. On a personal note, I and other un-churched black female acquaintances are routinely asked what church we belong to.
8. Ofelia Casillas and Margaret Ramirez, "North Lawndale Churches, Are They Causing More Harm Than Good?" *Chicago Tribune*, May 17, 2009 (http://articles.chicagotribune.com/2009-05-17/news/0905160012_1_storefront-churches-dozen-pastors-entities).
9. Ibid.
10. Christopher Winship, "Maintaining Legitimacy: Church-Based Criticism as a Force for Change," *Sacred Places, Civic Purposes: Should Government Help with Faith-Based Charity?* eds. E.J. Dionne and Ming Hsu Chen (Washington D.C.: Brookings Institution, 2001), p. *96*; Omar McRoberts, *Streets of Glory: Church and Community in a Black Urban Neighborhood* (Chicago: University of Chicago Press, 2005), 57-59.
11. McRoberts, p. 57.

12. "City Council Considers Limit on Downtown Storefront Churches, Times Daily.com, November 23, 2009; Bill Smith, "City Eyes Limit on Churches," *Evanston Now*, October 25, 2010 (http://evanstonnow.com/story/news/bill-smith/2010-10-25/city-eyes-limits-on-churches).
13. Ibid.
14. Martin Kuz, "That is What God Deserves: $60 Million Cathedral Opens Today," *Los Angeles Daily News,* April 28, 2001.
15. Ibid. "The evidence is everywhere. Businesses - from pizza shops to hair salons and gas stations - blanket the boulevard, where land now sells for $50 a square foot. Several business owners have told Blake that the church's presence persuaded them to set up shop." It should be noted that pizza shops and hair salons don't drive major revenue streams or the development of living wage jobs.
16. Patrick Kerkstra, "Home Improvement: Church Celebrates $50 Million Expansion of Sanctuary," *L.A. Times,* June 29, 1998 (http://articles.latimes.com/1998/jun/29/local/me-64700).
17. "Black Congregation Buys the Forum in California, Making Structure One of the Largest Churches in the U.S."*Jet Magazine*, April 16, 2001, 16-18.
18. Anthony Pinn, *By These Hands: A Documentary History of African American Humanism, 90.*
19. I will explore this further in subsequent chapters.
20. Grace Wyler, "Believers in the Pews—and the Polling Booths," *Newsweek Magazine*, June 23, 2008 (http://www.newsweek.com/2008/06/22/believers-in-the-pews-and-the-polling-booth.html).
21. Stuart Pfeifer, "Man Accused of Fraud May Get Life in Prison under California's Three Strikes Law," *L.A. Times*, September 1, 2010 (http://articles.latimes.com/2010/sep/01/business/la-fi-three-strikes-20100902).
22. Debbie Gruenstein Bocian, Peter Smith et al., "Dreams Deferred: Impacts and Characteristics of the California Foreclosure Crisis," *Center for Responsible* Lending, August 2010; See also, Bocian, Wei Lei, et al. "Foreclosures by Race and Ethnicity," *Center for Responsible Lending*, June 18, 2010, 4-6.
23. Ibid.
24. The income gap between blacks and whites have increased since the end of legal segregation. Younger blacks have less mobility than their parents. See Julia Isaacs, "Economic Mobility of Black and White Families," *The Brookings Institute*, November 2007 (http://www.brookings.edu/papers/2007/11_blackwhite_isaacs.aspx). Blacks also have significantly

less accumulated family wealth than whites. Dalton Conley, *Being Black, Living in the Red: Race, Wealth, and Social Policy in America*, (Berkeley: University of California Press, 1999).

25. Adelle M. Banks, "Faith-based Programs to Help Shape Bush Legacy," *USA Today*, January 13, 2009, (http://www.usatoday.com/news/religion/2009-01-13-bush-faith-based_N.htm).
26. Amy E. Black, Douglas L. Koopman and David K. Ryden, *Of Little Faith: The Politics of George W. Bush's Faith- Based Initiatives* (Washington, DC: Georgetown University Press, 2004), p. 3.
27. Ibid.
28. Ibid.
29. For commentary on the way this has played out in the larger sphere of black politics and social welfare see Bruce Dixon, "Top Ten Reasons Why Black Leaders Are Ignoring Obama's Good Cop Bad Cop Attack on Social Security," *Black Agenda Report,* November 18, 2010 (http://www.blackagendareport.com/?q=content/top-ten-reasons-why-black-leaders-are-ignoring-president-obamas-good-cop-bad-cop-attack-soci).
30. Bruce Dixon, "The Black Church and the Hollowing out of Black Politics," *Black Agenda Report*, January 16, 2008 (http://www.hartford-hwp.com/archives/45a/723.html).
31. Ibid.
32. The probe was launched by Republican Senator Charles Grassley and targeted six prosperity gospel televangelists for alleged violations of non-profit reporting requirements and excessive income.
33. These ads have been funded by groups connected to the Georgia Right to Life organization.
34. 51% of Americans characterize themselves as "pro-life" versus 42% who characterize themselves as "pro-choice." See "More Americans Pro-Life than Pro-Choice for the First Time," *Gallup Poll,* 2009, (http://www.gallup.com/poll/118399/more-americans-pro-life-than-pro-choice-first-time.aspx).
35. James Croft, "A White House Briefing for the Non-Religious Community," *The New Humanist Blog*, February 27, 2010 (http://thenewhumanism.wordpress.com/2010/02/27/a-white-house-briefing-for-the-nonreligious-community).
36. Dan Mears, "Faith-based efforts to improve prisoner reentry: Assessing the logic and evidence," *Journal of Criminal Justice, Volume 34 Issue 4, July-August 2006, pp. 351-367.*

37. A 1987 study of Prison Fellowship Ministries found that, overall, the likelihood of re-arrest after one year was the same for PFM participants as for non-participants. The Polis Center, "Responsive Communities" (http://www.polis.iupui.edu/ruc/printable/140.asp.).
38. Matt Larimer, *Speechless Tales of a White House Survivor* (New York: Random House, 2004), p. 209.
39. Lawrence Jablecki, "A Critique of Faith Based Prison Programs," *The Humanist*, Sept. 1, 2005, p.3.
40. During his tenure with the organization in the 1990s, NBC president Henry Lyons was sentenced to jail for graft and corruption. Disgruntled with the conservatism of the NBC, a breakaway group called the Progressive National Baptist Convention was formed in the 1960s to focus on the social justice and activist orientation of MLK. The PNBC is one of the few Baptist institutions that ordains women.
41. According to email correspondence with Sikivu Hutchinson from Kenneth E. Hollins, Chairman, Commission on Jail and Criminal Justice for the National Baptist Convention.
42. Michelle D. Mitchell, Gabrielle L. Hargrove, et al. "Coping Variables That Mediate the Relation Between Intimate Partner Violence and Mental Health Outcomes Among Low-Income, African American Women," Journal of Clinical Psychology, Vol. 62(12), 2006, pp. 1-18;" Prayer is Key Stress Reliever for Black Women," *Emerging Majorities Magazine*, December 2004.
43. Hedges, *American Fascists*, 177-8.
44. Jeff Sharlet describes the World Prayer Center in *The Family: The Secret Fundamentalism at the Heart of American Power* (New York: Harper Perennial, 2008), 301.
45. Despite high profile cases in which Christian Science adherents have been convicted for using prayer healing to "treat" their terminally ill children in lieu of medical treatment, the Senate healthcare provision would have effectively sanctioned this practice.
46. Tom Hamburger and Kim Geiger, "Healthcare Provision Seeks to Embrace Prayer Treatments," *L.A. Times*, November 3, 2009.
47. Ibid.
48. See for example Robert Putnam, *Bowling Alone: the Collapse and Revival of American Community,* New York: Simon and Schuster, 2000. Also, "Trends in Civic Association Activity in Four Democracies: The Special Case of Women in the United States" Robert Andersen, Edward Grabb

and James Curtis, *American Sociological Review*, 71: 376-400 2006. The former concluded that Americans have significantly decreased their engagement with community, civic and political groups, while the latter concluded that this was primarily true for working women.

49. Eddie Glaude, Jr. "The Black Church is Dead," *Huffington Post*, February 24, 2010 (http://www.huffingtonpost.com/eddie-glaude-jr-phd/the-black-church-is-dead_b_473815.html).

50. Ronald Neal, "RIP The Myth of the Black Church is Dead," *Religion Dispatches,* March 9, 2010 (http://www.religiondispatches.org/archive/atheologies/2331/updated_with_response%3A_the_black_church_is_dead%E2%80%94long_live_the_black_church).

51. Glaude, p. 1.

52. Jonathan Walton, "The Black Church Ain't Dead! (But Maybe it Should Be)," *Religion Dispatches*, March 9, 2010 (http://www.religiondispatches.org/archive/atheologies/2331/updated_with_response%3A_the_black_church_is_dead%E2%80%94long_live_the_black_church).

Chapter 4

Black Infidels: Secular Humanism and African American Social Thought

It is not too much to say that whoever wishes to become a truly moral human being...must first divorce himself from all the prohibitions, crimes, and hypocrisies of the Christian church. If the concept of God has any validity or any use, it can only be to make us larger, freer, and more loving. If God cannot do this, then it is time we got rid of Him.

—James Baldwin, *The Fire Next Time*

Saturday afternoon, like clockwork, the street corner preachers on Crenshaw and King Boulevard in South Los Angeles take to the stage. Decked out in flowing robes and dreadlocks, they fulminate into their mikes about the universe, God's will, and unnatural homosexuals to a motley audience of drivers and passengers waiting for the next express bus. Members of the Black Israelites, they are part of a long tradition of "prophetic witness" and performative religiosity in urban African American communities. This particular corner of black America is a hotbed of social commerce. Kids who've just gotten out of school mingle jubilantly as pedestrians flow past fast food places, mom and pop retailers, street vendors and Jehovah's Witness' hawking *Watchtower* magazines. The Israelites have become an enduring part of this shifting tableaux. Exclusively male and virulently sexist and homophobic in their rhetoric, they are tolerated in many African American communities, in part because of the visceral appeal of Black nationalism. In addition to articulating a vision of religious zealotry, the Israelites are also performing a caricature of black masculinity, one which links the "scourge" of homosexuality and fallen women to the destruction of the black family.

In previous chapters, I've argued that organized religion, specifically Christianity, has functioned as a gender defining mechanism for African Americans. The legacies of slavery, the Enlightenment, and scientific racism have racialized gender, such that Western notions of masculinity and femininity pivot on hierarchies of race. Forged in Enlightenment ideology, "New World" notions of civilized sovereign white manhood and idealized white womanhood were predicated on the antipode of the dark savage Other. Hence, African Americans utilized Christianity to disrupt this regime. Christianity enabled African Americans to stake a claim to being human and to being American. It provided ontological meaning and context to the Holocaust of African slavery. And it also prescribed a rigid hierarchy of masculinity and femininity based on heterosexist norms. These norms aligned African Americans with European ideals of family and domesticity. Despite centuries of racial apartheid, African Americans have struggled to achieve these ideals.

It is precisely because of these regimes of power that non-theism and secular humanism are problematic for mainstream African Americans. While there is tolerance for the very public bigotry of the Black Israelites, African Americans collectively view atheism and atheists as distasteful (according to the 2006 article "The Atheist as Other," African Americans have some of the most negative views of atheists among all groups.)[1] Performer Steve Harvey's charge that atheists have no morals underscored how much atheism is associated with otherness and deviance. In a racist culture, the otherness and deviance associated with atheism is at odds with the elusive quest for assimilation. Granted there have been few politically prominent African American atheists to provide cultural context and validation for black non-belief. However, aversion to secular humanism devalues the humanist legacy of African American social thought.

A belief system that encompasses atheist, agnostic, freethinking, and skeptical world views, secular humanism holds that humankind ultimately rises or falls on its own. Instead of demanding moral obedience to deities and supernatural forces, secular humanism frames morality in terms of principles of justice, fairness, and equality. Reason and the scientific method are the most viable ways of understanding the natural world. The afterlife is a fiction concocted by human beings to assuage fear of death and the unknown. And the dogmas and "moving goal posts" of many organized religions (i.e., a God or Gods as responsible for both suffering and freedom from suffering) often inhibit the quest for knowledge and respect for human potential.

Radical or progressive humanism is specifically concerned with the liberation struggle of disenfranchised peoples. Organized religion is one of many powerful forces solidifying inequity based on race, gender, class, and sexual orientation. Racism, classism, sexism, and heterosexism are amplified and reinforced by economic injustice institutionalized under global capitalism. Hence, humanism is especially relevant for people of color living in conditions of structural inequality in which the state serves only the human rights of the wealthy.

In his article "Anybody There? Reflections on African American Humanism," Anthony Pinn maintains:

> Humanism... is a way of ordering our world and our lives through giving equal attention to human failure and human potential as the launching platform for more sustained engagement with community and dignity.[2]

For Pinn, the cultural context of black humanist influence is critical. Contrary to the belief that black humanists are alien interlopers derailing the black Jesus train, he stresses that "African Americans who embrace humanism...do not live in isolation. They are able to draw on the wisdom of African American humanists who have come before them...who have embraced this perspective...before it was labeled (as such)."[3]

So, instead of being an abstract trope with no bearing on everyday black experience, humanism is a vital lens for critical consciousness. In contrast to the bigoted dogma of the Black Israelites, the work of Jeffrey "P-funk" Mitchell, public philosopher and You Tube pioneer (he touts having had the first videos on the web addressing atheism), speaks to this legacy. Since 2006, the L.A.-based Mitchell has been documenting his engagement with everyday folk on atheism and faith. Using the handle "Atheist Walking," Mitchell conducts free-ranging philosophical inquiries into Christianity's contradictions with a rolling camera and a satirically raised eyebrow. Often adopting the role of the bemused interlocutor, he delves into "atheist spirituality," biblical literalism, and the paradoxes of faith.

In one of his online videos set at a bus stop, Mitchell comments, "I want people to look at each other with the same reverence that they look at God and realize that 'we' did this, we made this happen." The "we" represents will, agency, and motive force; qualities that many believers attribute to

God as omniscient architect and overseer. "God's plan" or divine providence is then rendered inscrutable. Non-believers are compelled to ask if individual actions (for good or ill) are determined by God, or if human beings simply act on their own volition in a universe overseen by God. Since time immemorial, non-believers have questioned God's control over those who commit evil acts, or wondering whether hell is the only "medium" for justice. By refusing to invest supernatural forces with authorial power over human affairs, humanism emphasizes human responsibility for the outcome of our pursuits. Morality is defined by just deeds, fairness, equality, and respect for difference, not by how fervently one claims to adhere to "Godly" principles.

However, in communities plagued with double digit unemployment and cultural devaluation, self-sufficiency and ultimate human agency may be perceived as demoralizing if not dangerously radical. As a child preacher steeped in the fiery oratory of the Black Church, writer James Baldwin recounted his growing cynicism about spreading "the gospel." Lamenting the grip of religion on poor blacks, Baldwin said, "When I faced a congregation, it began to take all the strength I had not to...tell them to throw away their Bibles and get off their knees and go home and organize."[4] In Baldwin's view, worship saps collective agency. For Baldwin, religiosity is not just a liability but existential surrender. In a nation in which "God decreed" that "white people hold the power," the seeds of religious skepticism come from deconstructing institutional racism and white supremacy. In *The Fire Next Time,* Baldwin reflects on the economic degradation of his Harlem community. Boys and girls coming of age in an apartheid era of limited opportunity could "choose" one of two soul-killing paths: the "Avenue" or the church. Growing up in an ultra devout, God-fearing home with an authoritarian father who "became so holy" because "he believed what white people said about him," Baldwin's default escape hatch was religion.[5] White supremacy demanded that African Americans be complicit in their own negation. A Christian morality based on the theft of black liberty was an integral part of this negation. As a teenage preacher, Baldwin recalls the power he enjoyed in the pulpit, seduced by the emotional and spiritual rapture of being "saved." He vividly details his growing recognition of how corrupt this power was. For, "the fact that I was 'young brother Baldwin' increased my value with those same pimps and racketeers who had helped to stampede me into church in the first place."[6] Circling like vultures over dead flesh, "they were waiting for me to come to my senses and realize what a lucrative business I was in."[7] Being "young brother Baldwin," a hot prodigy in the pulpit, gave him a sense of power and authority, partly freeing him from his washed-up father's tyranny. In this universe he flourished, drunk with bible thumping performance art, courted, admired, and deferred to, given license to act with impunity because of his "holy" status.

Then, he begins to read. Reading is "fatal," for it signaled the "slow crumbling of my faith, the pulverization of my fortress."[8] Reading gives definition to his unrest, shape to the dialectic of the intellectual and the ecstatic raging within. Studying scripture, he begins to understand how his sense of certitude and moral superiority came from the othering of "infidels." Because his Jewish friends weren't "saved", they were destined to burn in hell regardless of the kind of lives they'd led on humble Planet Earth. Because black Christians and the Black Church demanded the same blind emotional servitude as white Christians, they were no better morally. The Black Church could not offer sanctuary nor sustenance, nor genuine charity or fellowship because it ran on fear.

Baldwin experiences a near epiphany about faith's futility in an all night prayer session. Lying in a wretched heap "on the floor":

> ...The saints sang and rejoiced and prayed. And in the morning, when they raised me, they told me I was 'saved.' Well indeed I was, in a way, for I was utterly drained and exhausted, and released, for the first time, from all my guilty torment. I was aware then only of my relief...I could not ask myself why human relief had to be achieved in a fashion at once so pagan and desperate. And by the time I was able to ask this question, I was able to see that the principles governing the rites and customs of the churches in which I grew up did not differ from the principles governing the rites and customs of other churches, white. The principles were Blindness, Loneliness, and Terror, the first principle necessarily and actively cultivated in order to deny the two others.[9]

Baldwin's journey underscores the intimate connection between socioeconomics and faith. Had it not been the "Avenue" or the church, then what? He speaks of men going into the service and returning ruined. He laments college graduates scrubbing floors. He swaggeringly declares that girls became "God's decoys" for boys slouching toward the wreck and ruin of the Avenue.[10] Girls, "single-minded" and duty-bound to making good black men and pleasing Jesus, keep home and hearth in clenched fists. As females, they are both earthbound and heaven-gazing. They must tame, civilize, and domesticate to sustain moral order. They must defer to the raging voice of original sin, knowing that it is their special God decreed lot in life to save the boys from their natural selves.

Baldwin's imagery smacks not just of determinism but the slow grind of enterprise. Faith is redeemer and parasite, codifier of gender norms and symptom of racial apartheid.

So when Baldwin, on the cusp of the bloody 1960s, fantasizes about telling his congregation to throw away their bibles and organize, he presages the era's existential dilemma. If white supremacy is ordained by God, then black liberation cannot be. If all men are *created* equal, then some will by definition be more equal than others, and others will not even be deemed human. Creation signifies an agent, an invisible standard, an implicit hierarchy. The "chosen people" make "God" in their image, not the other way around.

The street corner Israelites' "prophetic" visions of black macho nationhood hinge on this. And Baldwin highlights how organized religion is about competing versions of being chosen. Allegiance to this view of "chosen-ness" makes black liberation struggle impossible. So while activism and faith are not incompatible, blind faith is particularly insidious for black people because of the legacy of Jim Crow.

Much of the debate amongst European and European American religious skeptics and non-believers is fixated on religious cosmology versus science/evolution. However, African American religious skepticism has a broader mandate. Because African Americans have historically been excluded from the very category of the human, they have had to negotiate their relationship to Western notions of being human. The racist backlash to the election of Barack Obama is a stark example. Never has the old racist joke about what a black man with a Ph.D. (or in this instance an Ivy League law degree) is called been so relevant a commentary on white Middle America's psyche. Obama's flogging demonstrated how deep the legacy of African American dehumanization extends, the caricature of King's iconic little white and black kids holding hands up in flames. During the 2008 presidential campaign, right wing groups trotted out images of primitivism, terrorism, and foreignness to cast Obama as a politically dangerous anti-American racial Other. Obama was a bone in the nose savage, a joker in white face going after American freedoms, a turban wearing Muslim, and a watermelon-eating darkie evoking Birth of a Nation grotesques. After his election, these images were a recurring theme in the fear-mongering anti-government rhetoric of such far right factions as the Tea Party. Far from ushering in a new era of "post-racialism," as some political observers claimed, Obama's election was a firm reminder that white terrorism was alive and well. Indeed, the Secret Service reported that assassination plots and other threats to President Obama's life were at a record high. According to the Southern Poverty Law Center, far right paramilitary organizations also increased. The fact that Obama did not win a majority of the white vote underscored the intractability of racial divisions along party lines. Traditional schisms between the heavily "Red State" Republican white South and Midwest and the "Blue State" Northeast and West were minimally disturbed by Obama's victory. So while his election symbolized a quantum leap in *possibility* for racial equity, the narrative of uncomplicated progress that many would like to ascribe to it was undercut by the reality of racism and racial segregation.

It is within the context of over 400 years of liberation struggle that African Americans enter into the discourse of humanism. As I have argued in previous chapters, African Americans adopted European American cultural traditions and practices like Christianity as a means of survival and self-definition. Enlightenment ideology established a racial hierarchy in which Africans were subhuman and African culture was the antithesis of European civilization. Racial slavery was justified because of the alleged mental and spiritual inferiority of Africans, an empirical "fact" institutionalized by the emergent field of scientific observation. Similarly, Judeo-

Christian ideologies of racial hierarchy, in which Africans were perceived to be the so-called Children of Ham (doomed to enslavement because of Ham's sins against Noah), provided a "moral" context for white supremacist justifications of slavery. This complex relationship to the category of the human informed African Americans' embrace of Christianity. To be moral beings with *human* worth and value, African Americans had to identify with and reshape the corrupt ethical universe of the oppressor.

Insofar as the question of what it means to be human was a cornerstone of black liberation struggle—especially as it pertained to the contradictions inherent in Western epistemological formulations of the human—it has always been steeped in humanistic inquiry. Race, as defined by Western science, has been at the center of Euro-American notions of what it means to be human. According to evolutionary biologist Joseph Graves, "Eighteenth century Enlightenment scholars never doubted that God and science declared the existence of races and that there should be hierarchical relations between them. According to this thinking, the European stood at the pinnacle of human perfection and all other races were to be measured against him."[11] In America, the Africanist presence allowed the new white man to explore possibilities of being and becoming sovereign, free, and ultimately, human.

In Europe, the Africanist presence was conjured up in 19th century exhibitions of black bodies, most notably that of the so-called Venus Hottentot, aka Sarah Baartman. Baartman was a South African Khoi woman who was literally paraded all over Europe and displayed as a human artifact/oddity in salons and museums by the European scientific establishment. This was a common practice in an era of heightened Enlightenment exploration of race, racial difference, and sexuality. Like many Africans staged for public exhibition in 19th Century Europe before her, Baartman became an object of scientific investigation. She was poked, prodded, measured, assessed, and ultimately dissected in death by British and French empiricist wizards like the esteemed scientist Georges Cuvier. She was marshaled as resident other to determine the exact nature of her "difference" from "normal" (i.e., white) men and women. This standard only had weight and relevance in the context of Baartman's grotesqueness. Her deformations provided white femininity with its mooring as the standard of feminine beauty. Her sub-humanity gave her white male examiners a biological compass (and canvas) that was then translated into immutable racial difference. The sexual deviance signified by her enormous backside literally functioned as an epistemological frame and cover for her interpreters' own cultural biases and assumptions. In performance, she became the long sought "missing link." Her anatomy affirmed white racial superiority and captured inexplicable gaps in the ascent from "savage" to "civilized." Through the lens of the European male scientist, looking, seeing, and interpreting were transparent enterprises.

Western history's Exhibit A is the white man as impartial, objective, disengaged observer, hovering with the angels. Small wonder then that white Middle America has awoken to Obama—his imperialist policies aside—as its most visceral nightmare. Colonialist practices in which the bodies of African, Asian, and indigenous peoples were used by the scientific establishment to "measure" racial difference and verify social pathology helped advance Western rationalism and empiricism. European scientists typed and classified virtually every inch of the black body in the quest for some immutable marker of racial difference. In his book *The Race Game*, Joseph Graves details how scientists like eugenics pioneer Francis

Galton used psychometry, "the measurement of human intelligence," to validate the theory of black inferiority and white European superiority. African American human rights activist Ida B. Wells, along with Frederick Douglass, criticized the exhibition of "primitive" indigenous peoples and African "savages" in the 1893 Chicago World's fair. The fair was designed to highlight the social, scientific, and technological advances of the U.S. By exalting the U.S.' excellence, these exhibitions illustrated clearly demarcated boundaries between civilized and savage.

Black women's bodies were the proving ground. Caught in the crossfire of science and superstition, black femininity has been critical to defining Western notions of "the human." When the famed abolitionist preacher and activist Sojourner Truth dramatically rolled up her shirt sleeve to show her arm during her historic "Ain't I a Woman" address at the 1851 Women's Rights Convention in Akron, Ohio she was rebuking notions of genteel white womanhood *and* degraded black femininity. Although there is some dispute about her exact words, her declamation, "I have plowed, I have planted and I have gathered into barns. And no man could head me. *And ain't I a woman?*" was a resounding critique of European Christian ideals of cloistered, protected femininity. Truth's challenge was issued to the white male ministers in her audience. Festering with resentment, they violently objected to the blasphemy of women speaking in public. In celebrating her flesh and challenging the gendered division between body and intellect, men's space and women's space, Truth made a *humanist* intervention into the dualities of Western empiricism and Judeo Christian dogma. Truth's abolitionism was informed by a fiery religious world view. Yet her critique of gender inequity laid the foundation for black feminist freethinking analysis of Christianity.

Indeed, it is impossible to fully evaluate the African American civil rights legacy without a consideration of its humanist influences and implications. Although theologians and historians have historically emphasized the influence of organized religion on African American civil rights resistance, Black humanist scholars point to another tradition. Both Norm Allen, Jr. and Anthony Pinn have critiqued the exclusion of humanist influence from appraisals of African American social thought and civil rights resistance. Whilst acknowledging the role of African American Christian ideology in black liberation, these scholars believe the influence of humanist principles of rationalism, social justice, skepticism, and free thought must be foregrounded. Indeed, the absence of evidence for organized religion's truth claims led thinkers like Frederick Douglass, W.E.B DuBois, and A. Philip Randolph to form a secular humanist view of social justice.

Pinn's book *By These Hands: A Documentary History of African American Humanism,* chronicles this intellectual tradition. At an 1870 Anti-Slavery Society convention, Frederick Douglass proclaimed, "I bow to no priests either of faith or of unfaith. I claim as against all sorts of people, simply perfect freedom of thought."[12] Douglass' comments were in response to black preachers' insistence that he "thank" God for Emancipation. His failure to be appropriately devout elicited a firestorm. After his speech, a group of prominent black preachers passed a Resolution censuring him, holding, "That we will not acknowledge any man as a leader of our people who will not thank God for the deliverance and enfranchisement of our race, and will not vote to retain the Bible...in our public schools." This rebuke was perhaps one of the first documented instances of the black "authenticity police" trying to silence an eminent thinker. Generations before the poverty pimps of the prosperity gospel, black Christian carte blanche had already begun to rear its ugly head.

Douglass' standoff with black preachers foreshadowed the combustible politics of questioning the religious establishment. Things invariably got dicey when it came to authentic black leadership. Skeptic leaders like labor activist and Brotherhood of Sleeping Car Porters (BSCP) founder A. Philip Randolph utilized religion to reach the black masses. Although Randolph was widely believed to be an atheist, he understood the appeal religious themes had for a black constituency born and bred on religiosity.[13] Randolph relied on black churches and religious organizations for political outreach and community support. BSCP meetings and forums were frequently held at or supported by local black churches across the nation. Insofar as the BSCP's platform drew on religious themes, Randolph's acknowledgment of and respect for religion can perhaps be viewed as a form of cultural competence. However, throughout his career as publisher and editor of the influential journal the *Messenger*, Randolph provided a platform for vigorous critique of Christianity's role in black liberation struggle. In 1927, the journal sponsored an essay writing contest titled "Is Christianity a Menace to the Negro?"[14] As a socialist and vocal critic of "orthodox" Christianity, Randolph was constantly plagued with accusations of being an infidel. Of course, known infidels couldn't be effective black leaders. According to Cynthia Taylor:

> In the beginning the *Messenger* editors set out to attack all that was 'narrow and medieval in religion,' especially the Negro Church's accommodation to Jim Crow. Randolph himself redirected this counterproductive editorial policy in order to reach out to progressive-minded allies inside and outside the Negro Church. With the demise of radicalism by the 1920s,

> Randolph and other *Messenger* editors nonetheless kept up the debate on 'orthodox' black Christianity by offering religious alternatives to their readers...In this process, Randolph insisted that religious ideas and institutions were not so sacrosanct as to be excluded from democratic debate...In the *Messenger's* last phase...he consciously distanced himself from atheism while still challenging the Negro Church's position.[15]

Taylor also notes that Randolph's distancing from atheism was influenced by anti-communist sentiment that would crescendo in the post World War II era. Randolph was especially sensitive to the charge; he believed that being smeared as a non-believer was also motivated by racism. Being a non-believer, black, and part of the radical left was a lethal combination. Like many radical organizers aligned with communist and socialist politics during this period, Randolph was the subject of an FBI probe and frequent smears by the mainstream media. As the organizer of the first planned March on Washington in 1941, his later vision of community organizing was both socialist and humanist. Equitable living wage jobs, decent affordable housing, and full enfranchisement were basic human rights. The absence of these rights in the twentieth century U.S. made a mockery of its claim to democracy. In the context of Randolph's political organizing, Christianity became a lingua franca for black solidarity and not a litmus test.

Frederick Douglass' skepticism was of a different tenor. As a towering intellectual pioneer of the African American free thought and secular humanist traditions, he challenged the moral hypocrisy of white Christianity in both the United States and Europe. His journey from a committed Christian to a questioning agnostic was compelled by decades of critical observation and lived experience. For Douglass, white slaveholders' moral piety was especially obscene given the savagery of beatings, rapes, and family separations. Angered by what he viewed as Blacks' passive acceptance of the message of Christian deliverance from earthly suffering he noted, "I dwell here in no hackneyed cant about thanking God for this deliverance." Instead, he believed that "man is to work out his own salvation." And it was only through the individual's will and self-determination that uplift was possible.

Douglass' experience is a powerful example. Then, as now, the overwhelming association of religiosity with authentic blackness makes it difficult for atheist or agnostic black secular humanists to be vocal. In the introduction to *The Black Humanist Experience,* Norm Allen notes, "Humanists often feel…that they are a misunderstood and despised minority. Many are afraid to come out of the closet due to fear of being ostracized…by intolerant religionists."[16]

On websites and in chat rooms, many African American secular humanists who identify as atheists or agnostics express anxiety about "coming out" to friends and family. Sites such as Atheist Nexus and Think Atheist have become virtual meeting spaces for atheist, agnostic, and skeptic African Americans who believe that they would be stigmatized for their views in real time. During the late '90s Internet radio host Reginald Finley, aka the "Infidel Guy," began hosting a weekly online radio show focusing on atheism and free thought. Facebook and other forms of social networking allow black non-believers to connect in greater numbers than would otherwise be possible. Over the past year, organizations like Black Atheists of America, my own Black Skeptics Group, and African Americans for Humanism have sprung up or regrouped to address the need for community and visibility. Neurophysiology graduate student Mark Hatcher started a

Secular Students' chapter at Howard University, making it the first of its kind at a historically black college or university.

For my own part, I have had difficulty publishing an article on black humanism in the local black Los Angeles press. The assistant editor of one paper told me that the editor thought I was too "biased" against religion. Again, tacit religious belief is often a prerequisite for black social acceptance. David Burchall, founder of the now defunct Secular Community in Long Beach, California struggled to attract African Americans due to this factor.[17] Burchall's organization provided secularist individuals of all backgrounds and perspectives with a welcoming community meeting place. Burchall stated that he "rarely meets a black person who says he or she is an atheist."[18] In this regard, invisibility fuels isolation and reinforces social conformity among secular African Americans. Agnostic/ atheist Ivori Patterson fears coming out for professional reasons, especially since "I'm doing a short-term internship and looking for other work of the like in order to boost up my resume before I begin applying to law schools. The problem here is that I've been networking with some high profile people that belong to the same parish I used to attend. Do you honestly believe they'll continue to stick their necks out for an atheist?"[19] Thamani Delgardo, a health care professional and agnostic who grew up in the Black Church, said she is reluctant to come out as a non-believer because: "I'm afraid that my family members will think less of me and will be very disappointed."[20]

As the Religious Right has become more vociferous, black atheists have been challenged by a sociopolitical climate that has grown more showily hyper-religious, evangelical, and superstitious. Given the tenor of religious hysteria, it is not surprising that more atheists know their way around the Good

Book than Christian true believers. After years of passing as good Christians, benign "spiritualists," or even certified Holy rollers, many black non-believers come equipped with biblical ammo, ready to smack down the most obscure Old Testament absurdity. It pays to be equipped when the Bible is the most popular book in black America and black literacy levels are obscenely low. According to a 2005 Pew Survey, a majority of African Americans Protestants believe creationism should be taught in public schools rather than evolution.[21] Many also believe that secular liberals have "gone too far" to keep religion out of schools and government.[22] Consequently, black humanists argue that religious dogma has jeopardized African American academic progress, particularly in math and science. It is because of religious dogma, Delgardo says, that young African Americans believe "God will make a way for their survival, so they may drop out of school, have children with no visible means of supporting them, or simply not plan for their financial future because they believe god will handle the hardships and the details that rationalists plan for." The believer's devaluation of the present is a secular humanist point of contention. The belief that human agency is not a sufficient foundation for action, and that assuming ultimate responsibility for one's life and destiny is beyond the purview of "mere" human beings, is especially harmful for black Christians.

Commenting on the stranglehold religiosity has had on African American progress, black humanist James Forman said, "As a Negro growing up in the United States, I believe that the belief in God has hurt my people. We have put off doing something about our present condition because we have believed God was going to take care of business in heaven."[23] As a former head of the Student Nonviolent Coordinating Committee (SNCC), Forman's belief system had a profound influence on black civil rights resistance. Many of the principles of activist struggle, such as the focus on social justice and community organizing, multiracial coalition building, and political action through modeling, mentoring, and leadership building, reflect a progressive humanism. In 1969, Forman protested at Riverside Church in New York, demanding reparations for white churches' collaboration in the slave trade. The protest reflected his belief in the complicity of organized religion in the African slave holocaust—which is still perceived as a radical notion in the era of a resurgent Confederacy.

Forman challenged the role redemptive suffering played in black activism, identity, and community organizing. This challenge was also a powerful theme in the work of Harlem Renaissance writers. The Harlem Renaissance period was one of the most fertile eras for black secular humanist and skeptical thought. From the 1920s to the 1940s, Langston Hughes, Zora Neale Hurston, Nella Larsen, and Richard Wright explored the problematic role of the Black Church in African American culture. Larsen's 1927 novel *Quicksand* questions the cultural, social, and emotional dominance of the Black Church in African American communities from the standpoint of a biracial woman grappling with her apostasy and her place in life. Larsen vividly chronicles the claustrophobia of female domesticity and religiosity in a small rural town. Her mixed race protagonist Helga Crane emerges as a fiercely independent critical thinker whose ambiguous racial identity informs her frustrated quest for subjectivity. The daughter of a white Danish woman and an African American man, Helga's inability to meaningfully connect with either part of her heritage propels her on a nomadic emotional journey. For much of her young adult life she travels: teaching in a black Southern college town, working in Harlem, discovering long lost white relatives in Copenhagen, and finally settling uneasily in a small religious black community in rural Alabama.

Initially lamenting blacks' passive acceptance of the "White man's God," Helga's quest takes her from skepticism to Christian conversion to atheism.[24] She despairs when she discovers that she is unable to make her way on her own, deterministically trapped in an era and a cultural context where marriage is the only "proper" path for women. In a harrowing scene with orgiastic overtones,[25] Helga seeks shelter from the rain in a church after rejection by Dr. Anderson, a former colleague she was ambivalently attracted to. Drawn into the congregation's vortex of fire and brimstone, she is literally taken over by its exhortations of salvation. Distraught over her lack of purpose in life, she latches onto the church's minister, marries him, moves to Alabama, and quickly descends into the drone of domestic life. Helga's transition from single urbanity to married drudgery signifies a retreat from selfhood. She submerges her desire for independence, capitulating to a life of childbearing, childrearing, and family caretaking. At first, the simple devoutness of her adopted community seduces and lulls her. Yet, as she gradually grasps the depth of her submission to a life of unrelenting domesticity, it begins to repel her. Here, religiosity and domesticity are linked as emblems of oppression. Her internal conflict over the dominance of religious belief in the lives of African American working class folk reaches a fever pitch after a long tortured convalescence from childbirth. For Helga, "Religion after all, had its uses. It blunted the perceptions. Robbed life of its crudest truths. Especially it had uses for the poor—for the blacks. How the white man's God must laugh at the great joke he played on them. Bound them to slavery, then to poverty and insult, and made them bear it."[26]

Helga's observations have particular relevance for contemporary black women. She deftly links the imperialism of God belief with the socioeconomic degradation of black communities; communities whose "ghetto pathology" would be labeled "matriarchal" decades later. Conversing with Sary, a mother of six, she wonders how women can bear the burdens of all their family and domestic responsibilities. Sary responds that one must simply trust in the "savior" to be delivered in the afterlife. Sary is one of a stream of domesticated rural black women who cater to Helga's husband, the town preacher. Black women's entanglement in the cult of the male preacher becomes another example of provincial insularity. Helga's dissatisfaction with recurring suffering, sacrifice, and deferment ultimately leads her to conclude that there is no God.

Like James Forman, Helga's rejection of the Christian entreaty to take the possibility of redemption "on faith," despite unrelenting earthly evil, misery, and suffering, becomes the catalyst for her retreat from religious dogma. After the book's publication, Larsen's probing exploration of the ministry was uneasily received by some.[27] As a woman who "did not believe in religion" herself and was considered unconventional for the period, Larsen defied the bourgeois prescriptions of black middle class womanhood. Challenging religious faith bucked conventional gender norms epitomized by the sacrificial good woman. A recurring theme in both Larsen's *Quicksand* and her 1928 novel *Passing* is the gulf between society's narrow expectations and her female protagonists' sense of self and subjectivity. In this regard, *Quicksand* is a stunningly contemporary indictment of black parochialism and moral repression. And in the final scene of the novel, Larsen lowers the emotional boom on the reader with a devastating evocation of the price Helga must pay for her "complicity."

Larsen's cautionary tale resonates in an era in which black women are increasingly imperiled by domestic and sexual violence, persistent health challenges, and the often crushing burden of single parenthood. That this landscape has deepened in the context of heightened black religiosity is a testament to Christianity's contribution to black female dehumanization. Indeed, Larsen's depiction of the reverence black women bestow on community preachers provides vivid insight into the cultish nature of female idolatry. The women of the town in *Quicksand* practically revel in Helga's descent into domestication. By becoming one of them, her status as a potential threat to the town's social order diminishes. Distorted female self-image compels women to fixate on the preacher/pastor figure as a God surrogate whose human foibles are excused as part of the "stresses" of leadership.[28]

While Larsen's skepticism played out through her fiction, Zora Neale Hurston chronicled the evolution of her doubt in a 1942 essay, "Religion." Hurston notes that "as early as I can remember, I was questing and seeking."[29] For Hurston, the "group think" of organized religion conflicts with her fundamental sense of intellectual independence. The daughter of a preacher, Hurston admits that "When I was asked if I loved God, I always said yes because I knew that that was the thing I was supposed to say."[30] Though her family was invested in the church, doubt nagged at her in all the inexplicable details of life that were just chalked up to "God's will." When she began to study world religions, she saw that they shared the common theme of divine deliverance from earthly suffering. She then concluded that faith merely allowed the masses to deal with their "fear of life and its consequences."[31] The craving for some omnipotent source of all life's mysteries gave meaning to the unknowable, even though an all-powerful God was ultimately a human creation. Like popular entertainment, blind acceptance of religious contradictions dulled one's critical faculties, uniting believers in a bond of ritual and bigotry against non-believers.

Despite her blasphemous thoughts as a youth, Hurston fondly recalled church revivals, where "hell was described with dramatic fury...and everybody was warned to take steps that they would not be a brand in that eternal burning."[32] No reflection about being raised in the Black Church is complete without evocations of fire and brimstone. For African Americans in Baptist, Pentecostal and African Methodist congregations, the performative aspect of churchgoing is especially rewarding. Acts of testimony, witnessing and getting saved allow churchgoers to participate in rituals that require maximum audience participation. These rituals function as a public articulation and advertisement of their devotion to God and hope for salvation.

In his 1940 piece "Salvation," Langston Hughes took square aim at the performative nature of churchgoing and the act of getting saved. Hughes details an encounter during a special children's church service he attended at age 13, in which he was practically browbeat into accepting the "light of Jesus." While his friend Westley submits to the pastor's entreaties to come to Jesus, Hughes remains unmoved. Conflicted by his inability to actually feel the spirit or see Jesus, he agonizes over the congregation's overzealous encouragement: "I began to be ashamed of myself, holding everything up so long. I began to wonder what God thought about Westley, who certainly hadn't seen Jesus either...God had not struck Westley dead for…lying in the temple. So I decided that maybe to save further trouble,

I'd better lie too."[33] Hughes' decision to go with the flow to please others was the beginning of a lifelong struggle with the compulsory nature of black religiosity. Expressing his feelings of betrayal, he concludes, "I didn't believe there was a Jesus anymore."

Fear of being different, and being deemed less holy, forces Hughes to betray his own sense of what is true. The heavy emphasis on public conformity to Christianity as a badge of belonging and moral worth is one of the most problematic issues for black skeptics. Non-conformist African Americans are quickly marginalized as not racially "representative." For example, in *Quicksand*, Helga Crane's harshly candid assessments of organized religion are largely confined to her personal thoughts in the book. By remaining silent about her beliefs, she, like other African American non-believers, plays the game of presumed faith, thereby reinforcing religiosity as the default position in black communities.

Hence, black children don't have any publicly visible alternative models to organized religion. Commenting on the early indoctrination of children into religious belief, the 19th century atheist, suffragist, and abolitionist Ernestine L. Rose said:

> It is an interesting and demonstrable fact that all children are atheists and were religion not inculcated into their minds they would remain so. Even as it is, they are great skeptics, until made sensible of the potent weapon by which religion has ever been propagated, namely, fear. [34]

Jermaine Inoue, Los Angeles-based media director for Black Atheists of America, recounted how his aunt quizzed him on the Bible with "a switch in her hand."[35] "Tom," a black atheist from Dallas, likened religion in the black community to a "play toy for babies (i.e., the uneducated)."[36] Christian moral authority allows the powerful to do "whatever they want to without resistance."[37] In black Christian communities, the skepticism of children is squashed by biblical literalism and intolerance. Non-belief means the flames of hell are already licking up your legs. Membership in religious fraternity has its privileges. So at an early age, children learn not to question or publicly ponder the "truths" of organized religion. Although they may see non-observant religious relatives, particularly males, not going to church, unquestioned belief remains an expectation.

For young girls, conformity to the moral code of Christianity is particularly onerous. Those who don't comply with the moral double standard of chaste behavior and submission to males are targeted. While "promiscuous" or sexually provocative behavior in boys is encouraged, girls with these tendencies are quickly put in their place by peers, labeled "hos," "bitches" or (in the case of gender-nonconforming girls) "dykes." Policing the sexuality of young women of color begins at the school yard level, in the media, the community, and the family. While some would argue that this is as much a matter of secular as it is religious censure, its Judeo Christian roots are undeniable. The distorted self-worth and self-image of many African American young women speaks to the continued dominance of Judeo Christian European based gender hierarchies of desirability and attractiveness. Because of the slave legacy of racial and sexual dehumanization, black women in particular are judged through the harsh prism of European ideals of feminine beauty. The historical association of white femininity with moral worth and virtue still shapes contemporary stereotypes of young black women as promiscuous and sexually rapacious. While feminist historical scholarship and cultural criticism have disrupted these stereotypes, there has been virtually no secular humanist critique of the racialized construction of femininity.

The obscurity of black public figures or mentors who hold atheist/skeptic/agnostic views contributes to the tacit acceptance of organized religion in general and Christianity in particular. While most of the aforementioned thinkers are giants of twentieth century African American intellectual thought and literature, they have very few counterparts in contemporary letters. When it comes to explorations of religious skepticism, African American intellectual and literary inquiry has not produced a body of literature that rivals that of the early-to-mid twentieth century. The socially conservative tenor of African American communities has marginalized skeptical, agnostic or atheist analyses of black politics and culture. This highlights the historical and cultural amnesia of the times. Bible thumping blacks who invoke religion at every opportunity would be surprised that some of the most influential figures in "black history" were dirty infidels.

As one of the foremost scholars of black liberation struggle, W.E.B. DuBois often drew on religious themes and imagery in his work, most notably in his landmark *The Souls of Black Folk.* However, according to Anthony Pinn, DuBois' intellectual allegiance was to rationalism and skepticism. Following a trip to the Soviet Union, DuBois wrote an essay on his appreciation for Russian civil society. Proclaiming himself a freethinker, he expressed approval of the prohibition on teaching religion in Russia's public schools. The "fairy tales" of organized religion were destructive because they conditioned children to strive for a fictitious afterlife, rather than make the best of the world at hand. For DuBois, this was a "moral disaster." He had experienced religious intolerance after having been criticized as a teacher at a Black Methodist school for not leading his class in prayer. Like Hurston and Douglass, DuBois' skepticism deepened with his intellectual maturation. Consequently, he said, "From my 30th year on I have increasingly regarded the church as an institution which defended...slavery, color caste, exploitation of labor and war."

This critique has special resonance for Kwadwo Obeng, author of *We Are All Africans: Exposing the Negative Influence of the Judeo-Christian-Islamic Religions on Africans*. A native of Ghana, Obeng is a former Jehovah's Witness who broke from the sect after rigorous independent study of the Bible. In his book, he acknowledges the constructive role Christianity played in African American communities during the slave era, when it provided a cultural and philosophical context for black human rights resistance. Yet he cautions that contemporary Christianity is a mere diversion for black folk. Poor blacks have few avenues for systemic redress of racism by either self-serving black preachers or "Christian-identified" black politicians. As "the church has become part of our DNA, Black politicians feel they need to wrap Jesus all around them to be successful."[38] A recurring theme with black atheists and humanists is that the business of organized religion has been particularly detrimental to poor blacks, who tithe millions to churches while their communities collapse. They point to the rise of "prosperity gospel" as an example of the Black church's betrayal of the social justice legacy of Martin Luther King.

As a result, many black atheists and humanists oppose the political deference shown to faith-based initiatives. As I discussed in Chapter 3, faith-based initiatives provide churches and other spiritual organizations the license to discriminate against those that don't adhere to their principles. Gabriel Lockett, vice-president of the Secular Students' Alliance at the University of Maryland, decried the "lax accounting practices within churches," and wondered "why (there isn't) the same scrutiny of faith-based organizations as there is of other 501c 3's?"[39] As part of a younger generation of black secular humanists, Lockett identifies as an atheist and believes that black visibility in the secular movement must increase. Like many black atheists, he was raised in a Christian household. He was initially hesitant about coming out due to fear of "emotional backlash" from his family. Now active in secular causes, he believes that African Americans would benefit immensely from a more enlightened view of social morality. For Lockett, "if we eliminate the 'God Debate' from the conversation we can focus on the common bonds of humanity...oftentimes I hear 'not my problem' or 'I'm doing me' a mentality that is fostered in the church."[40]

Mark Hatcher of Howard University's Secular Students organization has seen a shift in public discourse due to the popularity of political satirists like Jon Stewart and Stephen Colbert. He is "happy that Stewart and Colbert are out there because they're making it cool to talk about these things. It's making it easy to talk about these things because of their extremism. It's not as much of an issue because a lot more people are talking about the outrageousness of religious fundamentalism."[41] The "us versus them" policing of morality in the Black Church is especially problematic for black atheists and humanists. Obeng believes that the moral authority of organized religion is most suspect when a solidarity of bigotry is forged, for "why else would the Mormon Church, the Catholic Church, Southern Baptists, Islam, (Rick Warren's) Saddleback Church...band together to deny those with a different sexual orientation the civil right of marriage?"[42] Similarly, black secular humanists say, the patriarchal tenets and biases of religions like Islam, Judaism and Christianity prevent women from becoming self-actualized beyond roles as caregivers. As the recipient of the American Humanist Association's 1997 Humanist of the Year award, author Alice Walker spoke of how women's self-actualization was a casualty in her strict religious Southern upbringing. Recounting how her mother was the backbone of her community's church—but had been taught to believe Jesus, and, by extension, God, was a blond white man—Walker assailed the Earth-denying aspects of Christianity. "The truth was," she noted, "we already lived in paradise...This is what my mother, and perhaps other women knew, and this was one reason they were not permitted to speak. They might have demanded that the men of the church notice Earth. Which always leads to revolution."[43] Affirming her belief in the sanctity of the natural world and the here and now, Walker affirms her "faith" in "womanist" self-actualization, free from the sanction of Gods or masters.

Chicago-based instructor Kamau Rashid believes that "Freethought is an extension and expression of the struggle that African Americans have waged for self-determination. In fact it represents a heightened phase of such a struggle wherein one of the final stages of 'conceptual incarceration,' the belief in a God or gods, is discarded for a belief in the human potential, for a belief in ourselves."[44]

In a religion-besotted culture that has enshrined pastors and preachers as the unquestioned arbiters of moral worth, Rashid's identification of freethought and humanism with black self-determination is a paradigm shift. Faced with complex socioeconomic challenges in an era of limited opportunity, African American communities have, in some instances, turned to religious dogma as a general anesthetic. The legacy of Douglass and others demonstrates that secular humanist tradition has been vital to black liberation struggle. Yet, when it comes to building alternative models of humanist community, non-theist African Americans face deep political challenges.

Endnotes

1. Penny Edgell, Joseph Gerteis, Douglas Hartmann, "Atheists As 'Other': Moral Boundaries and Cultural Membership in American Society," *American Sociological Review*, 2006 Vol. 71 (April:211-234), 223.
2. Anthony Pinn, "Anybody There? Reflections on African American Humanism," Association of Unitarian Universalist Humanists, 1997 (http://www.huumanists.org/publications/journal/summer-fall-1997/anybody-there-reflections-on-african-american-humanism).
3. Pinn, *The African American Religious Experience in America* (Westport: Greenwood Press, 2006), p. 73.
4. James Baldwin, *The Fire Next Time* (New York: First Vintage International, 1993), 39.
5. Ibid., 4.
6. Ibid., 38
7. Ibid.
8. Ibid., 34.
9. Ibid., 31.
10. Girls saw the profligacy represented by the "Avenue" and "understood that they must act as God's decoys, saving the souls of the boys for Jesus and binding the bodies of the boys in marriage. For this was the beginning of our burning time..and 'It is better,' said St. Paul…to marry than to burn.'" Ibid., 17.
11. Joseph Graves, *The Emperor's New Clothes: Biological Theories of Race at the Millennium* (New Brunswick; Rutgers University Press, 2002), 3.
12. Ibid., p.
13. Clarence Taylor, *Black Religious Intellectuals: The Fight for Equality from Jim Crow to the 21st Century* (New York: Routledge, 2002), 13-15. Taylor argues that Randolph framed black labor and civil rights resistance in terms of religious triumph/redemption rather than in terms of class struggle. Cynthia Taylor argues that Randolph publicly denied he was an atheist perhaps out of political expedience; the "charge" atheist and communist were often yoked together to discredit progressive leaders. See Taylor, *A Philip Randolph: The Religious Journey of an African American Labor Leader* (New York: New York University Press, 2006), 80-82.

14. Cynthia Taylor, 70.
15. Ibid., 84-5.
16. Norm R. Allen, Jr., *The Black Humanist Experience: An Alternative to Religion (*New York: Prometheus Books, 2002), Introduction.
17. Author interview with David Burchall, January 2010.
18. Ibid.
19. Patterson, January 2011.
20. Author interview with Thamani Delgardo, January 2010.
21. Pew Forum Study on Religion and Public Life, "Public Divided on Origins of Life," August 30, 2005, 10; Gallup Poll 1991. According to the Pew report, "White evangelicals and black Protestants are the only religious groups expressing majority support for teaching creationism instead of evolution in public schools."
22. Ibid., 5.
23. Pinn, "Anybody There? Reflections on African American Humanism."
24. Nella Larsen, *Quicksand and Passing*, ed. Deborah McDowell (New Jersey: Rutgers University Press, 1986), 133
25. Michael Lackey has characterized this scene to a rape scene. See Lackey, *African American Atheists and Political Liberation*, 73-95.
26. Ibid.
27. George Hutchinson, *In Search of Nella Larsen: A Biography of the Color Line* (Boston: Harvard University Press, 2006), 281.
28. I will address this in greater detail in Chapter five.
29. Zora Neale Hurston, "Religion," from *African American Humanism: An Anthology*, 146.
30. Ibid., 148.
31. Ibid., 153.
32. Ibid., 148.
33. Langston Hughes, "Salvation," from *African Americans for Humanism: An Anthology*, 120-21.
34. Ernestine L. Rose, *Women Without Superstition*, 82
35. Jermaine Inoue, Interview Questionnaire, November 2010.
36. Interview Questionnaire with Anonymous subject, November 2010.
37. Ibid.

38. Kwadwo Obeng, *We Are All Africans: Exposing the Negative Influence of the Judeo-Christian-Islamic Religions on All Africans* (Minneapolis: Two Harbors Press, 2008), 8.
39. Gabriel Lockett, Interview Questionnaire, December 2009.
40. Ibid.
41. Mark Hatcher, Interview with Author, December 2010.
42. Obeng, 1.
43. Alice Walker, "The Only Reason You Want to Go To Heaven Is That You Have Been Driven Out of Your Mind," *On the Issues: The Progressive Woman's Magazine,* 1997 (http://www.ontheissuesmagazine.com/1997spring/sp97walker.php).
44. Kamau Rashid, Interview Questionnaire, May 2010.

Chapter 5

Not Knocking on Heaven's Door

When I was a child, I spoke as a child, I understood as a child, I thought as a child; but when I became a man, I put away childish things."

—I Corinthians 13:11

The first few minutes of the 1960 revival movement film *Elmer Gantry* are a paean to the spit and gleam of Burt Lancaster's klieg light teeth. Dancing shamelessly like a character unto themselves, they tell you everything you need to know about 20th century divinity and the meteoric rise of the evangelical shaman as American idol. Based on Sinclair Lewis' 1927 novel, the film chronicles the arc of a white Middle American rogue's pursuit of Jesus Inc., represented by a beatific revivalist preacher named Sister Sharon Falconer. Lancaster tears into the title role with lupine brio. Barely ten minutes in and Gantry has landed at a Negro church, dirty and disreputable, freshly sprung from a hobo brawl on a musty boxcar from central casting. Gantry's old time religion is lock stock with sex, lies, moonshine, and doe-eyed indolence—before his date with destiny he staggers around half-heartedly, selling cheap vacuum cleaners, toasters, and any other sundry fare he can get his hands on, desperate for a quick fix, a ticket out of obscurity. Is there no better place then for a miscreant white man to jam his foot through the door of redemption than a Negro church?

If Hollywood cinema is America's shepherd, then yes. In the 1980 film the *Blues Brothers* ex-cons Jake and Elwood Blues embark on their back flipping "mission from God" with a send-off from preacher James Brown and choir member Chaka Khan. Robert Duvall's turn as a misunderstood "apostle" in the 1997 film of the same name begins and ends in steamy clapboard black churches. In Jim Crow America white people enter black sacred spaces strategically, innocently, their presence seemingly unquestioned. They enter and are indelibly transformed, their souls becalmed, the lynch rope that would surely greet a black interloper in a World War I era white church unthinkable. In *Gantry* Lancaster hears the peals of "On My Way to Canaan's Land" as he walks along the train tracks. He follows the sound, entering a church service going full bore. The singing stops as he enters. Gradually, as he lends his powerful tenor to the song, the all black congregation's initial wariness gives way to "acceptance." Of course, images of black folk rapturously belting out gospel songs are standard American pop culture fare. But the Gantry scene intrigues because of the striking figure of a little girl standing next to him in the congregation. She gives Gantry the once over, her disrupted body language conveying caution and bewilderment with the inimitable honesty of a child. The quizzical little girl is the visual anchor of the scene. She provides a critical gaze, a resistant spectatorship. All the adults are swept up in the euphoria of the moment; grinning, clapping, and singing at the top of their lungs with the soulful abandon that only Hollywood's Negroes know. Here, the Negro church is a crucial point of spiritual entry for the dissolute white man. The embodiment of natural primitive spirituality and devoutness, Negroes are an important space of projection for Gantry's personal journey from ignominy to (partial) redemption. The film charts Gantry's successful finagle into Sister Sharon's good graces. He becomes her spiritual lieutenant and lover and a quasi folk hero in the lily white corn-fed world of Pentecostal tent revivals. Tellingly, there are virtually no other people of color featured in the entire movie after the Negro church scene.

Thus, the little girl in the church scene is compelling as a silent commentator on the reality of black subjectivity and black childhood in the midst of racial apartheid. Yet she is also a symbol of the complex social rituals of faith in black communities. These rituals are a tacit part of traditional African American upbringing. The camera frames her shock at the white interloper's presence but it also suggests her potential defiance. Even in the sanctuary of the church, black children were taught very early on that whiteness signified power; that white space carried a special authority and terror, and that Jesus looked not unlike Elmer Gantry.

Blue-eyed Jesuses float spectrally from my childhood. It was a period in which the LAPD's murder of a single black woman in her own home solidified Los Angeles' police state status. In the still smoldering political climate of the seventies, the walls of friends and relatives' homes were often graced with the somber "trinity" of Martin Luther King Jr., John F. Kennedy, and an ethereal blue-eyed Jesus. Still, attending all-black elementary schools in South Los Angeles, discussions of "faith" were not that frequent. However, it was presumed that all black folk were religious in some respect. Because of the prominent street presence of Black Muslims other religions were fleetingly visible, yet Christianity was unquestioningly the default position. Coming from a rare secular African American household, dominated by a formidable literary and historical library, the Bible was something I was only cursorily familiar with. During a brief foray into world religions, my father brought home a copy of the Koran, but the Bible was essentially an alien mysterious document. Fleeting fascination with a storybook bible depiction of Moses' epic battle with the Pharaoh and the parting of the Red Sea was one of the few vivid childhood memories I have of the Technicolor majesty of Old Testament lore.

So when I was practically cornered and (sharply) questioned one day by "Angie," a school bus acquaintance, about whether I attended church on a regular basis I was embarrassed to confess that I didn't. The questioner had more than an impartial interest. She was a pastor's daughter and a sixth-grader, well-known for her "sage" advice and counsel and commentary on the knuckleheaded exploits of back of the bus screw-ups. My non-churchgoing flippancy and oddball upbringing were greeted with eye-rolling incredulity. Seeing a lost soul and potential convert, she recommended that I check in with the Bible and begin to "talk" to God. Painting a picture of God's benevolence and 24/7 accessibility, she encouraged me to practice this new form of supernatural correspondence as soon as I had a moment to myself.

I have vivid memories of attempting this experiment in the privacy of my own room. I balanced an inward sense of the futility of the enterprise with an earnest hope that it would yield something. If "God" was in fact omniscient, why would I have to talk with him, her or it? Why wouldn't my deepest thoughts and desires already be known? And how did this relate to my own actions? How would I in fact know that I'd been heard or acknowledged? And what about that jealous unforgiving God of the dimly remembered interminable sermons I'd had to sit through at my grandparents' church?

Wouldn't He be pissed off at my fairly new and grudging entry into his global 24/7 psychic Tower of Babel? For ten years, while all those other folk were praying and going to church and dutifully dropping their tithing envelopes into the collection plate, I was morally adrift in a loving household filled with books. This, then, is the rub for the non-religious and non-theist. Why is it necessary for children raised in secular homes to be indoctrinated with the codes and mores of any given religion when they are already steeped in a moral life? And why would anyone want to be associated with a religion that made such an arbitrary and artificial distinction, condemning children as sinners? Why, indeed, would children be compelled to profess belief, especially when they look around them and see that the world is overpopulated with adult believers flaunting their immorality?

So "talking" to God in the safety of my room, I was unmoved. In the pell mell world of elementary school cliques and neighborhood bullies, every day was a lesson in moral judgment. The temptation to lie, cheat, steal and/or knock someone upside the head for no apparent reason other than malicious fun is present at every turn. Prayer only offers a quick and dirty escape hatch from the messy human circumstance of immoral acts. Without the reinforcing compass of God my evangelist friend Angie worried that I would fall into an abyss of amorality. I would be paralyzed, unable to distinguish the delicate ethical nuances of sticking a grasshopper leg in the ear of a snoozing classmate or informing on a neck craning cheater cribbing answers from my spelling test.

What would it mean for children to view morality within a context in which both the common humanity of different individuals is not only emphasized but *value* is placed on the complexity of those differences? For children in a Christian tradition, the insularity of prayer is a linchpin of becoming moral. Prayer—atomized, isolated, viewed as one small drop radiating through a big God-roiled pool—is something that even little kids can do with minimal effort or expenditure. Prayer becomes a moral device, a tool, and a treadmill. If I send out well wishes for a certain person, cause, or catastrophe, it will reverberate and have some tangible effect. Prayer gives one a temporary pass for not actually doing something in the real world or fundamentally changing my perceptions of "others." For a few inexpensive moments a day I can plug my chip into the circuit board of the divine, holding out hope for resolution. For a few inexpensive moments I can hope that God takes care of the HIV/AIDS infected ten year old in my fifth grade class whose homeless parents can't afford to buy food much less the latest designer shoes, IPod or Sidekick. I can then go blithely on my way without having to linger on whether there actually is a higher power that can make such a whiz bang change. I can weigh the inequitable human social order with the mystery and moral justice of the divine. For, if this social order is not human inspired, then naturally there must be some moral reason why the child suffers. There must be some causal connection between the child's condition and the moral failings of the parents. The hand of God must be somewhere, benevolently pulling the strings.

I have a vivid memory of the first time I became aware that children could die. It was early evening in the leisurely dusk of summer. After eating with my mother at a local coffee shop, we passed by a newspaper vending machine outside. A child victim, kidnapped, murdered, and disposed of like garbage, stared ominously out at me from the front page of a newspaper in grainy black and white. I remember my sense of horror when my mother told me that the child, who was approximately my age, would never see his parents again. Associating death with old people, I was stupefied by this seeming contradiction. Alone in my bed that night, my friends' prayer-saturated social universe smacked me down, and I wondered how "God" could have countenanced such unspeakable evil.

Decades later there is an aching space where this child's life would have been, his personhood, his bundle of tics, idiosyncracies "frozen" at abduction. Violent death by homicide at an early age is a grim reality for many youth of color. Gangsta rap romanticizes it and dishes it up for the voyeurism of white suburbia. Mainstream media ignores it or relegates it to social pathology. Every semester when I ask my students if they've had a young friend or relative die violently at least half will raise their hands. Their tattoos, notebooks, and Sidekick phones are filled with vibrant mementoes for the dead. It is not necessary to go to Iraq, Afghanistan or some other theatre of American imperialism to experience the devastation that the killing fields of disposable youth inflicts. Yet, there is God at the precipice, dangling children and fools over the side. In the midst of sudden death there is refuge in the belief that the Cecil B. De Mille epic doomsayer of the Old Testament must have a special place in his heart for this tender constituency. Pied Piper religionists pat children on the head and whisper into their dewy ears that the murder of an innocent child is part of God's plan. They dish out divine providence like hard candy. They lure sweet-toothed youth with a ready "antidote" to the quandary of trying to make sense out of the senselessness and randomness of evil. The Wynken, Blynken, and Nod bedtime story of grand design is chased down with the simple carrot of eternal reward for slain innocents. The inexplicable is assimilated. Senseless evil, evil that befalls the good and stalks the innocent, is legitimized as part of the divine's hardscrabble boot camp for the living.

If it can be understood, it isn't God, said Augustine. In ambiguity then, prayer is the great equalizer and potential redeemer. As American children we grow up with recurring images of kneeling girls and boys, hands clasped solemnly in prayer. These images propagandize faith as a normal, natural phenomenon. The magic bullet of prayer is trotted out as an escape hatch from the small indignity to the unspeakably cruel act of wild-oats-sewing youth. Bad kids pray obsessively for forgiveness. Good kids pray strategically in crisp starched pajamas for family members, friends, and Fido to be delivered to the top of God's check list. Sinful thoughts can be defused by requesting a special audience with God. Good thoughts can be "deposited" into one's virtual piggy bank of moral worth.

Blasting the hypocrisy of this brand of yo-yo morality in the Doors' song "the Soft Parade," Jim Morrison bellows:

> When I was back there in seminary school, a person put forth the proposition that you can petition the Lord with prayer... *petition* the Lord with prayer...*petition* the Lord with prayer... You cannot petition the Lord with prayer!!!

Morrison's fierce monologue highlights the absurdity of prayer as a form of negotiation. Clearly, the more meditative personal and intimate benefits of prayer can be therapeutic to the believer. Yet, the assumption that prayer can be a bargaining chip in moments of crisis merely allows individuals to refuse to accept responsibility for their actions. Children who are indoctrinated into this escape hatch mentality are forced early on to reconcile an out of control, evil, morally rudderless world with the illusion of a forgiving tailor-made God who they can summon like hocus pocus. Picking and choosing morality and dividing the world into the Christian "us" and the immoral, unwashed secular/Muslim/Hindu/"them," "faith-based" children are socialized to see and enforce hierarchies of personhood rather than embrace fellowship.

Since God sees and "forgives" everything that is *petitioned,* the moral universe of Christian children is a tiny, confining funhouse of mirrors. In communities where death at an early age is considered unremarkable by mainstream media and policymakers, the deferment demanded by faith is an insurance policy against social oblivion. When death is near, it is easy to arm a child with the "faith" that their 15 year-old cousin, killed in a drive-by shooting, has gone on to a "better place." When death is near, the fear of retaliation for being a "snitch" compels crime witnesses to remain silent. As a result, homicide cases remain open indefinitely while perpetrators walk around free and clear in the same neighborhoods. Yet faith allows victims and witnesses to rationalize this seeming contradiction. God will punish the evildoer in the afterlife, granting the dearly departed everlasting peace and deliverance in heaven.

And, for the parents of a dead child, it is said that God doesn't give you more than you can handle. Having lost a child to a congenital disease, this is bitter refuge and rank fraud. This reductive homily has been especially tailored to domesticate and seduce women, saddled with a thousand obligations, the primary care of children and infirm relatives, dead end jobs with marginal pay. It is God's will that you be eaten alive by the "womanly" stress of always being expected to defer, sacrifice and persevere. And it is God's will that you must bite back your Eve-bequeathed rage in silent complicity.

In my infant son's final hours, I stared down at the phalanx of tubes that separated him from death. Soon, they said, he will be an angel. I could feel nothing but the obscenity of divine providence, the mockery of robust babies whisked from the delivery room to pink and blue splattered nurseries without incident, innocent of the antiseptic drone of the neonatal ICU.

But then, there is the stripped-to-the-bone eloquence of women waiting for deliverance: like that depicted in a story I read shortly after the 2010 Haitian earthquake about a homeless Haitian mother's heartbreaking quest for permanent shelter. Desperately she waited for God to "put something into her hand," to perhaps give her a sign that she won't be like scores of parents fated by this rudderless God to outlive their young children.

Pimps, Predators, and the "New" World Order

If morality is reduced to individual just rewards and punishments in the so-called afterlife, then the greater context of collective moral worth remains obscured. As a straight middle class girl in a homophobic heterosexist school community I was trained to dehumanize gay kids. After all, God, as we were fond of jeering to the suspected "fags" at my elementary school, created Adam and Eve not Adam and Steve. Historical leaders were straight, public figures were straight, normal families were straight, laws sanctified straight families, law enforcement protected male dominance over women and children in the home, and the exotic world of romantic love pulsed to the tune of boy conquers girl. This was our creed, our lifeblood, our moral universe, our cultural license for terror. This was the moral universe that claimed the life of Carl Walker-Hoover, an eleven year old African American Massachusetts boy who committed suicide in April 2009 after the adult leaders at his school failed him. Like scores of youth who are targeted for being gender non-conforming, Hoover-Walker's pleas for help from school administration went unanswered. Coverage of his death barely made a dent in the mainstream media. Coverage of the bullying-related suicide of a white Massachusetts high school girl during the same period made national headlines. In 2008, the murder of gender non-conforming middle school student Lawrence King by a fellow classmate in Oxnard, California put anti-gay bullying in the public spotlight. Prior to King's murder, homophobic violence in schools elicited little media attention or national outcry.

Like most children growing up in the U.S. I was systematically taught to view lesbian and gay people as deviant, unnatural, and immoral. Because heterosexuality was the "norm," the absence of LGBT figures of color in textbooks and media reinforced the righteousness of my straight identity. It conferred me with an automatic self-esteem and self-image advantage LGBT youth did not have. Because I looked, talked, and generally played the part of a boy-obsessed straight girl, I was not ostracized for my attraction to the opposite sex. And because I lived in a community where the presumption of heterosexuality and hetero-normativity always trumped other gender identities, I was not targeted for social "extermination." At my elementary school a boy named "Luke," who was obsessed with Mrs. Beasley, a doll featured in the 1960s sitcom "Family Affair," was mercilessly harassed for being effeminate and mentally "off." Luke became a cautionary tale for little black boys bold enough to be themselves. For, in this state of identity warfare, we were constantly reminded to enforce clear lines of demarcation between male and female, to inflict terror on those who deviated from the gender script. Children who blurred gender lines like Luke were deemed less valuable, less normal, and, by extension, less human. Girls who didn't express a preference for and show some interest in deferring to boys had questionable gender identities. Boys who didn't exhibit an overt interest in girls—who didn't flirt with, compete for or harass them—were social suicides.

Why isn't it considered immoral when gender non-conforming children have no space in our culture? Why isn't it considered an indictment of American culture when they are reviled for the toys they play with and the clothes they wear, while their straight peers reap the social benefits of being silent, of being normalized? And why isn't it a moral failure when LGBT youth don't see themselves represented in school textbooks and media?

Power is "moral" when it is arrogated by authority figures that uphold these gender norms and boundaries as an unimpeachable truth claim. For example, images of war and militarism are constantly coupled with the masculine moral imperative of imperial conquest. In the midst of the Iraq War, the indelible image of George W. Bush's triumphal 2003 "Mission Accomplished" speech on a naval aircraft carrier evoked hard masculinity and American moral authority. Decked out in an alpha male flight suit, his sensationalized jet landing on the aircraft symbolized American technological, tactical, and geopolitical might. His GI Joe dress-up juvenilia was calculated to reassure a credulous American public of the righteous necessity of the war effort. As a result, Bush became one of the most successful manipulators of moral identity politics and the creed of violent masculinity in recent memory. While the administration of his spiritual predecessor Ronald Reagan was motivated by political deference to the fledgling Religious Right and brutal dominion over Latin and Central America, Bush ushered in a new era of post-Cold War imperialism. The "scourge" of radical Islam supplanted that of global Communism. The confluence of global "anti-terrorist" incursions and domestic culture wars made his administration the most draconian civil liberties violator since the McCarthy era. Under Bush's watch, the shrill flat earth, lock n' load "pro-life" white nationalism that glimmered during the Reagan years came to fruition.

Enforcing boundaries of race, gender, and sexuality has always been the province of moral "guardians" and "gatekeepers." And it is perhaps no coincidence that the Catholic Church sex abuse scandals emerged during this era of increased immoral right wing policing. In my brief experience as a Catholic school student, children were naturally taught to revere and attach importance to authority figures simply because they were "anointed" by or perceived as being closer to God. This neo-monarchical view of the laity imbues children and adults with a level of trust that has proven destructive. While the sex abuse epidemic in the Catholic Church has received much coverage, similar epidemics in Protestant churches have remained largely underreported. In an online article on the Chris Brown/Rihanna abuse incident, feminist anti-violence activist Kevin Powell recounted how he'd been approached for advice by a young woman who had been sexually abused by her pastor since she was five years old.[1] Similarly, a young woman of my acquaintance related that she had been repeatedly molested by her pastor after her parents had entrusted her in his care. Clearly, sexual abuse is an endemic social issue that is not peculiar to organized religion. However, the mindset of the religious sexual predator is markedly different from one operating in a secular context because of the presumption of righteous morals and a higher calling. Further, religious hierarchies (be they Muslim, Christian, Mormon, Orthodox Jewish, etc.) delineating masculine roles, responsibilities, and privileges perpetuate a culture of patriarchal entitlement and control. The Bible's sanction of violence against women (e.g., rape and forced marriage) provides theological justification for viewing and treating women like property. If women are deemed to be second class citizens in scripture, and consigned to helpmate roles in the church, why wouldn't male clergy act with impunity when it comes to sex and power? And if the culture of compulsory heterosexuality demands that men hew to rigid gender norms, it stands to reason that some closeted gay clergy will abuse their power by sexually assaulting young male parishioners. Indeed, the heterosexist cult of the exalted pastor is based on the belief that "real men" should be inscrutable. Real men don't have to answer for the way they exercise power and authority. Hence, the religious sexual predator rationalizes his behavior as being ordained by God. God confers him with ultimate authority and moral license. The religious sexual predator's mandate is part of a divine moral order that mere laypeople don't have access to.

While God works in mysterious ways, the devil is a little more transparent. Just ask New Birth Missionary Church Bishop Eddie Long. Accused in September 2010 of sexually abusing young men in his congregation, arch homophobe and macho man mentor of boys Long is one of the devil's more high profile black casualties. The Atlanta-based prosperity gospel preacher has blazed a trail as an anti-same sex marriage Christian soldier and self-proclaimed "spiritual daddy" to a nationwide army of wayward sons. According to Earl Ofari Hutchinson, after the death of Coretta Scott King in 2004, "Long's anti-gay phobia was so virulent that then NAACP president Julian Bond publicly declared he would not attend (her) funeral service at Long's New Birth Missionary Baptist Church."[2] Long was a prominent supporter of George W. Bush's anti-gay policies. His empire of niche ministries, books, gospel shows, and seminars powers a robber baron's lifestyle of expensive cars, lavish estates, and private jets. One of these niche ministries involves spiritual counseling for young men and "delivering" men from homosexuality. Long evoked themes of hyper-masculinity and required followers to treat him like a divinely ordained patriarch. The financial improprieties of Long and other good Christian evangelicals were scrutinized in Sarah Posner's 2008 book *God's Profits: Faith, Fraud, and the Republican Crusade for Values Voters.*

Some in the elite world of prosperity gospel mega churches have attempted to address the behavior of predator preachers proactively. Betty Price, spouse of Los Angeles-based mega church preacher Fred Price, even authored a book entitled *Warning to Ministers, Their Wives and Their Mistresses.* Price calls for ministers (and their assorted womenfolk) to come back to the true word of the Christian God. But the true biblical word of God merely provides the context for male sexual predation and abuse. Because the Bible explicitly objectifies, commodifies, and reviles women—denying them official roles of authority in the church comparable to men—Christianity is simply not a legitimate avenue for women to achieve full personhood. Half-stepping and pussy footing around the Bible's atrocities with "womanist" revisions will not make it so. In their book *Gender Talk,* Beverly Guy-Sheftall and Johnetta Cole argue that the tradition of preaching has itself been "sanctified" as a masculine space. In this regard, "there may…be a deep psychological resistance to the very idea that a group of men (even though they will be in the numerical minority in most Black churches) should have to sit and listen to a woman (preacher) telling them what to do and what not to do."[3]

From the time African American children become socially aware, the dominant culture reinforces the heterosexist perception that male clergy are above the law. Preachers are revered as founts of knowledge, wisdom and "reason." In middle to working class black communities the absence of formal religious training or education is no barrier to having the title "Rev" "Dr." or even "Reverend Doctor" slapped in front of one's name. Consequently, the strong preacher father figure is one of the most universally respected models of masculinity in African American communities. Available for counsel and succor to male and female parishioners, the "daddy" pastor's biblically sanctioned faith pimping spiritual ministry translates into emotional manipulation, psychological control, and sexual exploitation. Wayward women in personal crisis can only find their way back through the guidance of Jesus and the pastor as Jesus surrogate. The foibles and transgressions of these women (the moral failings of pregnant teens are an especially ripe target) become fodder for cautionary tales about immorality and falling from grace.[4]

One of the most popular entrepreneurs of this brand of paternalistic "motivational" counsel for women is T.D. Jakes. Jakes is the pastor of The Potter's House, a non-denominational mega-church in Dallas, Texas. Over the past decade Jakes has developed a cottage industry of books, tapes, and films promoting his relationships-focused message of spiritual and emotional uplift. His public speaking events attract thousands of adoring female acolytes. He has recently morphed into a frequent guest "expert" on all things black for cable talk shows. Jakes has called attention to the high incidence of intimate partner violence and sexual abuse in black communities. However, his thesis on the essentialist nature of feminine and masculine roles is decidedly retrograde. As Shayne Lee notes in her book *T.D. Jakes: America's New Preacher*, Jakes "argues that though it was a mistake of the past for men to oppress women, the mistake of the future is 'this spirit whereby the woman imitates the masculine strength and we lose the creative edge of her feminine perspectives.'"[5] Jakes' notion of the woman as help mate and caregiver to beleaguered men plays into tired stereotypes of the male as provider and female as emotional safe harbor.[6] According to Lee, womanist theologians like Dolores Williams have criticized Jakes' sexism under the guise of female uplift shtick. Much of Jakes' prosperity gospel success has been powered by the millions he's raked in profiting from women's hunger for an antidote to the spiritual emptiness they feel in a morally "challenging" social climate. Over the past decade a bevy of cartoonish Tyler Perry-influenced melodramas hawking redemption in ninety minutes has popularized the theme of "coming to Jesus" as an essential part of female gender identity. What does this example of invulnerable masculinity and unquestioned moral authority convey to children?

There are those who would protest that Christianity is not to "blame" for these norms of masculinity. Certainly, if we look around mainstream American culture there are plenty of secular examples of hierarchical, authoritarian, controlling masculinity. They are a key part of what made this nation great; feared the world over as a kick ass, empire building superpower. Yet blacks' Christian religiosity and the de facto Christian socialization of black children should be examined vis-à-vis the culture of violent masculinity that shapes the lives of many youth of color.

A small item I read in a local throwaway newspaper about the case of a Los Angeles African American pastor who'd been accused of trying to kill his wife is an insidious case in point. The pastor was arrested after attempting to shoot his spouse on a public street. The article speculated on what might have compelled a respected member of the church community to commit such a violent public act. Incredibly, the article's concern for the female victim was eclipsed by in depth commentary from associates who knew the pastor to be a good "man of God." Having learned nothing from the global pedophile priest epidemic, our stridently Christian culture still routinely uses the assignation man or woman "of God" to shut down debate about how religious authority gives license to those who act immorally. Indeed, how many times has the public been told that a certain person could not have committed a heinous act because he was a good man of God, a devout Christian, and a churchgoer who could regurgitate scripture on demand? And how many times have predators, thugs, and hardcore career criminals been given a figurative pass or viewed as above suspicion because they were churchgoing Christians doing the Lord's (dirty) work? Conversely, how many times has one heard the caveat that a certain person could not have committed a heinous crime because they were a humanist, atheist or agnostic?

In the real world, polls consistently show that non-believers are far more moral and ethical on major values issues than their religious counterparts.[7] The Bible Belt, with its emphasis on abstinence- only education, continues to have the highest rates of out-of-wedlock births, teen pregnancy, divorce, and HIV/AIDS contraction. A 1999-2000 Barna study found that non-denominational Christians and Baptists generally had higher divorce rates than atheists and agnostics.[8] The majority of cities in Forbes' top 15 cities with the most violent crime rates in the U.S. are also in the Bible Belt. In a survey of highly religious societies versus non-religious ones, researcher Phil Zuckerman concluded that religious fundamentalist nations have higher rates of poverty, disease, and homicide.[9] Hence, "countries with the high rates of organic atheism are among the most societally healthy on earth, while societies with nonexistent rates are the most destitute."[10] Given that there is no empirical evidence that disproportionately connects atheists with immoral acts or heinous crime why do such attitudes persist? More to the point, what implications do these attitudes have for African Americans seeking alternative models of morality and social justice, based upon black humanist traditions? How might these models begin to address the crisis of gender equity?

"Post-Feminism" and Colorblind Lies

There is a painful truth that needs to be faced in contemporary black communities: namely, that violent masculinity and patriarchy are "sabotaging" black sustainability. For some progressive thinkers, violent masculinity is a symptom of larger ills, i.e., racism, white supremacy, and socioeconomic and political disenfranchisement. But what these phenomena actually have in common is the violent territorialization of women's lives and women's bodies. From sex trafficking to gender wage disparities to anti-abortion terrorism to the triple burden of household work, wage work, and child care, the territorialization of women's lives and bodies informs racial hierarchy and economic inequality. Yet in the U.S. these issues are rarely considered in the context of racial justice or human rights. Writers Beverly Guy- Sheftall and Johnetta Cole decry the lack of emphasis on gender equity and anti-sexism in black communities. The failure to connect the dots between black communities' sanction of violent masculinity and black-on-black homicide, gang violence, and intimate partner violence has stunted African American self-determination.

The complete and total internalization of sexist belief systems is reflected in the self-image of young women of color. In a perversely sad imitation of the mainstreaming of the word "nigger" among young black males, it is not uncommon to hear young women of color refer to themselves as "bitches" and "hos." Not surprisingly, whenever I conduct an annual series of workshops on sexual assault awareness training young women are some of the staunchest defenders of the view that "slutty" women in tight revealing clothes are just asking to be raped. Like men and boys who believe that males are entitled to rape "slutty" women because they can't "control" their "natural" sexual urges, some young women will argue up and down that the burden of responsibility rests solely on a woman's shoulders. Raised in a schizoid culture where female hyper-sexuality is both elevated and demeaned, young women get mixed messages about the relationship between sexuality and feminine identity. In the 2009 documentary film *Straightlaced,* a high school aged white woman talks about the pressure teen girls feel to be viewed as desirable and attractive. If you dress in revealing clothes, she says, you're considered to be a "slut." However if you dress modestly you might be considered a "prude" and "no one will want you." Slut/ whore if you do; prude/Madonna if you don't.

At every turn Christian models of femininity define and constrain young women. In the South L.A. schools where I teach, a popular past time consists of outing "loose girls" in a clandestinely circulated list of campus "sluts." Some of the girls on campus even enjoy being the moral gatekeepers of such nonsense. When a "loose" girl was caught in the act of giving oral sex on a cell phone camera she was hounded out of school, while the guy she was "doing" scored points for being a stud. Defining who is and is not a "slut" gives girls social power and moral authority in a climate that affords them with precious little of either. Deluged with ad after ad hocking make-up, hair products, lingerie, accessories and other beauty "enhancements," young women and girls can't escape the message that their primary "market" value lies in being physically attractive and sexually desirable to men.

However, the double-edged sword of the Madonna/ whore dynamic is even more insidious for women of color. Because of the premium placed on the white beauty ideal, African American, Asian, Native American and Latino women have never had the luxury to occupy the Madonna role. In mainstream film and TV, black women are typically trotted out as the hand-on-hip "bitch" or all-purpose caregiver to hapless whites, Latinas are reduced to prostitutes or domestics, and Asian women frequently wind up being arm-candy for white male action figures. The multi-billion dollar global beauty industry reinforces these stereotypes by promoting light skin, long straightened hair and Barbie-size proportions as the beauty standard all women should aspire to. Youth filmmaker Kiri Davis poignantly addresses the impact of this imagery on young black girls in her 2007 short "A Girl Like Me." Davis' interviewees cited cultural stereotypes of black women as loud, aggressive and "un-feminine." In an especially heartbreaking moment, Davis re-enacted the 1946 doll test—which was part of a study conducted by psychologists Kenneth and Mamie Clark used as supporting evidence for the 1954 Brown vs. Board of Education ruling—with young black children. The children were presented with a white doll and a black doll and asked to identify which of the dolls was ugly or attractive, smart or dumb. They overwhelmingly identified the white dolls as having the most positive traits.

In 2010, a university researcher recruited by CNN conducted a more extensive survey with white and black children which produced similar results. The majority of the white children associated darker skin with low intelligence, unattractiveness and "bad" behavior. The uncensored responses of the white children starkly contradict race neutral "colorblind" approaches to child-rearing in which young whites are supposedly taught "not to see" race.[11] By ignoring the pervasive racial cues of a dominant culture that normalizes whiteness, parents that adopt a colorblind approach with their children merely validate racial hierarchies.[12] Clearly, rearing white children to be colorblind doesn't prevent them from becoming prejudiced. For example, in a 2006 study conducted by researcher Birgitte Vittrup:

> The avoidance of race was something Vittrup also picked up in her initial test of parents' racial attitudes. It was no surprise that in a liberal city like Austin every parent was a welcome multiculturalist...But...in the original surveys hardly any of these white parents ever talked to their children directly about race...They might have asserted vague principles, like 'Everybody's equal' or 'God made all of us...they wanted their children to grow up colorblind but Vittrup could see from her first test of the kids that they weren't colorblind at all. Asked how many white people are mean these children answered 'Almost none.' Asked how many blacks are mean, they answered 'Some' or 'A lot.'[13]

As 24/7 consumers straight out of the womb, children learn quickly that whiteness is the norm and other ethnicities are merely window dressing or exotic exceptions. When the majority of cartoons, video games, books, toys, greeting cards, and Hollywood blockbuster tie-in products feature whites as the main characters or central figures—sympathetic, romantic, heroic, desirable and all points in between—how could white children believe otherwise?

The CNN segment was also noteworthy in its focus on black girls' sense of self-image. For example, some of the younger respondents commented that they wanted lighter skin because they felt lighter-skinned girls were viewed more favorably by teachers and other adults. One little girl was particularly vehement in her insistence that light skin was better, pointing shyly to her own dark brown skin as undesirable.

To be sure, the segment was yet another potent reminder of the need for counterprogramming on the part of parents of color. Yet it was also a stark indicator of the moral imperative *white* parents have to teach their children about the beauty, value, cultural worth, and importance of communities of color to American society. It is not sufficient to regurgitate the bromide that everyone is the same and hence tacitly valuable as individuals. An influential classroom experiment gives historical perspective on why. In 1968, white elementary school teacher Jane Elliot's "Blue Eyed" experiment demonstrated that the dominant culture's social cues about intellectual worth translated into either low or high self-esteem depending upon whichever racial group was identified as "normative."[14] Responding to the assassination of Martin Luther King, Elliot wanted a creative way to teach her all-white class about the insidiousness of racism. Dividing up her class according to eye color, she initially showed preferential treatment to the blue-eyed children and denigrated the brown-eyed children as dumb and inferior. The "dumb" brown-eyed children underperformed and misbehaved while the "bright" blue-eyed children exhibited greater confidence, arrogance, and high academic performance.

This self-fulfilling prophecy of good performance and underperformance was a direct result of the way the children were perceived and treated by Elliot. Internalizing Elliot's negative views and judgment, the brown-eyed children floundered. The blue-eyed children prospered and viewed themselves as naturally superior.[15]

The implications are similar for gender socialization. Twenty years ago, the term "bitch" and "ho" were extremely offensive epithets. Casual references in hip hop, rap, and popular music have desensitized younger generations to their use. The decline of feminism as a political movement has precipitated a backlash against anti-sexist discourse. And in high schools across the nation, the mainstreaming of pornography in virtually every aspect of mainstream media has demystified sex. "Sexting" explicit images over cell phones is commonplace, performing oral sex is viewed as a "harmless" alternative to intercourse, and feigning lesbianism for the voyeuristic gratification of young men is socially acceptable. Skyrocketing oral STD rates amongst African American girls and the growth of a pre-teen prostitution industry in urban black communities are symptomatic of this shift.

The national atmosphere of both anything-goes sexual permissiveness and "moral" repression is a paradoxical pill to swallow. From a humanist standpoint, the normalization of violence against women is a threat to every woman, man, and child of color. Clearly this is not exclusive to communities of color. But off the chart rates of homicide, domestic violence, sexual assault, and STD contraction rates point to a crisis of both institutional resources *and* moral values.

When the Bible is the most read and respected book in Black America, and these issues remain a salient feature of black communities nationwide, women must ask themselves who does a Christian morality based on exclusion and hierarchy really serve? Whenever I speak to young men about their sense of masculinity, I always begin with a question about their relationships with women that they love and respect. When we talk about their role models, the majority of them identify their mothers or another female relative.

However, when we talk about the high incidence of rape and sexual assault in black and Latino communities, young men have difficulty translating their love and respect for the women in their lives to the idea of humanizing young women. From the time the first blue onesie is slapped on them at the hospital to the time they don their first oversized white t-shirt they are taught that when they walk down the street, it is their prerogative to catcall a woman or girl about her appearance, destination or relationships. They know that when they gather amongst themselves that talking trash about women or girls is an expected ritual of male sociality. They know from the media, their peers, their families, and communities that slapping or hitting a girl is an acceptable way to express anger or frustration. They know that sexually harassing or even assaulting a girl or woman will be soft-pedaled with a hundred other names that absolve them of responsibility for their actions. They know that their behavior will rarely be challenged. They know that there is virtually no moral standard in the dominant culture that tells them that women are human beings with inalienable rights.

Any formulation of humanism that does not begin with a fundamental critique of the global implications of patriarchy and an affirmation of the inalienable human rights of women is bereft. Why is it that when it comes to an assessment of the pervasiveness of violence in the U.S., critiques of gender hierarchy and patriarchy continue to be marginalized? First, there is still a fundamental acceptance of the premise that male violence is inherent rather than learned. Parents justify allowing young boys to play with violent toys and video games on the grounds of biology. Girls are "predisposed" to salivate over play stoves and play houses. Boys are hard wired to like rough n' tough toys. According to this logic, the multi-billion dollar toy marketing and advertizing industry merely reinforces biological determinism.

In their 1999 article on the Columbine High School shooting, Sut Jhally and Jackson Katz argue that the human, social, and economic costs of male violence are rarely considered from a national perspective:

> What these school shootings reveal is not a crisis in youth culture but a crisis in masculinity. The shootings - all by white adolescent males - are telling us something about how we are doing as a society, much like the canaries in coal mines, whose deaths were a warning to the miners that the caves were unsafe. Consider what the reaction would have been if the perpetrators in Littleton had been girls. The first thing everyone would have wanted to talk about would have been: Why are girls - not kids - acting out violently? What is going on in the lives of girls that would lead them to commit such atrocities? All of the explanations would follow from the basic premise that being female was the dominant variable. But when the perpetrators are boys, we talk in a gender-neutral way about kids or children, and few (with the exception of some feminist scholars) delve into the forces - be they cultural, historical, or institutional - that produce hundreds of thousands of physically abusive and violent boys every year. Instead, we call upon the same tired specialists who harp about the easy accessibility of guns, the lack of parental supervision, the culture of peer-group exclusion and teasing, or the prevalence of media violence. All of these factors are of course relevant, but if they were the primary answers, then why are girls, who live in the same environment, not responding in the same way?[16]

Jhally and Katz deftly highlight a shopworn truism about the dominant culture's take on violence. Race (vis-à-vis the motivations of perpetrators of color) and class analyses are frequently invoked to account for the prevalence of violence in American society. Gender rarely if ever informs these appraisals. Presumably, only hand wringing feminists and a few sociobiologists are invested in examining violence through a gender lens. Gender is viewed as an obvious "ho-hum" factor that is not worth mentioning. Thus male violence is normalized as a permanent and immutable fixture of the socio-cultural landscape.

Neuroscientist Lise Eliot challenges this notion in her book *Pink Brain, Blue Brain.* Using careful analysis of scientific studies on "innate" sex differences she argues that there is "little solid evidence of sex differences in children's brains."[17] Instead, early exposure to environmental cues and factors elicit differences in the later development of children's brains. Adult perceptions of gender difference strongly influence children's behavior.[18] And social and cultural contexts which encourage regimentation between girls and boys also play a salient role. As early as one year of age children learn and replicate the nuances of gender identification associated with gender segregated play. Constant exposure to an environment in which girls are nurtured, coddled, and "protected" for being more fragile than boys actually produces subtle changes in the brain.[19] Evaluating the widely accepted testosterone as "trigger" for dominant aggressive behavior thesis, Eliot picks apart studies that attempted to correlate the influence of testosterone on rat behavior with that of humans. While rats are far more susceptible to testosterone in early life, humans have a far more complex hormonal and physiological structure: "the bigger the brain, the less instinctive the behavior and the more the brain's abilities are influenced by learning." The conditioning that a child's brain gets from real life interaction and stimuli can have long term implications for gender identity:

> In spite of our best efforts, moms and dads don't treat sons and daughters exactly the same. The two sexes start out a little bit

> different, and we, with our own lifetimes of cultural experience, react differently to them from their earliest days.[20]

Eliot reviewed studies on supposed sex differences in hearing, smell, and vision between infant boys and girls. She found little evidence to support the conclusion that these differences were anything more than slight.[21]

Clearly there will always be fierce debate about nature versus nurture within the scientific community. However, ask the average elementary or middle school student about the hardwired differences of girls and boys and they will preach them like the gospel. They square off in their separate recess and lunch lines and accept that the roughhousing playground antics of boys are natural and justifiable. Teasing, bullying, and sexual harassment of girls and "wimpy" boys is encouraged as an essential ritual of boyhood.[22] True to the arguments of Eliot and others, children become zealous enforcers of "normal" gender identity. They are just as invested in reproducing these models of exclusion as adults because they are tacitly instructed that there will be serious consequences if they don't. They learn early on that conformity is rewarded and difference is ostracized. Moreover, there are no countervailing forces in American public education that connect morality with social justice vis-à-vis race, gender, and sexual orientation.

For a child living in a predominantly Judeo Christian context, morality involves prayers, washing one's hands, not hitting one's younger sibling and being thankful for having food on one's plate. In short, the rote stuff of everyday life. It is presumed that routinization is easily digestible, while "higher order" thinking is not. In their infinite ignorance, adults often assume that children are able to discern difference but not ascribe a value to it. Time and again misguided adults will flatly state that "mommy's little man" Noah or "daddy's little girl"

Ashley do not see "color," "gender" or even sexual orientation when they are perfectly capable seeing it in crayons, animals, toys, and everyday objects. Constantly testing, experimenting, and evaluating, children are essentially scientists, establishing their own causal morality based upon adult cues and the inscrutable universe of childhood hierarchies. To secretly watch a child in imaginary play, cobbling together references from the babble of adults, cartoons, commercials, and other children, is to get a glimpse of a near alchemical process. In play children form relationships, exercise power and control, and improvise their own moral language based upon a syncretic understanding of the world around them. So if it is evident that children replicate what they see it should follow that they fail to replicate what they don't see. If it is routine in the dominant culture for girls to be grabbed and handled, for "effeminate" boys to be ridiculed and harassed as "fags," and Asian youth to be trotted out as kung fu mavens and nerd exotics, children will incorporate these belief systems into their behavior.

Morality *should* entail being taught to view "others" with dramatically different cultures, appearances, lived experiences, and sexual orientations as human beings with inalienable rights and innate human value. Certainly, when one examines the inroads of education reform movements such as culturally responsive pedagogy, this is the case. Yet conservative critics have done a brisk business in the media excoriating such teaching methodologies as "racist." In Arizona, recent debates around the value of multicultural education and ethnic studies programs exhibit this insidious divide. The passage of SB1070, a landmark anti-immigration bill signed into Arizona law by Governor Jan Brewer, precipitated draconian crackdowns on multicultural education in Arizona schools. Arizona legislators voted to eliminate ethnic studies programs shortly after the passage of SB1070.[23] The misguided belief that ethnic studies promotes racial division can be traced back to white mainstream America's colorblind mythos about the progressive nature of American social history. Central to this belief is the view that the U.S. is a true democracy based on freedom and individual liberty for all. Since the U.S. is a true democracy, historical portrayals that expose the contradictions of American social equality are partisan, revisionist, and "un-American." While big ticket historical "items" like slavery and Native American dispossession are lamentable, they are squarely in the past and have little relevance to the structure of contemporary American society. Consequently, conservatives argue that multiculturalism encourages a sense of entitlement amongst people of color that is fundamentally at odds with the American ethos of meritocracy.

Of course, part of the amoral genius of American cultural ideology has been the framing of imperialism and exploitation in the language of morality. The Iraq and Afghanistan Wars are informed by the legacy of the 19th century doctrine of Manifest Destiny, wherein American expansionism was framed as morally justified and inevitable. Slavery and the extermination of indigenous peoples exemplified the U.S.' moral right to subdue backward savage uncivilized (i.e., immoral) racial others through brute force and cultural conquest. Throughout American history, morality has been framed through the lens of expedience, whether it be driving out black residents from their homes during the brutal race riots of the Great Migration period or massacring innocent Native American children in the name of "justice." Few white Protestant denominations challenged the racist imperialist practices of the U.S. government on the grounds that they were immoral or "inconsistent" with Christian principles. Most viewed the slavocracy as their God-ordained birthright.

Centuries of human rights resistance by people of color led to the demise of American racial apartheid.[24] Many white radical and progressive activists played a crucial role in this history. Nonetheless, one of the reasons American apartheid endured for so long was because of the absence of white champions of equality within organized religion (the abolitionist movement notwithstanding) and other prominent institutions of white civil society. In fact, white religious abolitionists were influenced by the viewpoints of white free thinkers like Elizabeth Cady Stanton.[25] During the slave era white religious abolitionists represented a small subset of white religious voices and were not always unified in their allegiance to emancipation. For example, white abolitionist leader William Lloyd Garrison criticized the hypocrisy of mainstream white churches, often clashing with less radical white abolitionists who objected to his "disparagement" of the Constitution. White abolitionist Ernestine Rose attacked organized religion as an enemy of human rights. Abolitionists were the moral conscience for progressive white activists of the slave era. Indeed, the term "abolitionist" and "infidel" were often used interchangeably.[26]

The absence of a visible 21st century Religious Left is due to progressive institutions' failure to spearhead an activist moral challenge to the narrow corrupt "values" agenda of the Religious Right. The culture wars of the Reagan/Bush and George W. Bush eras have morphed into a white nationalist backlash. Though the anti-government, no taxes mania of this backlash may appear to be secular on the surface, it has deep roots in a fundamentalist Christian fascist agenda of social control.

In one of the final scenes in the film Elmer Gantry, Burt Lancaster rescues worshippers from the revival tent fire that kills Sister Sharon Falconer. When asked if he would carry on her mission he invokes First Corinthians' caveat about putting away childish things. It is implied that Gantry's revivalist ambition, and not necessarily organized religion, is one of the "childish" things he would "put away." The film's portrait of Christian venality is almost radical in a national climate dominated by the gospel according to Fox News demagogue Glenn Beck. In this, the most religious of post-industrial nations, being perceived as a real American and a true patriot is still inseparable from Christian faith. And for many young people, compulsory religiosity and its legacy of hate, bigotry, hierarchy, and repression is still a key part of their American education. By understanding the political and racial context of this legacy, humanists can radically redefine public morality.

*Name changed

Endnotes

1. Kevin Powell, "Ending Violence Against Women and Girls (The Remix)," *Newblackman*, February 13, 2009. (http://newblackman.blogspot.com/2009/02/kevin-powell-on-domestic-violence.html).
2. Earl Ofari Hutchinson, "Eddie Long: Victim, Hypocrite or Both in Sex Scandal?" *The Huffington Post,* September 23, 2010 (http://www.huffingtonpost.com/earl-ofari-hutchinson/bishop-eddie-long-victim_b_736542.html).
3. Johnetta Cole and Beverly Guy-Sheftall, *Gender Talk: The Struggle for Women's Equality in African American Communities* (New York: Ballantine Books, 2003), 109.
4. Marcia Dyson, "When Preachers Prey," Essence Magazine, 1998, 120-122.
5. Shayne Lee, *TD Jakes: America's New Preacher* (New York: New York University Press, 2005), 131.
6. Ibid., 131-136.
7. For example, the 2008 Barna report found that conservative Protestant Christians had higher rates of divorce than atheists and agnostics. Non-evangelical born-again Christians had slightly higher rates than atheists and agnostics. If Christian tenets were morally superior the stats for Christians would be dramatically lower in comparison to those of heathens. See Barna Group, "New Marriage and Divorce Statistics," March 31, 2008 (http://www.barna.org/barna-update/article/15-familykids/42-new-marriage-and-divorce-statistics-released).
8. "Christians are More Likely to Experience Divorce than are Non-Christians," Barna Research Group, December 21, 1999, Study no longer available at Barna website (http://www.adherents.com/largecom/baptist_divorce.html).
9. Phil Zuckerman, "Is Faith Good For Us," *Free Inquiry* 26, no. 5, August/September 2006 (http://www.secularhumanism.org/index.php?section=library&page=pzuckerman_26_5).
10. Ibid.
11. "Children Learn Attitudes About Race At Home," *CNN.com*, May 19, 2010 (http://articles.cnn.com/2010-05-19/us/doll.study.reactions_1_black-children-white-children-race?_s=PM:US).

12. See for example, Po Bronson and Ashley Merryman, *Nurture Shock: New Thinking About Children* (New York: Hachette, 2009) 28-50; Bronson and Merryman, "See Baby Discriminate," *Newsweek,* September, 9, 2004 *http://www.newsweek.com/2009/09/04/see-baby-discriminate.html).*
13. Bronson and Merryman, 49.
14. William Peters, *A Class Divided: Then and Now* (New Haven: Yale University Press, 1987), 1-10.
15. Elliot used a fictitious pseudo-scientific study to justify blue-eyed superiority.
16. Jackson Katz and Sut Jhally, "The National Conversation in the Wake of Littleton is Missing the Mark," *Boston Globe*, May 2, 1999, E1.
17. Lise Eliot, *Pink Brain, Blue Brain: How Small Differences Grow into Troublesome Gaps—and What We Can Do About Them* (New York: Houghton Mifflin, 2009), 33.
18. Ibid., 52.
19. In one illuminating study, babies were tested on a slope to demonstrate the level of steepness they were able to negotiate. Mothers consistently underestimated the steepness that their girl babies were able to negotiate, while mothers of boys were within a more accurate range of estimation for the steepness that their sons were able to negotiate. The study actually found that girl babies were able to negotiate a steeper grade than the infant boys.
20. Ibid., 56
21. Ibid., 59-65.
22. In my experience with sexual harassment training, middle and high school students are generally ignorant of the fact that slandering a boy for being a "fag" is a form of sexual harassment under the California Education Code.
23. Emily Gersema, "Arizona Ethnic Studies Ban Reignites Discrimination Battle," *Arizona Republic*, May 19, 2010, (http://www.azcentral.com/arizonarepublic/news/articles/2010/05/19/20100519arizona-ethnic-studies-lawsuit.html).
24. I make a usage distinction between the state of legal apartheid sanctioned by Jim Crow and other laws versus de facto segregation which is in some respects akin to apartheid.
25. Gaylor, *Women Without Superstition*, 104-133.
26. Ibid., 138-9.

Chapter 6

In God We Trust: Whiteness and Public Morality

When Newt Gingrich took to the stage at the 2010 Southern Republican Leadership Conference he had a simple message—the Obama administration was the fount of a "secular socialist" conspiracy. The adoring virtually all-white crowd gave him an amen-corner blessing and braced gleefully for more fire and brimstone. Ever since President Obama's election in 2008, the GOP has been relentless in its vilification of Obama as mortal enemy of American democratic traditions, free enterprise, and the moral authority of the United States in the so-called free world. Gingrich's canard was noteworthy because of its Cold Warrior style conflation of Obama's ostensibly liberal domestic policies and the lurking evil of secularism. The scorched earth culture wars that characterized the Reagan-Bush and George W. Bush eras made "secular" a dirty word. Secularism was blamed for everything from abortion, teen pregnancy, divorce, pedophilia, and political radicalism. In this latest iteration, secularism was once again code for being anti-American, anti-patriotic, and amoral. Gingrich's charge against Obama was part of a growing wave of anti-government hysteria incited by the far right Tea Party movement. Underlying this hysteria is the belief that secularism is the ideological linchpin of an administration caricatured as the architect of big government wealth redistribution.

According to a 2010 poll by Public Religion Research, a majority of Americans believe God has "granted Americans a special role in history."[1] It's a special Christian role; a Christian destiny in which white people have become the new discriminated against minority.[2] Historians such as Gary Wills, Robert Middlekauf, and Robert Boston have ably challenged the grossly misguided notion, popularized by John McCain and other conservatives, that the U.S. was founded as a fundamentally "Christian nation."[3] Nonetheless, this myth continues to cast long shadows on American politics, culture, and education. In March 2010 the Texas Board of Education proposed omitting references to the slave trade (substituting the term "Atlantic Triangular Trade") and revising historical representations of the separation of church and state in its textbooks.[4] Dominated by conservative Republicans, the most prominent members of the Board were a dentist and a real estate agent. No historians, sociologists or political scientists were consulted. The Texas debacle was significant because the state is one of the largest buyers of textbooks in the U.S. and has a broad national influence over school curricula. One of the most extreme examples of the backlash against "secularism" was the Texas Board's decision to omit Thomas Jefferson from "a list of figures whose writings inspired revolutions in the late 18th century and 19th century."[5] Jefferson was replaced with St. Thomas Aquinas, John Calvin, and William Blackstone. The National Rifle Association, The Moral Majority, and Gingrich's "Contract With America" manifesto were added to state content standards to restore "balance" to its left-leaning curriculum. Based on the Board's view that capitalism had gotten a bad rap, the word "capitalism" was replaced with "free enterprise." Ducking capitalism's association with robber barons and filthy lucre, "free enterprise" received a more nuanced definition—"including minimal government intrusion, taxation and property rights."[6]

The Texas Board's action and Gingrich's rhetoric exploited the old standby that secularism is seditious. When all else fails, demonize the heathens and let God sort them out. Tellingly, the Texas Board was much less vigorous about airbrushing Thomas Jefferson's slave-holding statutory rapist history than his status as a deist/skeptic. Owning slaves and having sexual license over them, though morally reprehensible in modern terms, was simply a perk of agrarian free enterprise. Just ask all the Civil War re-enacters and proud daughters and sons of the Confederacy drooling over new battle sites in Dixie.

The contradiction between "minimal government intrusion" and the depiction of the U.S. as a Christian-inspired, Christian-endorsing nation is one of the most pernicious. Conservatives crow over their allegiance to minimal government intrusion. They strut and swagger about the government keeping its hands off their guns and first amendment rights. Then immorally trample on a woman's human right to have her womb, body, and destiny free from state incursion. Nationwide the Religious Right's well-oiled well-funded political lobby has successfully promoted parental notification and parental consent laws that endanger pregnant working class teens. It has also bankrolled a shady network of fake reproductive services clinics (so-called crisis pregnancy clinics).[7] These centers vastly outnumber legitimate women's health care centers offering contraception, prenatal care, and STD testing in addition to abortions. As a result, many Southern and Midwestern women must cross state lines to find abortion clinics that provide a safe legal alternative to compulsory pregnancy, infection or death.

The individual's inalienable human right to exercise control and authority over her own body is distorted with fascist language like "fetal rights" and "pro-life."[8] But in reality, "what lies at the heart of the issue of abortion…is not the killing of babies (which is scientifically wrong in the first place) but the chaining of women in oppressive relations in which their essential role is reduced to that of being the property of men and the breeders of their children according to…theocratic interpreters of 'god's will.'"[9] As atheist writer Ophelia Benson argues in her book *Does God Hate Women?* "The control of women is dual. The goal is to deny access to women's genitals to all men in the world minus one and to guarantee access to one…God and the Prophet are simply a fig leaf for a brazen and naked form of sexual slavery."[10]

In conservative parlance, freedom from government intrusion has meant freedom for white males to bear arms, tax dodge, and avoid fiscal responsibility for public education and social welfare programs. Patriots like Kentucky Senator Rand Paul challenge the "excesses" of equal protection legislation like the 1964 Civil Rights Act because stuff like that stymies business and job creation. In this universe, a government in which there is no separation between church and state should rightfully be the handmaiden of Christian religious sacraments. Christian mores should supersede constitutionally protected rights for women, gays and lesbians and people of color. Muslim theocracies, however, are another matter.

The initial backlash against President Obama's health care reform legislation was partly due to the Religious Right's high profile propaganda apparatus. Powerful Christian evangelical groups like the Family Research Council and Campaign for Working Families joined the Conference of Catholic Bishops in a lobbying campaign against abortion coverage provisions.[11]

Speaking on a MSNBC segment, Family Research Council head Tony Perkins declared a government "takeover" of health care fundamentally anti-God and anti-Christian because, "Trying to give it off to the government is an abdication of personal responsibility." Fundamentalist mullahs of the Middle East would no doubt agree. Equitable access to health care is not ordained by God and should be tightly policed and controlled.

Across Middle America, town halls denouncing the plan were convened by the Tea Party and Republican elected officials. In one infamous exchange in South Carolina, a health care reform opponent shouted "keep your government hands off of my Medicare," swaggeringly ignorant of the fact that Medicare is in fact administered by big government. Noting the irony, *New York Times* columnist Paul Krugman remarked, Americans "hate single payer insurance…because they don't know they have it."[12] Hearkening back to the high-pitched rhetoric of the Contract With America era, "government" became the signifier for socioeconomic and political tyranny. Largely missing from mainstream media coverage of the debate were the voices of people of color. Indeed, health care reform opposition was almost uniformly white and conservative led. Many of the most prominent protests were dominated by Tea Party activists toting signs equating Obama's plan with "White Slavery." In the wake of the health care bill's passage, caveats like "taxed enough already" and shrill pledges to "take back the country" have become a popular rallying cry.

Liberal commentators like Sean Wilentz and Robert Scheer caution that dismissing the Tea Party as a white racist insurgency is too simplistic.[13] Wilentz locates the Tea Party lineage in the Cold War hysterics of the ultra-right John Birch Society.[14] Scheer identifies the tea partyers as an "authentic" populist response to the recession.[15] Yet,

Gingrich's characterization of Obama's policies as "secular socialism" relies on a tacit appeal to white nationalism, a sentiment that Tea Party pageantry has so masterfully exploited. Despite the Tea Party leadership's vigorous claim that it embraces disaffected people of color too, the majority of the movement is white, male, affluent, and over 45. According to a New York Times poll, Tea Party advocates believe that Obama's policies disadvantage the middle class and the rich and are fundamentally at odds with "authentic" American values. Moreover, a September 2010 survey by the Public Religion Research Institute concluded that "on nearly all basic demographic characteristics, there are no significant differences between Americans who identify with the Tea Party movement and those who identify with the Christian conservative movement."[16] The so-called libertarianism of the Tea Party movement is a carefully crafted mirage, designed to deflect attention from the authoritarian corporate apparatus that underwrites it. Scratch the surface and it's all about safeguarding an embattled Christian nation. As one Times poll respondent complained about Obama, "I just feel he's getting away from what America is...He's a socialist. And to tell you the truth, I think he's a Muslim and trying to head us in that direction, I don't care what he says. He's been in office over a year and can't find a church to go to."[17]

The connection between Christian religiosity and the notion that government is encroaching upon the freedoms of average white Americans has gained fresh currency in the conservative backlash against Obama. While the Tea Party movement has disingenuously resisted being identified as an arm of the GOP, prominent GOP leaders like Sarah Palin, John McCain, Mike Huckabee, and Gingrich have wholeheartedly embraced it. Three quarters of self-identified Tea Party adherents "usually support" Republican candidates.[18] Palin,

Gingrich, and the reactionary culture mavens at Fox News have fanned the Tea Party's "take back our country" flames with evangelical rhetoric that promotes belief in Obama's illegal "alien" status (a view associated with so-called "birthers"). Indeed, a CNN poll indicated that 27% of Americans and 41% of Republicans believe that the President is not an American citizen. This belief persists despite Obama's Hawaiian birth certificate, his very public very robust expression of Christian beliefs, and his administration's renewal of Bush's faith-based initiative program. Short of channeling Jerry Falwell, there is nothing further that Obama can do to establish his bona-fides. It's just that pesky African thing that's a deal breaker. For all his "first black president" mugging and big government pandering, Clinton was never demonized as a bongo playing bone in the nose savage. For the oracles of the neo-Confederacy, Obama's race *and* his policies are a toxic cocktail. They are antithetical to "real" American values, thus marking him as irredeemably other. According to Harvard professor Lisa McGirr, "the Tea Party uses a kind of code to talk about social values. For instance, when they emphasize a return to the strict meaning of the Constitution, they interpret that as a return to a Christian foundation." Thus, "when they talk about returning to the values of the Founding Fathers... they are talking about life as a social issue."[19]

The Tea Party and its thinly veiled religiosity is perfectly in line with what Chris Hedges has characterized as the "dominionist" orientation of the Religious Right. In his 2006 book *American Fascists* Hedges predicted that the dominionists, or the most extreme elements of the Religious Right, "wait only for a fiscal, social or political crisis, a moment of upheaval in the form of an economic meltdown or another terrorist strike on American soil, to move to reconfigure the political system."[20] Hedges' prediction has disturbing resonance in light of how the Tea Party movement has crafted an "anti-establishment" platform and a "populist" common man message to mine white anger over the economic recession. Appealing to the disgruntled white working and middle class, Tea Party propaganda about "Washington elites" airbrushes the movement's financial backing from arch conservative kingmaker elites like billionaire industrialists David and Charles Koch—men who are among the illustrious top 2% who control over 20% of the wealth in the United States.[21]

This seeming contradiction underscores why a mass movement based on class solidarity between the white working class and poor people of color remains a left-progressive pipe dream. Racial division between the white working class and poor people of color has always been mediated by a fundamentalist Christian conservatism (hearkening back to white Christian justification for slavery) based on white supremacy. The heritage of racial terrorism that characterized both the North and the South during the Jim Crow era was infused with the language and dogma of white religious destiny. Hence, it is no accident that regions with some of the deepest white poverty encompass the Christian Bible Belt. And it is no revelation that in public gathering after public gathering the constituency of the Tea Party movement remains steadfastly white, its moral rhetoric firmly tethered to the authoritarian agenda of the Religious Right.[22]

After Obama's election, some declared post-racialism and the Religious Right's political decline a fait accompli. The racist xenophobic tenor of public morality has demolished liberal-conservative delusions of melting pot racial harmony or colorblindness. Growing opposition to illegal immigration has exposed the deep well of white resistance to the "inclusive" vision of American democracy that Obama's candidacy appeared to represent in 2008. A new campaign to repeal 14th amendment guaranteed birthright citizenship to American born children of undocumented women has been engineered by demagogues of the far right. In its bid to "take back the country" the Tea Party movement's white supremacist blend of anti-secular, "anti-government" propaganda is perhaps the first gasp of a new Confederacy.

American Stars and Bars

In 2009 when the first round of health care reform protests emerged, so-called open-carry gun fanatics set the tone for the mobocracy to come. Flaunting their weapons at local bars they exhorted white "patriots" to stockpile guns, evoking the specter of an Obama driven apocalypse.[23] During the Clinton administration white-led militias were a familiar presence on the national scene. Sprouting like weeds in response to the killings of "political dissenters" by government agents in Ruby Ridge, Idaho and Waco Texas, contemporary militias of the 1990s were a hotbed of white supremacist, anti-government, milenniallist, Christian fundamentalist rage. The 1995 terrorist Oklahoma City federal building bombing and murder of 168 people was masterminded by militia zealots Terry Nichols and Timothy McVeigh. Yet although they were once a major force for anti-government revolt, "by early this century (the militia movement) had largely faded, weakened by systematic prosecutions…and a new highly conservative president."[24] The Southern Poverty Law Center (SPLC) characterizes the twenty first century resurgence of militia activity as the "second wave." Spurred by the election of a black president with a foreign name and liberal public policies, the second wave militia movement ably utilizes the language of siege and moral panic just like its predecessor. Conspiracy theories, paramilitary trainings, and anti-tax strikes are the currency of this revitalization. Shortly after the 2010 midterm elections, a deranged gunman who'd expressed anti-government sentiments and railed against the Federal Reserve murdered six people and critically wounded Democratic Congresswoman Gabrielle Giffords in Tucson, Arizona.

The resurgence of the citizen militia is yet another manifestation of the right wing assault on public morality. Militias like the "Oath Keepers," a Kentucky-based organization founded by a former aide to libertarian Congressman Ron Paul, train their members to prepare for a government dictatorship. Member allegiance is to the Constitution and not "politicians" who are subject to impose "unconstitutional (and thus illegal) and immoral orders."[25] These orders are deemed illegal and immoral because they violate the so-called sovereign citizenship of white Americans. In this view whites are a "higher kind of citizen," beholden to "common law" and not government rule. Conversely, African Americans are "14th Amendment" citizens.[26] Hence, "although not all sovereigns subscribe to or even know about the theory's racist basis, most contend that they do not have to pay taxes, are not subject to most laws, and are not citizens of the United States."[27]

In the midst of the worst recession in generations, these sentiments are often characterized as mere symptoms of the severity of "middle class" angst about the economy. Yet where are the people of color protestors and populist sympathizers, the black and Latino militias and lock n' load insurgents? With staggeringly high levels of unemployment and foreclosure in black, brown, and Native American communities people of color have profound grievances about the recession. In 2009 members of the Congressional Black

Caucus (CBC) approached the Obama administration about specific federal initiatives to redress recession fallout in inner city communities. Arguing that African Americans had been the most severely impacted by the recession, the CBC pressed Obama for aid to minority-owned businesses, struggling black homeowners, and black job seekers. In keeping with his strategic avoidance of racially charged themes and remedies, President Obama dismissed their recommendations. Ever the tactful "centrist" scrupulously attuned to the biases of the white electorate, Obama reasoned that all Americans would benefit from race neutral federal programs.

But as 2009 poverty figures indicate, a "high tide" does not lift all boats. While the Tea Party nationalists were storming Middle America, black and Latinos bore the brunt of the economic downturn. According to the U.S. Census Bureau 25% of African Americans and 25% of Latinos are living in poverty. With blacks comprising only 11-12% of the population these are criminally obscene numbers. Yet Tea Party propaganda does not delve into the implications of this crushing reality. And the policy initiatives and public rhetoric of the Obama administration, so besotted with the plight of Wall Street power brokers and Main Street's Joe Six Pack, have kicked talk of the poor and fighting poverty to the proverbial curb. Gone are the days when the Democrats, ala LBJ's War on Poverty or FDR's so-called second Bill of Rights, bowed to pressure from social justice movements on federal social welfare policy. Not wanting to be outflanked by the right, Obama has focused relentlessly on the plight of the middle class. In mainstream discourse the middle class is framed as white, angry, disaffected voters. This constituency has the most legitimate axe to grind about the recession.

As beneficiaries of the liberal social welfare programs the Tea Party vilifies, middle class people of color are marginalized. The "middle" equals white middle. The soaring black unemployment rate (across class lines) of 15% is immaterial. Reveling in nightly infusions from the corporate media, the freshly evangelized macho racist right's charge of socialist government expansion is now viewed as a "reasonable" critique of public policy. Tea Partiers have used Christian fundamentalists' language of moral panic to goad a white nationalist uprising obsessed with themes of enslavement.

Patriarchal imagery is a strong part of this equation. Patriarchal resentment and so-called white cultural disenfranchisement have always animated conservative mass protest and activism. During the 19th and 20th centuries "white slavery" was the catch all term for moral panic about the sex trafficking of white women. Sexual invasion became a metaphor for the imperiled white body as Nation. The association of the health care overhaul with this historical theme gives a telling glimpse into the mind of the macho racist. The specter of enslaved white people under the yoke of a black patriarch (ala the lawmaking blackface grotesques of the 1915 film *Birth of a Nation*) elicits visceral terror amongst white supremacists. True to their Confederate provenance, the Tea Partiers have begun to rally more vociferously for a return to States Rights. Before the ink was dry on the health care bill, 14 states lined up to contest its mandate that individuals' purchase health care coverage. After the 2010 midterm elections Republicans in Congress announced that they would introduce a bill to repeal so-called Obama-care. During the Tea Party's first convention, States Rights was the clarion call, with seminars on nullification—States Rights as trumping federal authority—and the heroism of Confederate president Jefferson Davis whipping up secessionist frenzy. Hijacking Christian fundamentalist propaganda, the Tea Partiers have succeeded in casting the "incursions" of the federal government as a grave moral transgression.

Ever since she was thrust into the national spotlight with her cartoonish Vice Presidential candidacy in 2008, Palin has been especially adept at using moral rhetoric to exploit white "class" resentment. During the 2008 campaign, she frequently harped on the difference between the values of real Americans living in small towns and the bankrupt inauthentic values of urban Americans. According to Palin, small towns like her hometown Wasilla Alaska are the "pro America areas of this great nation." Palin later retracted her comments, but scoundrel GOP Congress members Michele Bachmann and Robin Hayes also sounded this theme in patriotic refuge. Bachmann famously called for a McCarthyist investigation into all of the enemies of authentic American values in Congress. On the campaign stump for McCain and Palin, Hayes commented that "liberals hate real Americans that work and accomplish and achieve and believe in God."[28]

The association of small towns with God and country—and urban America with sin, debauchery, and amorality—has been a powerful theme in American social thought. Reflecting on his travels to the teeming cities of England and France, Thomas Jefferson lamented that urban cities were cesspits of moral decay. Abhorring the moral "chaos" of the industrialized city, Jefferson believed that private property was the ideal medium for realizing individual liberty and sovereign citizenship. A key aspect of sovereign citizenship involved providing white males with the freedom to cultivate their own plot of land with minimal intervention from the state. This freed them from the so-called tyranny of the majority. Manifest destiny, the belief that European Americans had a god-given right to conquer the "wilds" of America, solidified land ownership and colonial conquest as the U.S.' unique moral right.

The anti-urban ethos was deeply intertwined with constructions of racial otherness. This ethos is reflected in the way suburbs are privileged as the ideal place for raising families, educating children, and achieving the American Dream. Dysfunctional though suburbs may be in the classic WASP literature of John Cheever and Joyce Carol Oates, no one ever "escapes" to the city. Suburbs are a refuge from the urban other. Twentieth century urban reformers like Jacob Riis demonized the corrupt city as humanity's graveyard. Some cautioned that the ethnic enclaves of New York, Chicago, Boston, and Detroit were breeding grounds for white working class political radicalism and anti-American sentiment. Socialist movements of the 1920s and 1930s were largely propelled by white immigrants dissatisfied with the oppressive, economically disenfranchising practices of government and big business.

Did the descendants of those seditious white immigrants become Tea Partiers? And how did they morph from scary God n' country hating ethnics to Americana whites? Transportation politics played a key role in this special racial odyssey. Ferrying seditious urban white ethnics into newly created suburbs, early streetcars were just as much a "moral influence" as notorious early twentieth century white supremacist xenophobe Father Coughlin, the Fox Mafioso of his day.[29] According to historian Joel Tarr, streetcar development allowed white ethnics to move into working class suburbs and better assimilate into mainstream white Anglo America. Not only did some white ethnics escape the urban hub of white political "radicalism" and poverty but they escaped the first great migration of

African Americans to Eastern and Midwestern cities during the post World War I period. African American humanist thinkers like A. Philip Randolph were attracted to the urban North (Randolph moved to New York from rural Alabama in the 1910s) precisely because of its radical political and cultural promise. Yet white resentment of African American urban migrants boiled over into some of the worst race riots of the century. Scores of African American homes, neighborhoods and businesses were burned down and thousands were killed. Once associated with poor culturally "backward" barely white predominantly Catholic immigrant communities, Eastern and Midwestern cities became vital spaces for African American cultural traditions.

So if one closely examines the history of urban development in the U.S. it is not difficult to see why the terms "small town" or "small town values" have become euphemisms or shorthand for white supremacist notions of morality. I use white supremacist in the sense that the term "small town values" does not typically refer to predominantly African American rural towns in the Deep South or Latino towns on the border. The term "small town values" has a very specific racial coding. It is closely linked to the anti-urban sentiment that courses through American culture. For example, the association of people of color with crowded crime-ridden urban communities is deeply embedded in the mainstream American psyche. Terms like "urban music," "urban radio," "white suburban," and "mainstream" implicitly and explicitly rely on popular shorthand for racialized space.

During the twentieth century, suburbanization became the cornerstone for national identity and social organization. For white "ethnics," moving to the suburbs during the 1930s and into the post World War II period affirmed their cultural identities as white people.[30] Suburban homeownership became the linchpin of the American dream. The advent of the interstate highway system in the mid 1950s provided scores of white families with easy access to segregated suburban subdivisions, segregated jobs, and rigidly segregated schools.[31] Prior to that, restrictive covenants barred African Americans and other people of color from buying homes in white suburban areas. Instituted in 1934, the Federal Housing Administration's (FHA) practice of redlining urban communities and refusing to lend to integrated subdivisions allowed whites to gain easier access to suburban homes than African American homebuyers. Because the FHA was unwilling to lend in urban predominantly African American communities those areas fell into decline, and became national symbols of urban blight.

While FHA policies prohibited African Americans from buying homes in the suburbs, the Public Works Administration (PWA) provided poor and working class Americans of all races subsidies for public housing. The confluence of discriminatory FHA and PWA policies contributed to the development of a vast, substandard public housing apparatus. This apparatus has historically been associated with poor, "criminal" African Americans. Consequently, "like direct relief benefits, public housing was quickly typed in many places as 'welfare' for African Americans, as a handout for the 'feckless.'"[32] Moreover, due to the legacy of cultural propaganda promoted by reformers like Jacob Riis, urban blight was widely viewed as a symptom of low moral standards.

By contrast, much of the early marketing campaign for Southern California relied upon the language of redemption and uplift. Los Angeles was the first major city built on the model of suburbanism and sprawl. Streetcar development literally paved the way for the sprawling layout of the city, providing the foundation for its "autocentric" orientation. Real estate developers and city boosters vigorously promoted Los Angeles to white Midwesterners. With its relatively warm year-round weather, "eternally" sunny open frontier atmosphere and plentiful jobs in defense and manufacturing, L.A. had broad appeal for white Midwesterners looking for a new beginning. As Mike Davis, author of *City of Quartz,* notes, "every census from 1920 to 1960 recorded that Los Angeles had the highest proportion of native-born white Protestants of the largest American cities."[33] Dubbed the "port of Iowa" Southern California epitomized the so-called "good life." But the "good life" that white Midwesterners enjoyed was built on restrictive covenants, a racist police regime, and near feudal employment conditions. L.A. racial apartheid meant that African Americans were confined to South L.A., Latinos to East L.A., and Asians to East and Central L.A. The white residential idyll of Los Angeles was characterized by an abundance of single family homes far removed from the "congested, impoverished, filthy, immoral, transient, and heterogeneous city."[34] In this regard, L.A. was the modern manifestation of the Jeffersonian rural ideal.

Divine Destinies

There is a clear through-line between the notion of private space as moral and the conservative backlash to Barack Obama's election. As aforementioned, right wing pundits have become more and more vociferous in their criticism of big government and the Obama administration's alleged trespasses on the Constitution, individual rights, and the "Christian" ethos of American civil society. Professional heckler and Fox News commentator Glenn Beck is one of the most savvy practitioners of this brand of free enterprise demagoguery. In August of 2010, Beck elicited a furor amongst civil rights organizations when he decided to hold a rally at the Capitol mall on the 47th anniversary of the 1963 March on Washington. Alternately dubbed "Divine Destiny" and "Restoring Honor," the event drew thousands of mostly white participants. That same day, Beck bloviated on the Fox channel with an extended commentary called "Restoring History." Close at his side was David Barton, an amateur "historian" and professional snake oil salesman who has become the dean of the Religious Right's revisionist histories. Railing against all the haters who'd dare claim that the Constitution is secularist, Barton and Beck wondered aloud where inalienable rights came from if they weren't given by God. Throughout the program images of King and the March on Washington flashed on the screen, establishing a visceral connection between the gospel according to Beck and the legacy of the civil rights movement. In an inspired bit of stagecraft, Beck's studio audience consisted of a freshly scrubbed looking group of all white (save for two strategically placed young men of color) young people who hung on Beck and Barton's every word. True to form, Beck and his constituency at the Mall spun the anniversary to fit their egregious distortion of civil rights. Faith leaders of color were trotted out to provide a surreal dash of Kumbaya to an otherwise lily white confab. Most prominent among these tokens was Alveda King—the anti-abortion anti gay rights activist niece of Martin Luther King. In her remarks to the crowd King disgracefully proclaimed the Tea Party to be the true inheritor of the civil rights mantle.[35] As a King family representative her endorsement presumably gave the Tea Party street cred it was sorely lacking.

The Religious Coalition for Reproductive Rights blasted King's appearance at the march for the well-orchestrated political opportunism that it was. Condemning the entire Beck charade, the Reverends Carlton Veazey and William Fauntroy (one of the organizers of the 1963 demonstration) assailed King's "ludicrous" charge of abortion as black genocide and her "leadership of something she calls Freedom Rides for the Unborn."[36] Veazey and Fauntroy further criticized King and anti-choice religious activists for being allied with the Religious Right. National Black Pro-Life Union president Day Gardner scoffed at this charge, characterizing abortion in the black community as the "greatest civil rights battle of our time."[37]

Conservative appropriation of civil rights themes is hardly new. Right wing spin-meisters have always had a perverse genius for stealing and sanitizing civil rights language. In the Orwellian world of Glenn Beck, Sarah Palin, Bill O'Reilly, Sean Hannity, and Rush Limbaugh, health care reforms are "reparations" and the U.S. Department of Justice coddles black militants. The Religious Right pioneered these tactics long before the rise of the Fox mobocracy. Cunningly, anti-abortion propaganda was framed in both moral and civil rights terms. Aborted fetuses were sovereign citizens murdered by selfish pregnant sinners who didn't fear God enough to keep their legs closed. In her article "The Politics of Race and Abortion," Loretta Ross discusses how the right even attempted to pass a Roe v. Wade challenge bill entitled the Susan B. Anthony and Frederick Douglass Prenatal Nondiscrimination Act in 2008. Framing anti-abortion policy as "civil rights" policy has allowed the far right to "intimidate doctors who provide abortions for women of color, stigmatize women of color who choose abortions, and limit access to abortion services in our communities."[38]

The right crafts its fascist anti-human rights agenda from civil rights shorthand. King's historic declaration that individuals should be judged on the "content of their character," rather than their skin color, has been cynically deployed by conservatives of all hues to vilify affirmative action and any public policy that redresses racial disparities.[39] As Earl Ofari Hutchinson notes, "Starting with Reagan, Republican presidents realized that they could wring some political mileage out of King's legacy. They have recast him in their image on civil rights, and bent and twisted his oft times public religious Puritanism on morals issues to justify GOP positions in the values wars that they wage with blacks, Democrats and liberals."[40] Defining morality has been the common currency for these conflicts, with conservatives shaping the national dialogue on values from abortion to affirmative action to taxation. It is no accident that taxation has once again emerged as the defining issue of the Tea Party/ GOP platform. Despite the fact that government spending ballooned under George W. Bush, "no taxation without representation" has become the clarion call of the Obama era. Vilification of the public sector, be it public employees, public pension systems or just plain old "guv-mint," has a moral tenor. Here, average (white) citizens are unfairly penalized by taxation and profligate government spending that undermines free enterprise. Despite being the biggest beneficiaries of government programs in American history, whites are taught to see social mobility as earned. The ability to achieve wealth is a symbol of moral character rather than a function of unearned racial, gender, and class advantage. Any social institution that obstructs this ability is, by definition, immoral. Any social institution that seeks to address this nation's history of racism, sexism, and class injustice by protecting the civil rights of people of color is, by definition, authoritarian, i.e. "I didn't own slaves so why should I pay reparations?" Or so white mainstream thinking goes. Small wonder then, that in the town halls and coffee klatches of Sarah Palin's America, holding citizens fiscally responsible for social welfare is both a mortal and moral threat. An administration that supports tax cuts for the super-rich stifles entrepreneurialism. The wealthy are the authentically oppressed. And since white people comprise the majority of the super-rich white people are the *real v*ictims of racism and civil rights infringement. In Oceania war will always mean peace.

* * * * * * *

The moral ferocity underlying the right's theft of civil rights symbolism is most evident in the venomous backlash against Obama.[41] Utilizing the shrill tactics of the worst fascist propagandist, Beck has smeared *Obama* as a "racist" and "Nazi" who (despite having a predominantly white Cabinet and a white mother whose white family raised him) harbors a "deep hatred" of white people. "Restoring honor" is essentially code for restoring whiteness.[42] For many people of color this "rush" to honor signifies yet another reactionary attempt to ensure that the U.S.' white presidential legacy remains undisturbed. In other words, wake us from this nightmare in 2012 when proper moral order will be restored. With its implication of an America "blackened" and besmirched by evildoers there is also a strong gendered subtext to the call to restore honor. It evokes medieval contests for the honor of proper ladies, duels for the sexual purity and moral virtue of families. Honor has always been a commodity that men defined and controlled. In the 18th and 19th centuries honor was symbolized by the white virginal figure Columbia lilting over the rugged plains of America bringing civilization to the savages.[43] Typically portrayed as a young goddess-like white woman with outstretched arms and beseeching eyes, Columbia was used to advance Manifest Destiny. During the 19th century the "Manifest Destiny" of the United States was one of "God-ordained" expansionism. African slaves, indigenous peoples, Mexican nationals and other "non-Europeans" were deemed aliens and enemy combatants, anathema to the democratizing force of America. Under the 1790 Immigration and Naturalization Act "free white persons" of "good moral character" who had resided in the U.S. for two years were eligible for citizenship. Non-whites were excluded from this amnesty, further cementing the association of citizenship and national identity with whiteness. Using that "old time religion" to shepherd the flock, Beck's "Divine Destiny" revival deftly mined this history. Reeking of sulfur, hubris, and the visionary charlatanism of 1920s revivalist Aimee Semple McPherson, Beck claimed that the Divine Destiny event would provide "an inspiring look at the role faith played in the founding of America and the role it will play again in its destiny."

Decrying the cultural primitivism and backwardness of the Muslim world, twenty first century Christian fascists continue to put the lie to American exceptionalism. After the uproar over the proposed Islamic Center near Ground Zero in 2010, the Islamophobic vitriol of demagogues like Beck, Sarah Palin, and Newt Gingrich paid off in cold blood. The stabbing of a Muslim cabdriver in New York and hate attacks against Islamic centers in Tennessee and California (the latter committed by a group in Fresno calling itself the American Nationalist Brotherhood), were just two of the tragic but all too predictable results of the nationalist chest beating that masqueraded as empathy for the victims of 9/11.

Throughout American history, recourse to the transparent word of God has always been the last refuge of scoundrels wielding the Bible and the bayonet as protections from the ungovernable horde. Thus, it is fitting that this naked evocation of the language and legacy of Manifest Destiny comes during a period when the right has launched a campaign to repeal the 1868 14th amendment. The 14th amendment was originally designed to grant birthright citizenship to freed African slaves. As Kevin Alexander Gray wrote in *Counterpunch,* "in the Reconstruction period, as now, racism and white supremacy loomed large in public debate. Back then, opponents of the amendment talked about 'public morality' being threatened by people 'unfit for the responsibilities of American citizenship.'"[44] Now the self-appointed defenders of public morality have come full circle, drunk on a cocktail of xenophobia, anti-immigrant hysteria, and jingoism.

In 2009, Republican Congressman Nathan Deal, one of the staunchest critics of the 14th amendment's provision of birthright citizenship, introduced the Birthright Citizenship Act of 2009 into the House. The statute would deny citizenship to children born in the U.S. to undocumented women, stripping away yet another civil right that ostensibly distinguishes the U.S. from fascist governments. Emboldened by the anti-illegal immigration forces of Arizona's SB1070 legislation, some in the Republican right (including the "maverick" John McCain, one- time advocate for immigration reform) have stepped up in support of hearings to repeal all or part of the 14th amendment. As Constitutional scholars are quick to point out, the 14th amendment is the foundation for the equal protection clause that undergirds much of civil rights policy in the U.S. Without it states would be free to exercise their own judgment on what constitutes equal protection under the law. Anti-14th amendment forces are a powerful reminder of the connection between slavery and expansionism. In the midst of a burgeoning slave regime, cultural propaganda demonizing and dehumanizing indigenous Mexican populations provided American imperialism with the aura of moral righteousness. Writing in support of the U.S.-Mexico War in an 1846 *Brooklyn Daily Eagle* editorial, "radical" poet Walt Whitman proclaimed: "What has miserable, inefficient Mexico—with her superstition, her burlesque upon freedom, her actual tyranny by the few over the many—what has she to do with the great mission of peopling the new world with a noble race? Be it ours, to achieve that mission!"[45]

Back in the good old days of docile slaves and vanquished savages, there were no ambiguities about who deserved to be granted rights. God ordained the universality of European American experience, civilization, and moral worth. Non-white peoples either submitted to the Enlightenment principles and values of the culturally superior West or were extinguished. And States rights were white citizens' last vestige of protection from the trespasses of big government. So it is no mystery then why the ideology of 19th century expansionism and evangelical Christian revivalism has gained fresh currency amongst a "reloading" white nationalist insurgency. As the freshly inked graffiti on the vandalized Islamic Center in Fresno proclaimed, "Wake up America, the Enemy is here."

Endnotes

1. Public Religion Research, "Old Alignments, Emerging Faults: Religion in the 2010 Election and Beyond," November 17, 2010 (http://www.publicreligion.org/research/?id=428).
2. Ibid. Forty four percent of Americans believe that discrimination against whites has become just as bad as that against "minorities." Seventy five percent of those identifying with the Tea Party believe this to be case. White evangelicals were the only religious group with a majority (57%) that believed discrimination against whites was just as significant as that against minorities.
3. Gary Wills, *Head and Heart: American Christianities* (New York: Penguin Press, 2007); Robert Middlekauf, *The Glorious Cause: The American Revolution, 1763-1789* (New York: Oxford University Press, 2007); Robert Boston, *Why the Religious Right is Wrong About Separation of Church and State* (New York: Prometheus Books, 1993).
4. James C. McKinley, Jr., "Texas Conservatives Win Vote on Textbook Standards," *New York Times,* March 13, 2010 (http://www.nytimes.com/2010/03/13/education/13texas.html).
5. Ibid.
6. Ibid.
7. See for example, *Crisis Pregnancy Centers: An Affront to Choice,* National Abortion Federation, 2006 and *Crisis Pregnancy Centers Revealed*, NARAL Pro-Choice Virginia, 2010.
8. In Colorado anti-abortion advocates put a proposition on the ballot designed to confer unfertilized eggs with individual rights. It was narrowly defeated.
9. Avakian, *Away With All Gods*, 182.
10. Ophelia Benson and Jeremy Stangroom, *Does God Hate Women?* (Continuum: New York, 2009), 97.
11. The Family Research Council hosts the hugely influential annual Values Voter Summit, which features conservative Christian-aligned politicians.
12. Paul Krugman, "Why Americans Hate Single-Payer Insurance," *New York Times,* July 28, 2009 (http://krugman.blogs.nytimes.com/2009/07/28/why-americans-hate-single-payer-insurance).

13. In July 2010 the NAACP elicited a firestorm when it passed a resolution calling on Tea Party leadership to repudiate the racist sentiments and propaganda that have gained prominence in the movement.

14. Sean Wilentz, "Confounding Fathers," *New Yorker,* October 18, 2010 (http://www.newyorker.com/reporting/2010/10/18/101018fa_fact_wilentz?currentPage=all).

15. Robert Scheer, "Payback at the Polls," *Truthout*, November 3, 2010 (http://www.truth-out.org/robert-scheer-payback-polls64788).

16. Robert P. Jones and Daniel Cox, "Religion and the Tea Party in the 2010 Election: An Analysis of the Third Biennial American Values Survey," Public Religion Research Institute, Washington DC (October 2010), p. 5. According to this survey Christian conservatives constitute 31% of the GOP's base while Tea Party identified conservatives are 20% of the GOP's base.

17. Kate Zernike, "The Party Avoids Divisive Issues, *New York Times*, March 12, 2010 (http://www.nytimes.com/2010/03/13/us/politics/13tea.html?ref=tea_party_movement).

18. Jones and Cox, "Religion and the Tea Party in the 2010 Election," 4.

19. Ibid.

20. Chris Hedges, *American Fascists: The Christian Right and the War on America* (New York: Free Press), 2006, 21.

21. See for example, Jane Mayer, "The Brothers Trying to Bring Down Obama," *The New Yorker*, August 30, 2010, 44-55.

22. Kathleen Hennessey, "Republicans Seek to Address Issues of 'Values Voters," *Los Angeles Times*, September 18, 2010, A8. During the 2010 Values Voters Summit GOP and Tea Party stalwarts sought to assure Christian conservatives that both had they would preserve their traditional anti-choice, anti-gay, Creationist agenda.

23. On the heels of a Supreme Court ruling that said citizens have an "individual right to keep a loaded handgun for home defense," Arizona, Tennessee, Georgia and Virginia enacted laws allowing guns in bars and restaurants. See Malcolm Gay, "More States Allowing Guns in Bars," *The New York Times*, October 3, 2010 (http://www.nytimes.com/2010/10/04/us/04guns.html?_r=1&src=twr&scp=6&sq=guns&st=cse).

24. Southern Poverty Law Center, "The Second Wave: Return of the Militias," (Alabama: Southern Poverty Law Center, 2009), introduction.

25. Ibid., 7.

26. Ibid.; I discuss the implications of the backlash against the 14th Amendment's birthright citizenship provision later in this chapter.

27. Ibid.

28. Lyndsey Layton, "Palin Apologizes for 'Real America' Comments," *The Washington Post*, October 22, 2008.

29. Joel Tarr, "From City to Suburb: The Moral Influence of Transportation Technology," Alexander Callow ed. *American Urban History,* (New York: Oxford University Press, 1973), 202-212.

30. For further discussion on the complex dynamic of the suburbanizing of whiteness see, David R. Roediger, *Working Toward Whiteness: How America's Immigrants Became White* (New York: Basic Books, 2005), 8, 9, 224-234.

31. The Federal Housing Administration refused to provide mortgage loans to residents wishing to live in integrated subdivisions, citing close proximity of "inharmonious racial or nationality groups" as being an undesirable condition for lending. This practice institutionalized the redlining of inner city communities and residential segregation.

32. Roediger, 225.

33. Mike Davis, *City of Quartz: Excavating the Future in Los Angeles* (London: Verso, 1990), 326.

34. David Brodsley, *L.A. Freeway* (Berkeley: University of California Press, 1981), 72-74; Robert Fogelson, *The Fragmented Metropolis: Los Angeles, 1850-1930* (Cambridge: Harvard University Press, 1967), 43-62.

35. According to Earl Ofari Hutchinson, King "has been on the campaign circuit for more than a decade pushing a discriminatory, anti-gay marriage, anti-abortion, hard right family values message." From, "How Alveda King is Turning Martin Luther King's Dream into a Nightmare," *The Grio,* August 27, 2010 (http://www.thegrio.com/politics/mlks-niece-turns-a-beautiful-dream-into-a-nightmare.php).

36. Carlton Veazey, "The Religious Right Insults King's Legacy," *Street Prophets*, August 27, 2010 (http://www.streetprophets.com/storyonly/2010/8/27/132225/448).

37. Steven Ertelt, "Black Abortion Advocates Attack Alveda King, Say Martin Luther King Not Pro-Life," *LifeNews*, August 27, 2010 (http://www.lifenews.com/nat6662.html).

38. Loretta Ross, "Trust Black Women: The Politics of Race and Abortion," *Collective Voices*, Volume 5, No. 11, Fall 2010, 25.

39. Prominent black conservative Shelby Steele famously used King's aphorism as the title of his best-selling book which argued against the need for race-based remedies to discrimination.

40. Earl Ofari Hutchinson, "Glenn Beck Continues Crusade to Co-opt King," *The Grio*, August 23, 2010 (http://www.thegrio.com/politics/glenn-beck-continues-conservative-crusade-to-co-opt-dr-king.php).

41. One of the more venomous and intellectually sloppy tirades against Barack Obama was penned by Dinesh D'Souza, who accuses Obama of being a "Kenyan anti-colonialist." Dinesh D'Souza, *The Roots of Obama's Rage* (New York: Regnery Press, 2010).

42. Attendees at the Beck rally were instructed not to bring "political" signs or slogans, ostensibly to minimize the potential for the noxiously racist signs and slogans popular at Tea Party rallies.

43. According to Thomas J. Steele, Phillis Wheatley was one of the first to use Columbia "in such a way as to create a personification of America" in her 1776 poem "To His Excellency George Washington." Thomas J. Steele, "The Figure of Columbia: Phillis Wheatley plus George Washington," *New England Quarterly* (Vol. 54, No. 2, Jun., 1981), 264-266.

44. Kevin Alexander Gray, "Shooting Cans: The Racist Assault on the 14th Amendment," *Counterpunch*, August 13-15, 2010 (http://www.counterpunch.org/gray08132010.html).

45. Walt Whitman, *Brooklyn Daily Eagle*, 1846.

Chapter 7

The White Stuff: New Atheism and Its Discontents

Even with the best of intentions, a largely white male community can become a self-fulfilling prophecy.

—Greta Christina, atheist blogger

It was a common saying, even among little white boys, that it was worth a half-cent to kill a 'nigger,' and a half-cent to bury one.

—Frederick Douglass, 1845

Promising a taste of the immortal, churches are sanctuaries from death, decay, and the wanton other. They shield true believers from the specter of contact and engagement with the other. They sanctify identity through opposition, from pillar to post.

This was part of the ethos of the original Puritans, drunk as they were on sex and original sin. Giddy as they were over the carnality of the dark savage witch Tituba. Exercised as they were that their pure white daughters were beholden to and contaminated by a female slave of color.[1] Was it Tituba who brought seventeenth century Salem to its knees, or the rumor of her, the haunt of her resurrected in the cold stiff church pews of eternal Sundays? Feverish with the specter of Eve's serpent luring Adam out of Eden, it is this part of the American mind that regards black and brown ghettoes as graveyards, spaces to be passed over, rammed through, discarded, and demonized. In the blessed light of the steeple, we are saved, inoculated from the virus of history.

Navigating the wilderness of the Obama era, disaffected whites "cling" to religion as an antidote to the encroaching other. Secularism, big government, and Islam are a poisonous stew for white slavery. The basic freedoms that separate God-fearing Americans from the superstition shackled third world horde have been trampled by government jackboots. Whereas the Obama era is rife with unknowns and intangibles, the Ronald Reagan, George Bush, and George W. Bush eras offered white fundamentalists soothing clarity about race, gender, and sexual orientation. As Chris Hedges notes, "there runs through the fundamentalist belief system a deep dread of ambiguity, disorder, and chaos. Accordingly, the cult of masculinity keeps all ambiguity, especially sexual ambiguity, in check. It fosters a world of binary opposites: God and man, saved and unsaved, the church and the world, Christianity and secular humanism, male and female."[2] This longing for a restoration of "the known" animates Glenn Beck revivalism, the betrayal narratives of the Tea Party, and the millennialist fervor of the new militia movement. Yet this longing for the known is also the lifeblood of the Black Church, and it has had devastating implications for black cultural diversity and socioeconomic sustainability.

With blacks comprising 25% of the nation's poor, only economic justice can truly redress the cult of religiosity in African American communities. Our communities are filled with stories of women like "Ann," an out of work administrator profiled in a Los Angeles Times series on the unemployed.

Overqualified, under-housed, and too poor to afford dental care, Ann was nonetheless able to scrape together fifty bucks a month for the local church's collection plate. Would Ann's fears about the future be stilled by the revelation that there is no God? Would the prospect of being $16,000 richer in ten years diminish her need to believe?

There is little analysis of the relationship between economic disenfranchisement, race, gender, and religiosity in New Atheist or secular humanist critiques of organized religion. It is for this reason that much of New Atheist critique has limited cultural relevance for people of color. In fact, some New Atheist discourse exhibits the binaries Hedges identifies. Richard Dawkins has unpacked the evolutionary dimension of religious belief and adherence, arguing that contemporary reverence for supernaturalism of any kind fatally undermines reason and scientific inquiry. Sam Harris has barnstormed against the evils of Islamic and Christian fundamentalism, eviscerating, among other things, moderate believers' complicity in the "terroristic" precepts of Islam. Christopher Hitchens has lambasted the religious as fools and dupes. He has condemned radical Islam as medieval and shares Harris' contempt for its liberal apologists/enablers in the West. Hitchens has also been criticized by feminist atheists and skeptics for sexism and essentialist views of gender.[3] In a widely circulated web commentary, skeptic feminist Rebecca Watson called Hitchens on sexist comments he made about women comedians, including a racist homophobic reference to African American comedian Wanda Sykes.[4] In Hitchens' elite white alpha dog world, "the problem with many female comedians up until now is that they tended to be dykes or Jews or butch…and these are all forms of emulating male humor."[5] Watson and other feminist bloggers have also written extensively about the shrilly sexist comments and ad hominem attacks posted on popular websites like Richard Dawkins.net.[6] Dawkins does not directly moderate the comments on his site's forums.[7] And the Dawkins Foundation has been proactive about including the work of feminist writers like Ayaan Hirsi Ali, Greta Cristina, Ophelia Benson, and me on it. But the balls to the breeze swagger of Hitchens, atheist celeb Bill Maher, and male atheists in the blogosphere is merely part of the larger context of institutional sexism. It isn't earth shattering news that men feel uninhibited about strutting their sense of sexist entitlement under the guise of "free thought" "rational thinking" and "objectivity" in the anonymous comfort of the blogosphere. The dominant culture supports and normalizes this right. Who needs arcane religious tracts decreeing the inferiority of women and "minorities" when the history of modern science and rationality decrees it?

The totalizing narratives of Dawkins, Harris, and Hitchens (three of the so-called Four Horsemen; the fourth being the more even-handed Daniel Dennett) establish a clear line of demarcation between the religious and non-believers. Some secular humanist and religious critics complain that the Horsemen are so adept at railing against religion that they can't adequately define a vision of morality and ethics in an atheist universe. For example, Harris has argued that morality and ethics can be scientifically adduced. There is a universal template for what is "good" and what is "right." This essentially boils down to wellbeing. Good values are equivalent to unimpeachable empirical facts. They are not merely products of the cultural, social or historical context of a people, nation or culture. Taking aim at this notion, skeptic philosopher Massimo Pigliucci contends:

> if we let empirical facts decide what is right and what is wrong, then new scientific findings may very well "demonstrate"

> that things like slavery, corporal punishment, repression of gays, limited freedom of women, and so on, are "better" and therefore more moral than liberal-progressive types such as Harris and myself would be ready to concede. The difference is that I wouldn't have a problem rejecting such findings – just as I don't have a problem condemning social Darwinism and eugenics – but Harris would find himself in a bind. Indeed, he seems to be making a categorical mistake: what he calls *values* are instead empirical facts about how to achieve human wellbeing. But why value individual human wellbeing, or the wellbeing of self-aware organisms, to begin with? Facts are irrelevant to that question.[8]

Pigliucci has criticized the atheist/skeptic movement's fixation on science as the antidote to all social ills. The belief in science as magic bullet has been dubbed "scientism." Eugenics is an example of the divide between scientific observation and ethics:

> Contrary to rather politically correct fashion among biologists, I do not think eugenics was entirely an aberration based on pseudoscience. We know that many of the claims made by eugenicists were based on sloppy research or were simply unfounded. Nonetheless it is undeniable that eugenics is a logical consequence—applies to humans—of our understanding of natural selection. Humans do breed...and our genes behave in the same manner as those of cattle or crop plants...the real question, of course, is...should eugenics be practiced? The answer, given the moral standards of many human societies, is a resounding no. But this is an ethical, not a scientific conclusion.[9]

Pigliucci argues that one of the reasons scientism is problematic is because thorny uncertainties such as moral values, ethics, and ideology can't be quantified through empirical investigation. For example, notions of "wellbeing" come down to context and positionality. Anti-abortion anti-choice activists argue that the "wellbeing" of an unborn fetus supersedes that of the mother. The mother should be a host carrier prevented from exercising sovereign power and control over her body. Hence, it doesn't matter whether the fetus can exist outside of the mother's body. However, in this book I have argued that those who subscribe to this belief system seek to impose their immoral fascistic values on a woman's right to exercise sovereign control. But can "good" science police the woman's right to sovereignty in the name of unimpeachable empirical moral value? Harris maintains that "if there is real diversity in how people can be deeply fulfilled in life, this diversity can be accounted for and honored in the context of science… the concept of 'wellbeing' like the concept of 'health' is truly open for revision and discovery."[10] Nonetheless he comes out strongly against secularists' morally relativist "respect" for the ethics and principles of organized religion. He concedes that non-Muslim tolerance for such extreme (in the West's eyes) practices as veiling and female genital mutilation may derive from an anti-colonialist ethos. He simplistically allows that "the most common defense one now hears for religious faith… is that belief in (God) is the only basis for a universal conception of human values."[11] Clearly Harris should get out more. Such a notion ignores the material and social benefits organized religion confers on poor and middle class people of color in a racist capitalist context where the social welfare safety net is negligible. Moral value is shaped by systematized power and control that often defines the choices, investments, and social realities, i.e., the wellbeing, of the disenfranchised. An emphasis on wellbeing, or "utilitarianism," is an inadequate metric for determining moral value. For example, African women who participate in genital circumcision rituals might argue that they serve the "wellbeing" of their community and their female kin because circumcised women have a greater chance of being chosen as wives and potential mothers. Are women who invest in patriarchy, seemingly against their own interests, hardwired to do so, or are they merely socially conditioned to see their interests and that of violent patriarchal controlling regimes as one and the same?

Why people do seemingly paradoxical things, their motivations, and the manner in which these motivations reflect the way they make sense out of the world, are the province of science *and* philosophy. Yet to suggest that science *determines* morality, as the subtitle of Harris' book *The Moral Landscape* does, is folly. In many regards the idea that a person's "biological" race determined moral fitness (and hence moral values) was the premise of scientific racism. Your position on the racial food chain determined your sense of morality, a status which was preordained by "scientific" observation. Pigliucci argues

> Of course, I am in complete agreement that our *sense* of morality is an instinct that derives from our biological history, and that our moral reasoning is carried out by certain areas of the brain. But neither of these conclusions make evolutionary biology or neurobiology arbiters of moral decision making. Of course we do moral reasoning with the brain, just like we solve mathematical problems with the brain. Is Harris going to suggest that neurobiology will supersede mathematics? Of course our basic sense of morality has its roots in having evolved as social primates, but so do xenophobia, homophobia, and a bunch of other human characteristics that are not moral and that we don't want to encourage.[12]

The problem with Harris and other New Atheists who espouse scientism is that their work lacks context. They provide no sociological insight into why organized religion and religiosity have an enduring hold on disenfranchised communities in the richest, most powerful nation on the planet. Religion is only one apparatus for draconian repression and inequity.

Secular institutions that enforce and uphold oppressive hierarchies must also be actively challenged within a humanist framework. Modern capitalist inequities that permit criminally stratospheric wealth and obscene poverty buttress America's faith industry. So in the absence of an explicitly anti-racist, anti-sexist, anti-heterosexist and anti-imperialist critical consciousness there will continue to be a major divide between white atheist discourse and the lived experiences of humanists of color. And in the absence of community-based institutions anchored in humanist approaches to health, wellness, and sustainability, humanist atheists of color will have no "real time" foundation beyond insular white settings.

At the same time, it is important to acknowledge that the global visibility of the secular humanist and "New Atheist" movements has had some impact on notions of public morality. Dawkins' critique of the pathological hypocrisy of the Catholic Church and the U.S.' political deference to the Religious Right on science research and innovation has reached millions. The Richard Dawkins Foundation for Reason and Science supports and provides platforms for such organizations as the Black Atheists of America and African Americans for Humanism. And although non-believers are still feared and reviled by a majority of the U.S. population, recent research has shown that the younger so-called "millennial" generation is less religious—partly in reaction to the militancy of the Christian right. In 2009, president Obama became the first president in history to host a delegation of secular organizations for a brainstorming session at the White House.[13] Departing from the theocratic swagger of his predecessor, Obama's attention to this coalition was almost certainly due to the atheist movement's rise on the national radar.

That said, the broader question of how secular humanist and atheist perspectives can contribute to feminist, social justice liberation struggle remains. Many humanists and atheists of color look around and see a movement whose public face and official leadership is white and largely male. They look around and see conference after conference dominated by white males and females from the scientific establishment. They struggle to gain voice in a dialogue that has been reduced to the narrow lens of a handful of international superstars and academic elites. And though deeply critical of religious tyranny in their own communities, they chafe at white atheists' often paternalistic and ahistorical criticism of the role religion has played in African American, Latino, and Native American cultures.

In the preceding chapters I've argued that organized religion has been a bulwark against white supremacy and institutional racism. Organized religion enabled African Americans to achieve self-determination and community under conditions of racial apartheid. Judeo Christian religious practice was also a means of legitimizing enslaved Africans' claim to being Americans. It provided them with a foundation for a moral claim to citizenship and personhood. It continues to have a defining influence upon blacks' perceptions of themselves as Americans. It establishes "insider" status and racial authenticity. Consequently, it both binds African Americans to and separates them from the larger context of an American national identity based on the presumption of Christian moral and cultural eminence. Insofar as notions of public morality are always inflected through race, gender and sexuality, African Americans will always remain outside of these paradigms. African Americans who reject organized religion are even further marginalized as cultural and racial others.

The challenge for African American atheist humanists is in confronting these orthodoxies. Reflecting on the potential appeal of atheism and humanism for African Americans Kamau Rashid commented:

> Someone once told me that Ché Guevara said that "the job of a revolutionary is to discourage the very last vestige of faith that the people have in the existing system; and to expedite the bringing into existence of a new and honest system." I think that the key to promoting Atheism or Secular Humanism to and among African Americans is to demonstrate the innumerable failures of religious fervor to guide us in solving our most basic problem. Here we reside within a community where polls indicate high degrees of religious belief, yet the ethical or institutional mandates that this supposedly implies are nearly absent in reality. I'll use two examples: the relatively high rates of Black-on-Black violence in many American cities and the high rates of childbirths by young, never-married mothers. Perhaps Christianity didn't create these contradictions. But it certainly seems ill-suited to solve them as well. So I think that the key is to capitalize on the doubt, the anxiety, the longing for something that is based in reality that provides a sense of meaning, purpose, and direction for our collective energies.[14]

Rashid alludes to the "revolutionary" impetus and longing that must drive the shift from mental servitude to critical consciousness. Simply rejecting organized religion and exhorting others to do so is hardly a strategy for redress. Condemning the robber baron ways of faith predator preachers and their parasitic hold on the inner city will not convert impoverished believers like "Ann" to enlightened non-belief. It will not stem the tide of forked tongued showmen and ghetto hucksters nor break the long sordid chain of corruption that stretches from Father Divine to Reverend Ike to Elijah Muhammed to Eddie Long down to the gates of a Christian hell. It will not substantively address the twenty first century complexities of people of color living in a "white supremacist capitalist patriarchy" (to use bell hooks' term).

Hooks' term speaks to the multi-layered nature of African American lived experience. It also speaks to the challenge African American atheist humanists face. There is a visible black middle class but black poverty and incarceration have gone through the roof. Greater numbers of African American women are entering colleges and universities, yet K-12 black achievement reflects apartheid conditions in public schools. The Obama girls have emerged as national symbols of idyllic American girlhood yet there is the atrocity of a 7 year-old black girl murdered by Detroit police. In a white supremacist capitalist patriarchy there is no sanctity for black life and black children are not innocents. While missing white girls command national attention coverage (if any) of missing or murdered black children is generally confined to the back pages in the bloodlessly tiny print reserved for marginalia. In May 2010, Aiyanna Jones' murder by Detroit police officers after a military-style raid on her home generated rare national media attention. In the wake of the shooting neighbors and loved ones placed stuffed animals in front of the house in memoriam. Rows of stuffed animals stared out from Associated Press photographs of the crime scene in dark-eyed innocence. In black communities across the nation Aiyanna's death elicited a firestorm of outrage from activists critical of police misconduct and excessive force. Recalling New York, Los Angeles, Oakland and other cities where black lives have been cut down by trigger happy police officers, many condemned the murder as yet another example of law enforcement's criminal devaluation of black lives.

It is difficult to imagine a universe where the murder of a little suburban white girl would be tolerated as "collateral damage." It is impossible to fathom a historical moment in which innocence has not been associated with the lives of little white children. The media and public culture are designed to validate the basic humanity of white children. It is a reality which even the smallest black children, already struggling with a kind of DuBois-ian "double consciousness," see reflected around them. DuBois introduced this term in *Souls of Black Folk,* meditating on black liberation struggle at the turn of the twentieth century. Insofar as black identity and self-image were also disfigured by the norms of the dominant white culture, black subjectivity was dual. DuBois framed this dilemma in masculinist terms. Black self-determination was essentially a masculine journey. For "one ever feels his two-ness—an American, a Negro; two souls, two thoughts, two unreconciled strivings; two warring ideals in one dark body... The history of the American Negro is the history of this strife, this longing to attain self-conscious manhood, to merge his double self into a better and truer self."[15]

In the wake of both Reconstruction and the 1895 Plessy vs. Ferguson decision, DuBois' double consciousness also highlights black liberation struggle around who and what is human. Now, as the right wing backlash against social justice reaches fever pitch, the question of the "human" continues to define and terrorize African Americans in our struggle for moral and political agency. In the broader context of the "New Atheist" movement, this question is often marginalized as "other," undermining the possibility of any sustainable cross-racial alliances around humanist issues.

Writing in her blog "Unscripted," Institute for Humanist Studies managing director Mercedes Diane Griffin noted, "Most programs looking to address the lack of diversity within the Humanist movement are quite limited in their scope, often focusing solely on the low income African American community, ignoring all other communities of color (and economic strata within these communities) and rarely addressing the practical aspects of what feeds religiosity amongst the members of these communities."[16] Indeed, for many black humanists coming from African American communities where religion has become *the* opiate for a people under socioeconomic, political, and cultural siege, the reductive science worship of the white non-theist world is a problematic luxury. Throughout the history of Western science, scientific inquiry has been just as beholden to the social and political orthodoxies of a given era as religion. In many regards the black body has been the universal proving ground for the "verities" of science and European cultural ideology.

Certainly, the domination of white male scientists and science scholarship in atheist communities has occurred at the expense of a broader lens that emphasizes social justice. At the 2009 African Americans for Humanism (AAH) conference Center For Inquiry (CFI) field organizer (and current AAH Director) Debbie Goddard challenged the insularity of prominent atheist and Humanist organizations such as CFI, the Council for Secular Humanism, and Atheist Alliance International (AAI). Goddard noted that their virtually all-white all-male boards become a self-fulfilling prophecy of Eurocentrism.[17] In this regard, atheist and humanist discourse becomes an endless echo chamber. And the ideological priorities of the movement are reduced to evolution and the glories of the Enlightenment, the tyranny of religious belief, the "backwardness" of believers, church/state separation, and more doses of evolution. Questioning or deviating from the playbook, by historicizing the cult of science worship, is viewed with scorn by some non-theist whites unaccustomed to having their cultural privilege and assumptions challenged.[18]

Hence, the Eurocentric insularity of the American atheist and humanist movements is reinforced by the relative absence of people of color in prominent leadership roles. Over the past twenty years, the director of African Americans for Humanism has been the only full-time leadership position dedicated to promoting people of color in the traditionally white-dominated field of secular humanism. Author Norm Allen held this position until his dismissal in June 2010. Allen played a critical role in advancing humanist discourse in Africa and black humanist scholarship in the U.S. His unceremonious dismissal from AAH was yet another indicator of the vulnerability of African American leadership in the humanist sphere.

White Allies and Cultural Proficiency

The conference, sponsored by the Council for Secular Humanism, drew members from all the major doubters' organizations, including American Atheists and the American Humanist Association. The largely white and male crowd – imagine a Star Trek convention, but older came to hear panels by best-selling pamphleteers like Richard Dawkins and Sam Harris.

—on the 2010 Council for Secular Humanism conference,
the New York Times, October 15, 2010[19]

The counting starts as soon as we step foot in the convention hall. One, two, three, a negligible four, hovering tentatively at a vendor table, darting past with averted eyes. My friend and I can tick off the number of people of color at the 2009 AAI convention in Burbank, California on one hand. I have been invited to speak at the event but we savor the old familiar counting game ruefully, sardonically. Having both attended predominantly white universities and sat on nearly all white boards we've become experts in the anthropology of white settings. The laser-like stares that people of color elicit from curious whites in protected communities. The feeling of black hyper-visibility and invisibility. The specter of white folks' oblivion to the history and power of white crowds. The creeping sense of being transported back in time, to a galaxy not far away. Though a few minutes away from downtown Los Angeles' ethnic polyglot, Burbank is a largely white professional enclave dominated by TV studios, industrial parks, hotels, strip malls, awkwardly configured streets, and an airport. Like similar cities in L.A. it has a robust history of racial profiling and segregated schools. So, coming in to the convention we know the drill. But the thriving online community of atheists of color has led us to have higher expectations for some "real time" presence.

As in most social movements before them, people of color in the atheist and humanist movements are constantly being called on to school, teach, and otherwise "mentor" white folks wanting guidance on matters of race and "diversity." Such tutorials can get tiring and enraging for even the most patient native informant guiding her charge out of the "Eden" of innocence and white entitlement. Reflecting on her experiences working with predominantly white humanist organizations, Mercedes Diane Griffin of the IHS recounted the ritual of "turned heads" whenever she enters the room at humanist conferences. Accustomed to being the sole person of color at many of these confabs, she believes that the Eurocentric emphasis of humanist atheist discourse is symptomatic of the racial schisms within American society as a whole. Noting that the contributions of women are also given short shrift in leading secular organizations she commented that:

> (The) AHA and Secular Coalition of America…are best suited to normalizing humanism within the broader context. These organizations are the most progressive in terms of engaging

> women and younger people in the movement and in leadership roles. However many of the other organizations are dominated by older people and it is very much a good old boy's network. When women speak it's as if they're talking to the wall. People don't second their motions, people challenge their authority. The issue of women not being taken seriously in the humanist movement is very real. Women are not brought in as speakers, they're not in leadership roles. Humanist organizations need to adopt a concrete plan of action to make women visible in the humanist secular movement."[20]

Similarly, Naima Cabelle, a long time activist in the Washington D.C. secular humanist and atheist communities, notes, "I'm concerned about the entrenched white male establishment found in national secular organizations. There seems to be no room for any form of leadership other than their own; no room for any ideas other than their own. Likewise... too few African American atheists have come forward to actively support efforts to promote atheism, build alliances and friendships ***even with each other***, and to begin to work to build a foundation which promotes transparency, openness, diversity, and activism in the secular community."[21]

Being marginalized is not a revelation for most African American, Latino, Asian, and Native American folk accustomed to invisibility in all white institutions. For example, despite conservative claims of a left wing academic "mafia," buttressed by preferential treatment toward so-called minorities, American academia remains a largely white preserve powered by cronyism, favoritism, and affirmative action for white elites. The majority of tenured faculty, permanent administrators, presidents, and chancellors at American universities are white. The struggle that academics of color frequently face getting hired and getting tenure has negative consequences (particularly in predominantly white fields like science and engineering) for recruitment and retention of students of color. Tenure, publication, conference presentations, and participation in committees determine status, visibility, and career longevity in the academic community. All are key factors in the dissemination of scholarship. So it is no coincidence that many of the major figures and spokespersons in the humanist atheist movements come from academia (such as Oxford, Tufts, Stanford, and the University of Minnesota), where they have benefited from the ivory tower politics of faculty recruitment, hiring, and tenure. Yet for some reason many white atheist humanists believe that just being an atheist magically exempts them from the institutionally racist belief systems and practices of the dominant culture.[22]

Discussing her motivation for founding Black Atheists of America, Ayanna Watson contended:

> When I started Black Atheists of America, the number one criticism received was that there was no need to separate black atheists from other atheists. There is this belief that a group can fight for equality by ignoring the impact of yesterday's ills. We have members in both the atheist and humanist movements that do not realize that there are cultural differences between members within these groups. Because many members in these movements shut down the minute they hear a particular subgroup is recognized (i.e. - women of color), they do not even attempt to educate themselves on why the distinction is necessary.[23]

In other words, why the hell do we need to be culturally proficient when we're the masters of the universe?

Cultural proficiency is an approach that is used to train educators about the influence of culture on teaching and learning. It is based on the belief that there *is* a dominant culture that affords advantages and disadvantages to individuals and communities based upon race, gender, sexual orientation, and class. It holds that these advantages and disadvantages come from systemic institutional practices, and not what white anti-racism activist Peggy McKintosh has characterized as "individual acts of prejudice." In this regard "systems of oppression and privilege are the societal forces that affect individuals due to their membership in a distinct cultural group. Systems of oppression do not require intentional acts by perpetrators; they can be the function of systemic policies and practices."[24]

Becoming culturally proficient involves more than just acknowledging that racism exists, and being able, as a white person, to move on. More specifically it involves developing critical consciousness about how white supremacy (in concert with other systems of advantage and disadvantage) informs the way power and authority are constructed locally, nationally, and globally. Greta Christina summed up the prevailing attitude of whites irritated with critiques about the whiteness of the atheist movement as "How dare you accuse me of unconscious racism and sexism—I'm not the problem, the unique personality and culture of women and people of color is the problem?" Thus

> When we say things like, 'Sure our movement is mostly white and male—but that's not our problem...' What we're really saying is, 'White male atheists are the real atheists. White male atheists are the ones who count. The reason white men stay in religion, or have a hard time coming out as atheists—those are the real reasons, the ones we should be addressing. Women and POC (people of color)—they're special, extra, other. We shouldn't have to change our behavior to include them in the movement. This should be a One Size Fits all movement—a size that fits white men.[25]

And why would it be otherwise when American society naturalizes white supremacy? During the AAI convention an older white man approached me and lamented how wrongheaded religious blacks were. Speaking in a hushed confidential tone, he proceeded to tell me that religion was the primary cause of intimate partner violence among African Americans. It was a tragedy that more blacks didn't realize it. He was clearly an expert on all things Negro because he'd taken black history classes in college, a tidbit that he revealed in parting. In the era of Obama and hip hop, becoming an expert on blackness doesn't require any special talent. It is one avocation that many whites seem eager to claim as existential sport and national obsession, salting their dialogue, when they want to be bold, nasty or dangerous, with "black" dialect, "black" inflections, and "urban" pop culture references. Blackness is a body of knowledge, because as Frantz Fanon said ala DuBois, "the white gaze, the only valid one is already dissecting me. I am fixed."[26] In his classic meditation *Black Skin White Masks*, Fanon considers the violence of the white gaze as a means of asserting universal subjectivity, transforming black bodies into objects of knowledge. Hence, Western empirical traditions enshrine blackness as a known object while whiteness remains epistemologically "mysterious."

This dynamic is particularly acute in academia and the classroom. White students who "politically consider themselves liberals and anti-racists…unwittingly invest in the sense of whiteness as mystery."[27] For bell hooks:

> White students respond with naïve amazement that black people critically assess white people from a standpoint where 'whiteness' is the privileged signifier. Their amazement that black people watch white people with a critical 'ethnographic' gaze is itself an expression of racism. Often their rage erupts because they believe that all ways of looking that highlight difference subvert the liberal belief in universal subjectivity (we are all just people) that they think will make racism disappear…

> in white supremacist society, white people can 'safely' imagine that they are invisible to black people since the power they have historically asserted, and even now collectively assert over black people, accorded them the right to control the black gaze.[28]

In an educational context, cultural proficiency is a strategy that can be used to disrupt these encounters. Cultural proficiency involves recognition of how that "critical ethnographic gaze" has historically been denied the other. Organized religion provided black people with one "critical ethnographic" lens onto white supremacy. The reality of black religious experience is that it has been both racially liberating and *racializing*. This dialectical process occurred within the context of an Enlightenment tradition based on racial inequality. Anthropological and ethnographic traditions of studying and "understanding" the other were key to establishing the West's global cultural and economic dominance. In the hip hop era where neo-minstrel show caricatures masquerade as authentic blackness, this legacy is exemplified by whites who believe that "they know" black culture simply because they are familiar with mainstream stereotypes about black people. Tim Wise, the foremost white critic/interpreter of white supremacy, once noted that whites "swim in white privilege." Like fish in water, whites don't grasp or see the complexity of white privilege because they breathe it and live it 24/7. White privilege powers the predominantly white schools, neighborhoods, social networks, media, places of worship, and scholarly traditions that they inhabit and consume. It makes the systemic institutionalized nature of racial hierarchy invisible. And it marginalizes race and racism as part of the narrow, sectarian and supposedly divisive concerns of a "minority" lens.

Navigating a fantasy post-racial universe, these "invisible" cornerstones of white supremacy are not supposed to matter. It is not supposed to matter that an African American male infant has less chance statistically of going to college or even of living to the age of 25 than his white male comrade over in the next incubator. It is not supposed to matter that home equity for blacks and Latinos of all classes has historically been far lower than that of whites due to institutional residential segregation. These "blemishes" in the fabric of American liberal democracy are not supposed to matter because individualism and meritocracy are the currency of Americana. There is no evil intelligent designer separating one's exercise of free will from free enterprise.

DuBois characterized these disparities as the "wages of whiteness," a public and psychological wage granted to whites, regardless of class status, simply for being white. The wages of whiteness translate into everyday white privilege for even the most destitute whites. It entails the privilege of not having to worry about race unless you're walking around predominantly black and Latino neighborhoods in South Los Angeles, Detroit or the South Side of Chicago. It grants the privilege to know that "when I am told about our national heritage or about 'civilization' I am shown that people of my color made it what it is."[29] It allows whites the privilege to see people with their own skin color held up as natural leaders, visionaries, thinkers, and agenda setters in the science profession. The wages of whiteness implies that the very arc of European American intellectual, social, and economic progress has been shaped by the racialization of the Other. For example, as an artifact of a supremely barbaric and unenlightened aspect of the Enlightenment, Saartje Baartman's dissected backside was a key player in the birth of the objectivist researcher. Representing reason and rationality,

Baartman's interpreters were conferred with a personhood and subjectivity that afforded them "unraced" status.

Toni Morrison has defined unraced status as the ability to appear to be beyond racial classification or identification. Whiteness becomes the norm not only through racial segregation but through the discursive tools of defining value and worth. This status rests on having the right to write, analyze, classify, quantify, and have one's conclusions recognized as universal truths, rather than as the culturally contextual products of a racist colonialist legacy.

New Atheist discourse purports to be "beyond" all that meddlesome stuff. After all, science has been cleaned up to redress the atrocities of the past. The "bad" racist eugenicist science and scientists of back in the day have been purged. Religionists of all stripes are merely obstacles to achieving greater enlightenment in the generic name of science and reason. Race and gender hierarchies within the scientific establishment are immaterial when it comes to determining the overall thrust and urgency of the New Atheism. Non-believers who argue for a more nuanced approach to or progressive understanding of the political, social, and cultural appeal of religion are toady apologists. Religious bigotry and discrimination are deemed the greatest threat to "civilized" Western societies. As delineated by many white non-believers the New Atheism preserves and reproduces the status quo of white supremacy in its arrogant insularity. In this universe, oppressed minorities are more imperiled by their own investment in organized religion than white supremacy. Liberation is not a matter of fighting against white racism, sexism, and classism but of throwing off the shackles of superstition.

Some white secular humanists have sounded a cautionary note to this swagger. Greg Epstein, the Humanist chaplain at Harvard University, has criticized the New Atheist fixation with skewering religion in a vacuum. Epstein argues that "the single biggest weakness of modern, organized atheism and Humanism…has been the movement's own tendency to focus on religious beliefs, when the key to understanding religion lies not in belief…but in practice—in what people do, not just what they think."[30] In his book *Good Without God*, Epstein articulates a vision of socially engaged Humanism. He emphasizes the need to build culturally diverse secular institutions to meet the social, moral, and emotional needs of non-believers. He embraces community organizing as the most potent model for Humanist change. In his view, Humanism will only grow as a movement if non-believers have the same space for collective engagement, community service, and sharing of values as believers. This is the key to making Humanism sustainable. Tapping the fervor and passion of religious experience (minus dogma) can drive an enduring Humanist legacy.

Epstein cites a long tradition of civic engagement amongst Jewish secular humanist, Unitarian Universalist, and Ethical Society organizations as inspiration.[31] Paul Kurtz, venerable founder of the Center for Inquiry and Council for Secular Humanism, has also countered the New Atheists' totalizing views. In 2010, following the tradition of Humanist Manifestoes developed in 1933, 1973, and 2003, Kurtz drafted a "Neo-Humanist Statement of Secular Principles and Values" endorsed by humanists across the globe.[32] The statement advocates equal rights for women and "sexual minorities." It roundly condemns global warming skepticism, intelligent design, and other superstition-based dogmas. In a caveat to the New Atheists, Kurtz appeals for humanist tolerance of secular diversity:

> The "New Atheists" have been very vocal, claiming that the public has not been sufficiently exposed to the case against God and his minions. We agree that the lack of criticism is often the rule rather than the exception. We point out, however, that the community of religious dissenters includes not only atheists, but secular and religious humanists, agnostics, skeptics, and even a significant number of religiously affiliated individuals. The latter may be only nominal members of their congregations and may infrequently attend church, temple, or mosque, primarily for social reasons or out of ethnic loyalty to the faiths of their forbearers, but they do not accept the traditional creed. *Ethnic identities can be very difficult to overcome,* and may linger long after belief in a given body of doctrine has faded—sometimes for many generations.[33]

Although well-intentioned, Kurtz's caveat reflects a reductive view of so-called ethnic identity. Here, the implication that ethnic identities can be "overcome" (like a disease) suggests that they are remnants of a primitive phase of human development wherein religion was the primary vehicle for ethnic socialization. Under the veneer of "tolerance," Kurtz's notion merely reinforces New Atheist biases against ethnic identity as a barrier to rational enlightenment. This implies that ethnic identities are not a vital source of lived experience, cultural knowledge, community, and selfhood, but a hindrance. Hence, ethnicity is a "difficult to overcome" vestige from bygone eras of religious indoctrination. By conflating "ethnic" with "religious," and "identity" with "loyalty," Kurtz reinscribes ethnicity as static and monolithic. One could very well argue that while religious indoctrination and affiliation shapes *some* aspects of ethnic identity—and could be *interrogated* through critical inquiry, analysis and lived experience—the foundations of ethnic identity are far more complex and intersectional than Kurtz's declaration acknowledges. Indeed Kurtz's view veers toward the kind of hollow post-racial rhetoric which deems that ethnic identity is something that needs to (and can) be transcended or shorn.

Scratch the high-minded well-intentioned surface and Kurtz's assertion underscores the deficits of European American New Atheist and secular humanist analysis vis-à-vis the enduring power of organized religion. For communities of color, the lifeblood of organized religion is economic injustice. In comparison to third world nations, Americans live in a consumer "paradise" of easily attainable status commodities like cars, appliances, electronics, and clothes. With fifty different designer clothing brands at the local Walmart and fifty different DVD player brands at the local Target, even lower income Americans can bask in the illusion of classlessness. Consumerism and the meritocracy myth reinforce the belief that class differences amongst Americans are fluid. Given the right type of bootstraps pluck anyone can become a Bill Gates, Warren Buffet or Mark Zuckerberg, billionaire creator of Facebook. Yet only 1% of the population controls over 38% of America's wealth. Ten percent of the country "owns America," holding over 68% of the nation's wealth.[34] By contrast, Switzerland is the only nation that exceeds the U.S. in the percentage of wealth concentrated among the super rich.

It is no coincidence then that Western European countries are far less religious than the U.S. These relatively low levels of religiosity correlate with the fact that citizens of Western European countries enjoy a comprehensive social welfare safety net. On average, Western European health care, child care, unemployment compensation, job security, job benefits, and affordable housing subsidies provide a far higher quality of life and standard of living than that in the U.S. Western European cities generally offer more accessible pedestrian and recreational green space than the car dominated sprawl of most

American cities.[35] Miles of undeveloped brown zones and vacant lots are symptomatic of dead commercial development and so-called "park poor" urban neighborhoods of color. As in most arenas, racial politics and segregation determine available park space in the U.S. Having the ability to use a clean, safe, accessible park is a luxury that many white middle class families take for granted. Further, the bucolic carefree association that parks traditionally conjure up may not be shared by urban youth of color who associate neighborhood parks with crime and gang activity. According to a 2006 study conducted by the City Project, African American and Latino children in Los Angeles County have far less access to park space than do their white counterparts in the Valley and Westside regions of the county.[36]

Of course the piecemeal localized services provided by urban and rural churches don't compare with that of the wrap around socialized care in Western European countries. Insofar as churches operate as charitable organizations, the most progressive only provide stopgaps to the steamrolling regime of capitalism. Brutal extremes of wealth and inequality are driven by the gargantuan divide between American democracy and capitalism. These extremes provide fertile ground for the God industry and religious fundamentalism. In the Middle East, just as in the West, religious fundamentalism also thrives under conditions of extreme poverty and economic injustice. Martyrdom in the name of Islam is a "redemptive" path for desperately poor young men and women in the oligarchies of the Middle East. Mainstream portrayals point to religious fundamentalism as the primary cause of these terrorist acts. However suicide bombers are often motivated by outrage, frustration, and a sense of powerlessness over Western occupation.[37] Although the Neo-Humanist statement alludes to these extremes, there is no acknowledgment of the need for wealth distribution and anti-imperialism. The statement argues for the need to "move beyond progressive individualism" but privileges the market economy and "progressive taxation" as the most equitable remedies for income inequality.

If there is no reckoning with the role economic injustice and capitalist exploitation play in shaping hyper-religiosity among people of color then black humanist atheist critiques risk irrelevancy. Engaging in science fetishism without a social justice lens merely reproduces the white supremacist logic of the movement. As Greta Christina notes, "if a movement—however unintentionally—is being dominated by white men, then that movement will tend to focus its energies on issues that concern white men... at the expense of issues that concern women and people of color."[38]

Becoming culturally proficient on the race, gender, and class complexities of access and equity in the U.S. is essential for any potential white ally. First off is recognition of the fact that the U.S. has never been a meritocracy. Part of the Tea Party's seductive appeal for some white folks is its bird flipping revisionism about this nation's four hundred-plus year history of white rule. If you regurgitate the slogan "no taxation without representation" as a white citizen's anti-government call to arms you obliterate the history of black citizens unjustly taxed in a nation where they were systematically terrorized and disenfranchised. With no mooring in history, it stands to reason that white folk don't like it when it is inconveniently pointed out by ghetto interlopers that knowledge production and universal truth claims in the West have historically been marked as white. It's pro forma when white folk, ignorant of these historical traditions, insist that atheist discourse is implicitly anti-racist, anti-sexist, and anti-heterosexist because one, we say so, and, two, hierarchy is something only those knuckle-dragging supernaturalists do. It's paint-by-the-numbers entitlement time when some in the New Atheist movement go ballistic about the charge that racial and gender politics just might inform who achieves visibility and which issues are privileged in the broader context of non-theist discourse. It's not PC to suggest in the science-besotted circle jerk of atheist-supernaturalist smackdowns that Hottentot-obsessed traditions of scientific racism and fire and brimstone Judeo Christian religiosity went gleefully hand in hand for much of the West's enlightened history. It belies humanist delusions of pure objectivism to say that the "science as magic bullet" boilerplate will not enlarge the conversation to include those for whom organized religion has been a cultural and historical necessity. It is treasonous to argue that having the luxury and privilege to proclaim one's atheism, publish, command a global audience, and garner recognition for capsizing the sordid ship of religious tyranny is a white enterprise precisely because of the history of Western knowledge production. And it stomps on the myth of meritocracy to suggest that eminent white philosophers and scientists don't "focus" on race and gender because their identities are based on not seeing it.

During a teacher training session I conducted at a South L.A. high school I asked the predominantly white faculty why mainstream historical portrayals were male dominated. Some of the male instructors responded that men fought all the important military battles. Some of the female instructors retorted that *men* wrote the histories. A majority of the school's black and Latino student body are below proficient in language arts and math. Four year college-going rates for graduating seniors are abysmally low. From the moment they arrive on campus students are taught that only a privileged few will go on to college. Tracking based on ethnicity, language, citizenship status, and attitude, is tacit. Critical literacy, engaging with the politics of racism, sexism, and homophobia is considered dangerous. Beyond trotting out Martin Luther King, Rosa Parks or occasionally Cesar Chavez, very few students I encountered could name major historical figures or activists of color. For most young people, the civil rights movement began and ended with MLK's "I Have a Dream" speech. In this sense, the movement had no bearing on the overall context of democracy and human rights in the West. Racial disparities in student achievement were certainly not seen as part of the movement's unfulfilled legacy.

Not seeing themselves represented in the curriculum, youth of color begin to accept that history should be written by the victors; and that they are, in effect, Tituba. A radical progressive humanism recognizes that hand-wringing about diversity—be it in education, corporate America or cultural movements—without challenging the power dynamics of access and visibility, makes white supremacy a self-fulfilling prophecy. When *not seeing* difference becomes a matter of faith, a religion, a virtue, it is equivalent to telling all those uppity "missing links" and Titubas to sit down and shut up. In other words, let us write the historical record for you, because we know how it ends.

Endnotes

1. The female slave Tituba (whose racial origin is contested) was reputed by historians to be the instigator of the seventeenth century witch hysteria in Puritan Salem Massachusetts.
2. Hedges, *American Fascists: The Christian Right and the War on America*, p. 80.
3. "Bill Maher and the white dude privilege of New Atheists/Skeptics," *Skeptifem*, 11/19/09 (http://skeptifem.blogspot.com/2009/11/bill-maher-and-white-dude-privilege-of.html).
4. Hitchens wrote a piece in Vanity Fair opining on how women comedians weren't as funny as men because evolution didn't call for women to be funny. Men needed to be, and hence were, more funny because they had to use humor to attract women. See Christopher Hitchens, "Why Women Aren't Funny," *Vanity Fair*, January 2007 (http://www.vanityfair.com/culture/features/2007/01/hitchens200701).
5. Christopher Hitchens, "Why Women Still Aren't Funny," *VanityFair.com*, March 3, 2008.
6. Ibid.; see also Amy Clare, "Not Rational, Not reasonable, Not Funny," *The F Word*, 3/1/10 (http://www.thefword.org.uk/blog/2010/03/sexism_in_the_a).
7. In an online posting Benson discussed Dawkins' desire to address the sexist postings on the site: "I've been subject to sexist abuse from anonymous commenters on the main page…I know for a fact that Richard considers this kind of thing a serious problem because he emailed me to say so." *Heathen Hub Board*, February 27, 2010 (http://heathen-hub.com/blog.php?b=263.)
8. Massimo Pigliucci, "About Sam Harris' Claim that Science Can Answer Moral Questions," *Rationally Speaking*, April 6, 2010 (http://rationallyspeaking.blogspot.com/2010/04/about-sam-harris-claim-that-science-can.html).
9. Massimo Pigliucci, *Denying Evolution: Creationism, Scientism, and the Nature of Science* (Tennessee: Sinauer Associates, 2002), 161.
10. Sam Harris, "Moral Confusion in the Name of Science," *Project Reason*, March 29, 2010 (http://www.project-reason.org/newsfeed/item/moral_confusion_in_the_name_of_science3).

11. Ibid.
12. Pigliucci, "About Sam Harris' Claim that Science Can Answer Moral Questions."
13. Obama has frequently woven references to "non-believers" into his presidential rhetoric.
14. Rashid, April 2010.
15. W.E.B. DuBois, *The Souls of Black Folk: Essays and Sketches* (Chicago: A.C. McClurg & Co., 1903), 3-4.
16. Mercedes Diane Griffin, "Advancing a Humanist Respose to Issues Facing Communities of Color," *Unscripted* (http://unorthodoxparadox.blogspot.com/2010/06/advancing-humanist-response-to-issues.html), May 18, 2010.
17. Both the 2010 AAI Convention and the Council for Secular Humanism's Free Inquiry anniversary conference (the latter held in the heart of predominantly black and Latino downtown Los Angeles) "suffered" from the same Tea Party-esque composition.
18. For example, see the vitriolic responses to my December 2009 article, "The White Stuff," *Daylight Atheism,* December 2009 (http://www.daylightatheism.org/2009/12/the-white-stuff.html.).
19. Mark Oppenheimer, "Atheists Debate How Pushy to Be," *New York Times,* October 15, 2010 (http://www.nytimes.com/2010/10/16/us/16beliefs.html?_r=1).
20. Diane Griffin, Personal Interview, November 2010.
21. Naima Cabelle, Interview Survey, November 2010.
22. See for example Greta Christina's analysis on the denial of "unconscious" racism among white atheists. "Getting it Right Early: Why Atheists Need to Act Now on Gender and Race," *Greta Christina's Blog*, September 2009 (http://gretachristina.typepad.com/greta_christinas_weblog/2009/09/race-sex-atheism.html).; also "The Cultural Tethers of Organized Religion: Interview with Black Atheist Sikivu Hutchinson," *Greta Christina's Blog*, June 2009 (http://gretachristina.typepad.com/greta_christinas_weblog/2009/06/sikivu-hutchinson-black-atheist.html).
23. Ayanna Watson, Interview Questionnaire, November 2010.
24. Randal B. Lindsey, Kikanza Nuri Robins, et al. *Cultural Proficiency: A Manual For School Leaders* (Thousand Oaks: Sage Publishers, 2009), 5-6.
25. Christina, "Getting it Right Early: Why Atheists Need to Act Now on Gender and Race."

26. Frantz Fanon, *Black Skin, White Masks* (New York: Grove Press, 1952), 95.
27. Bell hooks, *Black Looks: Race and Representation* (Boston: South End Press, 1992), 21.
28. Ibid.
29. Peggy McKintosh, "Unpacking the Invisible Knapsack," *The Heart of Whiteness: Confronting Race, Racism and White Privilege (City Lights,* September 2005), 1.
30. Greg Epstein, *Good Without God: What a Billion Non-religious People Do Believe* (New York: Harper Collins, 2009), 174-5.
31. Ibid., 203-212.
32. Paul Kurtz, "Neo-Humanist Statement of Secular Principles and Values: Personal, Progressive and Planetary," March 2, 2010 (http://paulkurtz.net).
33. Ibid.
34. G. William Domhoff, "Wealth, Income, and Power," *Who Rules America?* University of Santa Cruz, September 2010 (http://sociology.ucsc.edu/whorulesamerica/power); and William Levy, "Recent Trends in Household Wealth in the United States: Rising Debt and the Middle-Class Squeeze," (The Levy Institute, March 2010).
35. This is not to idealize Western Europe but rather to emphasize the absence of such nationalized care in the U.S. Clearly deep racial and ethnic disparities exist in countries such as France, Germany and Britain where Muslim and African populations are discriminated against in access to employment and education.
36. Robert Garcia and Aubrey White, "Healthy Parks, Schools and Communities: Mapping Green Access and Equity for the Los Angeles Region." (The City Project, 2006), 3. "Unfair disparities in safe places to play go well beyond Los Angeles. While 87% of non-Hispanic respondents reported that "there are safe places for children to play" in their neighborhood, only 68% of Hispanics, 71% of African Americans, and 81% of Asians agreed, according to the Census Bureau survey 'A Child's Day." Almost half (48%) of Hispanic children under 18 in central cities were kept inside as much as possible because their neighborhoods were perceived as dangerous. The same was true for more than 39% of black children, 25% of non-Hispanic white children, and 24% of Asian children. Non-Hispanic White children and youth were most likely to participate in after school sports, with Hispanic children and children in poverty least likely to experience

37. University of Chicago Project on Security and Terrorism professor Robert Pape makes the argument that the U.S. military presence in the Middle East is the primary motivator for suicide bombings not religious zeal. Robert Pape, "What Triggers the Suicide Bomber," *Los Angeles Times*, October 24, 2010.

38. Christina, "Getting it Right Early: Why Atheists Need to Act Now on Gender and Race."

Chapter 8

The Road Ahead

All servants imported and brought into the Country. . . who were not Christians in their native Country. . . shall be accounted and be slaves. All Negro, mulatto and Indian slaves within this dominion. . . shall be held to be real estate. If any slave resists his master. . . correcting such slave, and shall happen to be killed in such correction. . . the master shall be free of all punishment. . . as if such accident never happened.

—Virginia General Assembly declaration, 1705

The boy's face, expressive beyond his years, is twisted in anguish. He is trying to talk to the class about being followed and harassed by the police. Ten minutes before the bell is supposed to ring, his gentle candor is marred by the jeers of a female classmate. Freaked out by his vulnerability, she mocks to keep him in check, for, in this familiar space of regimented desks, pristine whiteboards, paramilitary P.A. announcements, inscrutable teen hierarchies, and racial cliques, boys are not supposed to express pain. Boys, especially black boys, the universal symbol of savage criminality, are supposed to suck up their pain and keep moving. They internalize this message very early on and enforce it amongst themselves in a fraternity of silence. In some quarters the worst crime of an adolescent black boy is displaying vulnerability and being dubbed a "bitch nigga." A popular 50 Cent video runs down how BNs betray the masculine essence of hip hop. Young black men who don't display a hard cool pose are the ultimate subversion of mainstream black masculinity.

My male students know how to navigate this precipice without misstep. Our discussions are filled with outrage over their devaluation in the image industry. On the streets, in classrooms, in the news, and in movies they are still public enemies. In the Darwinian kingdom of Hollywood film, black characters are often the first to be maimed or killed off. If they are sympathetic/buddy characters they're avenged by the stalwart white hero. If they are villains they're tossed into the celluloid dumpster. Unless represented by Denzel Washington or Will Smith, Hollywood heroism, romance, and "true grit" are strictly the province of white male crusader action figures. And with rare exception, intellectualism, discovery, and invention—from the Western to the swashbuckling epic to the foreign intrigue film—are still marked as white male territories. As one of the most powerful vehicles of global propaganda, the Hollywood film industry has had a strong impact on shaping mainstream masculinity. At the same time, it has also made cultural critics of youth of color who see their lives reduced to an ever-enduring caricature of crime, inner city violence, hypersexuality, and anti-intellectualism.

There has always been a robust market for black pain in America; slavery, Jim Crow terrorism, and the cradle to grave prison complex being the biggest beneficiaries. Frederick Douglass once wrote that black lives were worth half a cent to white people. Growing up in the slavocracy, white children learned this edict early on. The preciousness of their childhoods, their sense of moral worth and personal esteem, rested on black pain. Their equilibrium depended on it, as they closed their eyes to the bloody violence inflicted upon the bodies of the slave children they played with and the women who'd nursed them, burped them, and wiped their asses. In this golden age of 18th century heroic secularist founding fathers, decorum and savagery went intimately hand in glove. In her book *The Hemings of Monticello: An American Family,* Annette Gordon Reed chronicles how Thomas Jefferson's every need was provided for by the slave Sally Hemings and her brother James. After much naysaying from white historians, DNA testing has proven a blood tie between the descendants of Hemings and Jefferson. During his seminal trip to Paris both James and Sally acted as Jefferson's "servants." This euphemism was given to them to make it easier for Jefferson to skirt France's anti-slavery laws. Jefferson's Paris stay is regarded as a critical period in his intellectual and political maturation. It further refined his views on individual liberty, citizenship, and democracy. So, although the Hemings' could have petitioned for their freedom in France, they did not. Portrayed by some historians as a conflicted opponent of slavery, racked with internal "existential" strife about the "terrible transformation," Jefferson only freed five slaves during his lifetime, three of whom were reputed to be his children with Hemings.

Douglass, of course, wrote with blistering sensitivity to the contradictions of a white "civil" society personified generations before by the slaveholder and slave-profiteer Jefferson. If Douglass were alive today he'd probably reel from the paradoxes of modern America. He would be in satirical awe of its affluent trophy black politicians, entertainers, and sports figures, and its outsized black homeless population. In a nation that prides itself on the boundless opportunities it bestows on its "minorities" he would have excoriated the fact that African American boys have a greater likelihood of being incarcerated than of going to college. There is a clear line from the dehumanization of Douglass' youth and the rise of the prison industry, a phenomenon that has had the most devastating impact on postwar African American communities. Black juvenile offenders are over six times more likely to be incarcerated than are whites who have committed similar offenses. Disproportionate suspension rates of black K-12 students also reflect and contribute to this disparity. Legal scholar Michelle Alexander has aptly characterized incarceration rates of African Americans as the "new Jim Crow." Based upon exhaustive research of prison data and the historical record, Alexander concluded that black offenders racked up more time in the modern criminal justice system than during the antebellum and Jim Crow eras.[1]

Negro spirituals are often characterized as a culturally unique reservoir for the expression of black pain. Religion and music have historically been its most popular vehicles. Faith is "marketed" as an antidote to and respite from pain. For those faced with unspeakable pain there is the sacrificial figure of Jesus nailed to the cross. We are told that Jesus died for our sins. We are instructed that Christian charity, departing from the brutal eye for an eye ethos of the Old Testament, really began with Jesus. We are ensured that Jesus, sacrificial lamb that he was, loved everyone. We are instructed to develop a personal, emotionally intimate relationship with him. However, the New Testament does not offer an alternative gender schema to the one enforced by the Old. No matter the alleged ambiguity of Jesus' relationship to his disciples, nor his purported encouragement of female followers to spread the gospel, the pecking order of Christ's "new" universe is remarkably similar to the old. Women's bodies are still the fount of sin and temptation. Women are still prohibited from leading men. Men are still the tempted protectors/owners of home, hearth, and women's bodies. The women of enemy tribes are still fair game for conquest through rape and forced marriage. Infidels who worship "false gods" are still evil and deserving of eternal damnation if they don't repent.

Rather than assuage black pain, Christian precepts enshrine and fetishize it. And women's bodies are the ultimate space of purity and impurity. Because of their uniquely debased position women must accept cultural scorn and personal sacrifice as their natural God decreed penalty. Since the Bible encourages colonial conquest of women's bodies and the coveting of female virginity, it's not difficult to understand why young males steeped in Judeo-Christian traditions are constantly pushed to conform to a code of hard masculinity.

"Dead Letters"

During a debate on women's rights in 1856 Ernestine L. Rose said:

> Do you tell me that the Bible is against our rights? Then I say our claims do not rest upon a book...Books and opinions, no matter from whom they came, if they are in opposition to human rights are nothing but dead letters.[2]

Certainly one of the pressing challenges of feminist atheist humanist freethinking activists is to liberate women from the tyranny of religious dogma. In her introduction to *Women Without Superstition*, Annie Laurie Gaylor notes that Elizabeth Cady Stanton, Margaret Sanger, and Sonia Johnson were all strongly committed to counseling women on the dangers of organized religion. Stanton said that her "heart's desire is to lift women out of all these dangerous, degrading superstitions, and to this end I will labor my remaining days on earth."[3] As one of the foremost 19th century feminist suffragists Stanton was heavily influenced by Rose's uncompromising atheism.

However, according to Rose biographer Carol A. Kolmarten, Rose was unsettled by Stanton's racist xenophobic opposition to the 15th Amendment, which granted voting rights to African American men.[4] Before the 15th Amendment's passage Stanton strenuously objected to granting voting rights to black men before women. Presenting the case for women's voting rights to white audiences, Stanton often drew on racist imagery depicting blacks, Asians, and non-Anglo whites as backward and culturally unworthy of voting rights.[5] As many black feminist historians have argued, the white supremacist, nativist views of early feminist leaders like Stanton and Susan B. Anthony were a major roadblock to interracial alliances with feminists of color. White suffragists' exploitation of white privilege and entitlement has cast a long shadow on third and fourth wave feminism. Nonetheless, the historical implications of this legacy continue to be ignored. For example, there has been little engagement with the white supremacist lens of mainstream feminism in white feminist atheist or humanist social critique.[6] In many respects, the misguided belief that atheism automatically constitutes an anti-racist anti-sexist stance parallels white feminist blindness to the fact that white women's experiences are not the center of the universe when it comes to gender justice.

It is for this reason that younger generations of women of color find little to identify with in feminism. When I talk to high school students about feminism or the women's movement I get blank stares and quizzical looks. Sadly, in an era in which sexual "freedom" has been equated with "feminism," the lessons of feminist activism have become "dead letters" lacking in cultural relevance to young women of color who view themselves as having little in common with white women. Mainstream depictions in textbooks and media reduce feminism to moldy images of high-collared white suffragists or Capitol Hill storming white abortion supporters. The contributions of women of color feminists (i.e., feminists in either name and/or deed) are marginalized. And the work of "rock star" feminist activist/critics like bell hooks and Angela Davis is either reduced to a strictly racial lens or framed as antagonistic to black liberation struggle.

Yet, as I have argued throughout this book, gender justice remains the most pressing unfulfilled challenge for African American communities. As they pray their brains out, black women are burdened with some of the highest health and wellness risk factors in the U.S. They are more likely to be killed in cold blood by a boyfriend or husband. They are more likely to contract HIV/AIDS from a boyfriend or husband. And in desperately poor communities they are more likely to lay down their burdens in churches where black patriarchs drive the leadership and black male parishioners are conspicuously absent.

Black atheist humanist belief offers a critical intervention into these culturally destructive models of masculinity and femininity. Seeking a rational refuge from centuries of moral indoctrination, black women atheists express the need to educate, if not proselytize, other black women about the culturally specific threat Christianity poses. Atheism and secular humanism are appealing to black women freethinkers who find even "liberal" interpretations of Judeo Christian and Muslim faith unpalatable. Commenting on the degree to which Abrahamic religions fixate on the woman as sexual and moral provocateur, black atheist Alfreda Howard noted:

> In about every religion the woman is the one igniting the war and causing men to go astray from god and his purpose, creating a stigma. With African American women we often get an even worse stigma because whites already tend not to value

> us and when we are in positions of power whites tend to fear us. We [get] called manipulative and Jezebels because of the negative images of women from the Bible and in other religious doctrines.[7]

Again, biblical stigmas against female sexuality are a double-edged sword for black women. In the mainstream mind, women of color are constantly relegated to the position of the "bad" fallen woman and temptress in contrast to the white virginal ideal. For example, in the decidedly Judeo Christian universe of Hollywood film, depictions of voracious black female sexuality and smothering black motherhood reinforce each other in an industry that has barely moved beyond Jim Crow. Over the past two decades mainstream Hollywood film roles for black women have rarely deviated from that of sex objects, caregivers to hapless white folks, and hard-driving mother figures. From comedian Monique's portrayal of the pathological ghetto mother from hell in the film *Precious* to Halle Berry's hackneyed turn as a violent hypersexual single mother in *Monster's Ball,* Academy Award winning depictions of black womanhood embody tired black female stereotypes that confirm all of white America's Moynihan Report-influenced beliefs about the "black matriarchy."

An inversion of traditional patriarchal European cultural norms, the myth of the black matriarchy goes hand in hand with stereotypes of black female religiosity. As I discussed in Chapter 2, images of the strong indomitable black woman who "rules the roost" in her home and community abound in American culture. These images are buttressed by the stereotype of black women's unswerving Christian faith, or, what journalist Jamila Bey characterizes as the "long-suffering, strong black woman who needs only herself and her Jesus to get through life."[8] This notion of the strong black woman who is nonetheless dependent on a patriarchal Jesus and the teachings of the good book is a contradiction that is seldom teased out in black feminist criticism. Womanist theologians might argue that the God or Jesus concept can be crafted to support women's resistance and agency. However, there is still no evidence to support the argument that the Bible articulates a vision of human rights based on gender justice.

Hence, critique of the mental enslavement that Christian dogma inspires is a recurring theme in black feminist atheist belief. In her journey to atheism, Alfreda Howard transitioned from a Methodist, Pentecostal, and Baptist religious background. Like many black atheists, Howard is deeply critical of the slave era origins of black Christianity. Characterizing black Christian belief as "brainwashing" Howard also sees parallels with black conversion to Islam:

> Blacks in religion still hold the slave mind of the Christian religion that was brainwashed into them by the white slave owner. When this is revealed to the[m] some go to Islam to justify their blackness...Most African Americans will continue to worship the Christian god because...they do not understand how to express their freedom; because they were told not to do or be [anything] all their lives by the white master.[9]

As an "out" atheist living in a small community in South Carolina, Howard has been discriminated against because of her beliefs. She describes having been denied housing by whites in her community who were in league with her family's church. She and her daughters were physically assaulted by a community member opposed to her atheism. She stressed that mental health and wellness resources in her community are intimately tied to the church. The church counsels that strengthening one's belief in and reliance upon God is the most legitimate antidote to depression. In several instances she was told that it was her fault that she was being mistreated by her family because she didn't believe in God.

Howard's experiences underscore the secular vacuum that exists in many working class communities of color when it comes to mental health and wellness resources. While middle class folks with health insurance are often able to access non-religious therapy and counseling services, poor and low income people of color must often rely solely on faith-based services. Further, the stigma that some African American and Latino cultures place on therapy and mental health support makes it difficult for many blacks and Latinos to admit that they need or want therapy. Despite the mainstreaming of therapy I can't count the number of times I've been told that black people "don't do therapy" or that therapy is a "white" luxury. Black women who shoulder the burden of child care, care giving, and supporting their families are triply challenged to devote time and energy for self-care. Again, long standing stereotypes of "indomitable" black matriarchs prevent some black women from exploring secular mental health alternatives. This message was reinforced in the 2010 Tyler Perry film of Ntozake Shange's play *For Colored Girls.* In one scene, a female neighbor tells a domestic abuse victim struggling with clinical depression as a result of the violent murders of her children by her partner that she is partly responsible for their deaths. The neighbor counsels her to stop mourning and go out into the world to educate others about her experiences. There is no acknowledgment of the extreme trauma she has suffered at the hands of her children's father/killer.

The scene highlights the cultural expectation that black women must overcome or downplay their own pain and trauma in service to others. Here, black women's needs as domestic violence victims are secondary to that of their families and the community.

While there is no overt religious reference in this scene, there is still the strong implication that self-healing, coupled with acceptance of "personal responsibility" for one's trauma, is the ultimate antidote and solution. Given this world view, it is deemed culturally acceptable and socially practical for black women to turn to prayer and/or the church for internal matters. Women who are already heavily involved in the church are presumed not to need emotional or psychological intervention because their needs are secondary and besides the Lord will provide.

During the 2010 "Science and Faith in the Black Community" dialogue sponsored by the Richard Dawkins Foundation and Howard University's Secular Students Association, I was approached by a woman who said that some Christian black women describe themselves as being "married" to Jesus. In the midst of stressful single parenting, work, and other family care giving obligations this is the most viable "relationship" alternative for some. Personalization of the Jesus relationship is a hallmark of evangelical faith. Evangelicalism contrasts with the hard line literalism and foreboding of fundamentalism. According to evangelicals the Gospel is "good news." Jesus becomes an intimate buddy figure, spiritual guide, and moral compass in life's turbulent storm. Relating to Jesus as an intimate allows for rapturous release and unbridled expression that might not be tolerated or understood by a living breathing partner. Projecting a desire for intimacy onto Jesus is a "safe" way for black women who feel demoralized and devalued on a daily basis to achieve comfort.

Spiritual marriage to Jesus is yet another example of the deep emotional investment that black women have in patriarchy and heterosexism. Because biblical scripture does not allow women any real equity with men in the church, the family or everyday life, an intimate relationship with Jesus is an alternative way for women to assert agency. As Naima Cabelle notes:

> African American women aren't often viewed as being fit for humanity not just in the wider society but often inside of our own communities as well. We are, of course, very useful. We are supposed to do what women are seen as being fit to do: nurse the sick, care for children and the elderly, work inside and outside of the home; finance, build, clean and maintain the church; help keep the church coffers filled by giving until it hurts and then hurts some more; keep the pews filled by making sure that we hound family, friend, and foe to come to church, and remember our rightful place is to help, not think on our own behalf and to carryout decisions, but not make them especially on our own behalf. We also play a significant role in the community with respect to community-building; political, social, and economic life...Yet, even as a substantial and disgraceful number of women remain on the bottom rung of society, we are always admonished not to go too far; not to seek liberation on our own terms but as our men dictate, and of course, don't show-off by stepping out in front of men.[10]

Ironically, as the oppressive hierarchies of mainstream Christianity become more and more irreconcilable with the lives of modern black women, a God and/or Jesus-based spiritualism has become more popular.[11] Spiritualism allows for greater personal improvisation. It gives believers license to "bend" the rules and flout the orthodoxies of traditional organized religions without crossing over to the "dark side" of atheism or humanism. Alice Walker and Ntozake Shange's womanist credos of "finding God in oneself" are increasingly the chosen path for those disgruntled with organized religion yet too faith-based to forgo supernaturalism entirely. Cabelle notes the unfortunate trend whereby "many of the African American feminists who are well-known seem to identify themselves as spiritual, angels, miracle workers, etc. Some feminists, regardless of color, claim to have turned religion on its head by rejecting male deities and embracing female deities...praying to goddesses and/or referring to themselves as being blessed even when they don't consider themselves as religious."[12] Consequently, some women of color who experience trauma from domestic violence, sexual assault, and emotional abuse take a spiritualist if not overtly religious approach to healing and wellness.

In many respects, the self-sacrifice and submission demanded of women by patriarchy is reinforced by America's prayer panacea. Studies have shown that African Americans in general and black women in particular, rely on prayer as a first line mental health strategy.[13] Indeed, when it comes to "perceptions of spirituality and IPV (intimate partner violence) focus group research reveals that some married women remain in an abusive relationship because they perceive leaving as breaking a covenant with God. Others perceive remaining in an abusive relationship and forgiving their partners as indications of being a strong Black woman a culturally idealized form of African American womanhood."[14]

Being the strong or sacrificial good woman is intimately tied with religion and spirituality. I was again reminded of the urgent need for humanist mental health and wellness alternatives at a black/Latina women's conference I attended on "breaking the silence" about domestic violence and HIV/AIDS. Several presenters portrayed faith-based mental health and wellness "remedies" as the most viable approaches to healing. Prayer will "right you," a woman who had been in a violent long term relationship declared to a literal amen corner of nodding heads. Relying upon prayer as an antidote to stress and trauma is a common coping strategy in communities of color, particularly for women of color. Race and gender-related stress are major contributors to stroke, hypertension, and obesity in African Americans. Yet those who question faith-based healing remedies and belief systems are often marginalized as being "white-identified" or elitist. In some quarters evidence-based therapy is slammed as something black and Latino folks simply "don't do" or can't realistically afford. Even when economic circumstances make therapy an option the cultural stigma remains. Black women with through the roof depression levels suffer the most.

Atheist men of color often express solidarity with women about the sexism and misogyny in Christianity. During a South L.A. community discussion on atheism in the black community hosted by the L.A. Black Skeptics, conversation about women's oppression grew contentious when some men wondered what it would take to make black women "less religious." There was much debate about whether black women were entirely responsible for their overinvestment in religion or whether larger societal and cultural forces kept them overinvested. One participant noted that there was little social pressure/onus on black men to exhibit the kind of religious devotion that black women exhibit in their everyday lives and relationships. Hence, because black men enjoy patriarchal privilege, the real issue should be transforming masculinity to make men more accountable for the care giving and nurturing roles that women are expected to fulfill. Merely criticizing the God-investment of black women without interrogating the dialectic of masculine and feminine vis-à-vis care giving and self-sacrifice is not sufficient to crafting anti-sexist humanist alternatives to religious community. Reflecting on the lack of black women in his campus student group, Mark Hatcher agreed that "There is a patriarchal aspect to being out as an atheist."[15] In Hatcher's experience, "A lot of (black) women are anchored to religion and they need to be absolutely on the same page to be friends."

Consequently, for some men, atheism and secular humanism is both a social luxury and a lens that provides them with a feminist critique of gender and power. As Kamau Rashid noted:

> African American women are the fodder of the Black Church, the floor mats of the Mosque, and the waste receptacle of the synagogue. I believe that black women have been victimized to a profound degree by organized religion. Their victimization by organized religion underscores religion's basic inhumanity and should compel, for critically thinking folks, the need for mass-defection.[16]

Echoing this sentiment, attorney Shawn Brown believes that, "rejecting organized religion is one of the most effective things that black women could do to achieve equality. Given that black women are the backbone of the black church, the power of the church to perpetuate patriarchy would end almost immediately upon black women's exodus from the pews."[17] A secular humanist reading of contemporary politics may compel a feminist view of women's self-determination. Male atheists such as Brown highlight the mortal threat which the Religious Right and its allies pose to women's right to control their lives and destinies:

> Anti-choice forces are almost universally drawn from religious groups. The rhetoric that they espouse is almost always couched in religious terms. It is absurd to be aligned with a system which offers itself up so readily to causes which are a mere pretext for controlling women.[18]

Controlling the bodies of women of color is still a robust business, one which Christian dogma thrives on and organized religion profits from. Yet there are few models of anti-sexist radical masculinity that secular humanists of color can draw on. Lamenting the gender imbalance in black churchgoing, atheist author Donald Wright wonders "where are the black men on Sundays?" As a former long time believer who became disillusioned with the church after witnessing his pastor's improprieties, Wright is deeply critical of the emotional co-dependency that Black Church hierarchies perpetuate. Writing on the psychology of black men in the church he says, "Many black men recognize 'the game' played by the preachers and choose to limit their participation but are uncertain…in addition to being in fear of losing their salvation."[19] As one of the few black male atheists who have published a book on their experience, Wright offers key insights into the miseducation of black boys in Christian schools. This process is also a critical part of male indoctrination into the sexism and misogyny of the dominant culture. As I have argued throughout this book, right wing "traditional family values" advocates have made lucrative careers slamming the dominant culture as a hypersexual cesspit of anti-Christian, anti-biblical influences. Yet religious prohibitions on female sexuality, fetishization of female chastity, and patriarchal obedience go hand in hand with hyper-sexuality and the violent degradation of women in American culture. Mainstream secular American culture takes its cue from a Judeo Christian ideology that socializes girls to be submissive, sexualized, and co-dependent while boys are trained to be violent, aggressive and invulnerable. The Religious Right's pretext of moral righteousness has always rested on the corrupt, savage, inhumane poetry of the Bible. The Bible's seductive hold on millions of educated and uneducated female believers of color shows no signs of abating.

Nonetheless, many of the most outspoken black atheist humanist activists are women. For many black atheist women, atheism's appeal lies in its deconstruction of the bankrupt mores, values and ideologies that prop up patriarchy, sexism, heterosexism, racism, white supremacy, imperialism, and economic injustice. Black women atheist humanists have a more nuanced view of the institutional valences of organized religion *and* secular society than European and Euro American atheists. As I have argued in previous chapters, many European and Euro American atheists promote a limited view of scientific knowledge as moral antidote that does not fundamentally challenge Western paradigms of power and entitlement. For some black feminists, atheism is the natural progression of their belief in and commitment to gender justice. Naima Cabelle describes having come to her awareness as a feminist, socialist, and atheist at the same time. For Naima it was simply a key part of her involvement in human rights activism.

As Jamila Bey notes:

> I am a feminist. I am an atheist. These two things work in tandem to make me a more fully human person who wishes the best for my sisters. It's hard to find misogyny or simple enforcements that hold girls/women back from the same opportunities and entitlements as their brothers where there is no religious rationale lent to the behaviors. I personally don't know how a woman who considers herself to be feminist/womanist could claim any religion other than Wicca or other goddess worship, because all of the major world religions are explicit in denying women the same treatment and esteem as men. When we cast off the oppressive mantel of religion, we are free then to take up the actual work of equality and fairness and justice. Women can't do this whilst being "protected" from reality and

> exposure to the world as religions would dictate. Humanist/ Atheist activism is about the greatest good possible.[20]

Black feminist atheist humanists are also frustrated by the lack of intersectionality between movements. Atheist Tanya McGumerait laments the fact that "the broad principles of the humanist community include statements about racial and gender equality but the atheist and humanist communities are far more concerned with issues like separation of church and state or science education and funding."[21] Nonetheless, she concedes that "this is somewhat understandable, given the growth and aggressiveness of religious conservatives in our politics, but it is still frustrating… at some point, if humanism is to live up to its stated mission of achieving the best of what is possible for humanity, it will need to understand and embrace the concerns of people of color, feminists, LGBTs, and the poor."[22]

Another reason atheism and humanism appeal to black feminists is because they open up possibilities for critical "self-reflection." The freedom to define one's identity, defying the conventions and dogmas of the dominant culture, is a hallmark of black feminist thought and practice. As Elizabeth Ross notes, atheism represents, "The ability to own my own values, my thought process through cultural critique (and) self reflection and digging deep."[23] For Ross, it complements all of her identities "as a woman, as black, as female, as bisexual, as human, as vegan, as radical, as decolonized."[24] Elaborating on this theme, freethinker Kamela Heyward-Rotimi mused that atheism can provide a progressive avenue for black women because the patriarchal nature of most organized religions "stifles their ability to grow as thinkers and full citizens of their respective societies."[25]

Attracting Blacks to Atheism and Humanism: Organizing and Agitating

For black feminist atheist humanists, translating these paradigms into a viable community movement is the next frontier. Diane Griffin of the Institute for Humanist Studies relates her frustration with the often all-encompassing social welfare net of faith-based institutions.

For Griffin, the importance of humanism is "how it affects the lives of people in the real world. I can be an atheist by myself. I don't need to be a member of an organization to not believe in any gods, I can do that all by myself. For me, humanism is all about social change." Even though she believes that faith-based initiatives are problematic, she is concerned that if they are dismantled there will be a vacuum in poor communities of color: "I went to school with scholarship money that came because my father was a pastor. I've gotten food from food banks…I understand that these churches do provide services that aren't available anywhere else. And so if we really need to free the minds of people we need to start with freeing their bellies…Many people believe because they have to believe. It is a coping mechanism to get them through the day…they don't have time to sit around and think about Darwin's theory of evolution.[26] The prominent role that black churches play in low to moderate income black communities was borne out in my interview with Pastor Seth Pickens of Zion Hill Baptist Church. Pickens related how his church provided tutoring, utility assistance, groceries for needy families, and recreation in the church gym, among other services. Critically conscious humanists recognize that meeting the practical needs of poor communities of color will drive greater mainstream interest in humanism. Humanist organizations can benefit from using some of the "best practices" of churches and community nonprofit organizations. Those seeking to forge the same kind of community resonance and interpersonal connections as faith-based institutions (without the element of fear, superstition, profiteering, and exploitative charismatic leadership) have a long uphill but winnable battle. Certainly educating other African Americans about the contradictions and immorality of religious dogma is a key part of this work. But the greatest contribution of black atheist humanist community will be the provision of safe secular passages for non-believing people of color. Humanist community-based organizations can provide culturally relevant education, mental health and wellness, and other social welfare resources that have traditionally been delivered with supernatural strings attached by faith-based organizations. Without the burden of religious dogma or the carrot of redemption, humanist organizations can nurture human rights and social justice work across boundaries of race, gender, sexual orientation, class, and ability status.

As a founder of the Los Angeles Black Skeptics Group, I've found that promoting humanist discourse and advocacy on a local level has been a major challenge. On the issue of black atheist visibility, Naima Cabelle cautions that "The assumption that every black atheist wants to be involved in the promotion of atheism will probably be the source of a great deal of disappointment. African American atheists may be as disinterested in supporting atheism or joining a secular organization as are most of their white counterparts."[27] Undoubtedly, there will always be varying levels of engagement within any community on any given issue. However, the question of what might uniquely appeal to greater numbers of African Americans and other people of color, unaware that a black freethinking tradition exists, remains. Making black secular community relevant to African

Americans will require more than an emphasis on science literacy and critical thinking.

With this in mind, the black secular community's moral obligation to social justice was the recurring theme of the Black Skeptics' first "Going Godless in the Black Community" roundtable in November 2010. Fifteen atheist/ humanists from a broad array of backgrounds, ages and world views attended. The discussion ranged from critiques of the influence of hyper-religiosity in the African American community to practical strategies for developing humanist resources and social welfare institutions. Participants did focus on the importance of instilling black youth with an appreciation for critical thought and questioning received dogma. Reflecting on his K-12 education in L.A. public schools Black Skeptics member Fred Castro said that he couldn't recall ever being exposed to humanist curricula or anything beyond a traditional Western Judeo Christian lens. Indeed, one of the most intense discussions I've had recently with students about homophobia veered into a scathing dismissal of the idea that humans "came from apes." Two young men took issue with my claim that scientific evidence overwhelmingly suggests that homosexuality has a biological basis (and is hence not a "lifestyle choice"). They retorted that scientists are just as wrong about people being born homosexual as they are about evolution. Their views are not isolated. As I noted in Chapter Three, a majority of African Americans believe in some form of creationism. One survey indicates that evolution denial and belief in creationism have actually increased among Americans in general over the past several years. So though hardly exclusive to African American youth, these beliefs have troubling implications for black achievement in science and science literacy. According to the National Assessment of Educational Progress (NAEP), African American middle and high school students have the lowest rates of science proficiency in the U.S.[28] Heavy religious belief amongst blacks is merely one small factor in this disparity. In urban communities of color unequal access to highly qualified science teachers, disproportionate focus on standardized testing, deep budget cuts, and poor college preparation resources are the biggest contributing factors.[29] Round this out with an absence of culturally responsive science education and it is no surprise that black students don't excel in or gravitate to science.

As the second largest school district in the nation, the Los Angeles Unified School District is particularly challenged by the absence of systemic culturally responsive education. With skyrocketing dropout rates and large numbers of youth who are homeless, in foster care, and/or on probation, the district has become an engine in the school-to-prison pipeline. Curriculum and instruction that is fundamentally anti-humanist, that emphasizes regimentation, rote learning, top-down teaching, and disconnection from the lived experiences and cultural knowledge of youth of color, makes critical thinking a liability. In his public appearances, renowned education analyst Pedro Noguera often cites an enraging conversation he had with an elementary school administrator. The administrator dramatically identified a disruptive young black male student as destined for a cell in the state's prison. Time and again, the low expectations of school faculty and staff become a self-fulfilling prophecy of academic failure for black students. Programmed to bubble in Scantron dots, regurgitate stock responses, and learn about the contributions of "great" white men (and a few "exceptional" people of color), students of color can either conform or be shipped out of school as discipline problems.[30] It is within this culture that bigotry thrives. If students are not taught that *their* home cultures have value, and are not encouraged to value difference across race, gender, and sexual orientation, then the culture of the school is toxic. It is no wonder that high incidences of "faith-based" bullying and harassment, degradation of young women, and a culture of violent hyper-masculinity prevail in many K-12 schools. Modern schools must have an explicit foundation of human rights and social justice to equip youth who already exist in apartheid conditions with the tools to succeed.

The oft-lamented "crisis" in public education underscores the need for anti-racist anti-sexist anti-homophobic humanist youth leadership initiatives. During the Black Skeptics roundtable, Atlanta-based activist Black Son spoke forcefully about having imbibed a culture of bigotry from the Bible, noting that African American youth are merely recycling the oppressive images and gender stereotypes they've been taught by "Christian" precepts. For example, under the terroristic conditions of slavery, black parents were often compelled to adopt harsh disciplinary practices with black children as a defense against institutional violence. These practices were reinforced and sanctioned by the Bible's endorsement of parental force. In a presentation at the 2009 African Americans for Humanism conference, atheist journalist Jamila Bey challenged biblical justifications of force for black disciplinary practices. Bey argued that black emphasis on corporal punishment in the home often influences violent behavior among some black youth. Hence, cultural and religious factors, coupled with the normalization of violence against women in mainstream media and the dominant culture, contribute to high rates of intimate partner violence and domestic abuse amongst African Americans.

On the flip side, parenting in a sea of religious conformity and finding secular private schools with multicultural student bodies were also topics of concern at the Black Skeptics roundtable. Children of color who come from atheist or agnostic households—especially those who are taught to openly identify that way—are often subject to ridicule and ostracism as cultural traitors. In a world of public school Christian Bible study clubs, "mandatory" flag pledges, and teachers who violate church/state separation by using and/or endorsing prayer as a coping strategy, black children who don't believe are marked as other.

Thus, developing the next generation of black humanists is very much a matter of cultural literacy. Because of the imperiled state of our communities, rejecting belief in god is not, as it may be for white atheists, an end in and of itself. Embracing humanism as a form of liberation struggle is paramount for African Americans, precisely because blacks' ironclad investment in organized religion is a function of capitalism, sexism, and institutional racism. These three factors operate in harmony with each other to deny African Americans and other people of color basic human rights. For example, when young black women become homeless due to domestic/sexual abuse, aging out of the foster care system, and/or having criminal records that don't allow them to find stable living wage employment, black communities are fundamentally destabilized. When black LGBT youth drop out of school, become homeless, and resort to "survival sex" to make a living on our first world American city streets they may do so because there are not enough secular institutions to care for them. Critically conscious humanism can be a path to liberation for all African Americans. For, how do LGBT black youth who have been told by "liberal/progressive" Christians that "god loves the sinner and hates the sin," reconcile this assurance with the anti-gay venom of Leviticus and Deuteronomy? In my interview with Mercedes Diane Griffin, she expressed frustration with the religious bent of many black HIV/AIDS organizations she encounters in her activist work. Desperately craving acceptance from the mainstream, many of these organizations embrace the faith-based initiatives approach and view atheism as a potential threat to their mission because they "want to remove the (homosexual) stigma of being amoral."[31]

It is not surprising that black gay organizations would overcompensate with Christian devotion. The dominant culture's historical view of African Americans as savage and immoral automatically makes any black organization that has an explicitly secular ideology suspect. White America's racist fixation on Barack Obama's religious affiliation is an obvious case in point. As I discussed in Chapter Two, black public figures must be tacitly religious or risk irrelevance. Since there is no precedent or context for secular black public figures the absence of black humanist and humanist of color organizations becomes a self-fulfilling prophecy. In the U.S. and Europe, it is far easier for whites to gain national visibility and political credibility as humanists or atheists without ostracism. By contrast, humanism is more prominent as a movement in Africa. Former African Americans for Humanism director Norm Allen has devoted much of his work to promoting humanism in countries like Nigeria, Ghana, and Kenya. African Humanism has become a counterweight to religious persecution and ritual killings, oppression of women, and state-sponsored homophobia. Although both Christian and Muslim indoctrination predominates in many African countries, African Humanist activists such as Nigeria's Leo Igwe have strongly criticized the colonialist origins of Christianity and Islam in Africa.

In the final analysis, African American humanism will only be viable as a movement if it is culturally relevant. In this regard, black humanists can learn from the lessons of feminism. Feminism was "rejected" by African Americans because it was (and is, albeit mistakenly) perceived to be a "white woman's thing." It was also a casualty of the emphasis on black male uplift as the solution to racism. Despite the tremendous gains that black women enjoyed as a result of feminist anti-racist organizing and legislation, there is still little acceptance of feminism as a social justice imperative for black communities. I contend that feminism is both a social justice imperative *and* a moral imperative for what ails black communities. Every day print newspapers tread silently past the deaths of black youth. Every week anguished families file solemnly into churches to memorialize the deaths of babies who will never go to college, know romantic love or seek their life's ambition. Every week more of them are sacrificed to hyper-masculine violence. Perhaps they were told that they were destined for heaven. Perhaps they wavered, harboring doubt in the face of the atrocity, the normalization of young death. Perhaps they died having the courage to disbelieve. In an excerpt from his book *Black Boy* Richard Wright related an exchange that he had with a young friend distraught over Wright's lack of belief:

> Richard think of Christ's dying for you, shedding His blood. His precious blood on the cross.
>
> Other people have shed blood, I ventured.
>
> But it's not the same. You don't understand.
>
> I don't think I ever will.[32]

Instead of devotion to an industry of false idols what would devotion, unswerving, non-negotiable, to the shared humanity of women and men look like? Would the death anniversaries of murdered innocents continue to multiply? Would there be so many unmarked monuments to the cult of redemptive suffering in black communities in Los Angeles, New York, Detroit, Chicago, and D.C.? Would the lust for what conscious rapper Chuck D has labeled "black death" drive global record sales into the tens of billions?

In 1955 fifteen year old Claudette Colvin refused to give up her seat to a white passenger on a Montgomery Alabama bus. Before her ejection from the bus she yelled that her "constitutional rights were being violated."[33] She was jailed and then released into historical obscurity. Pregnant, poor, teenaged, and dark-skinned, Colvin was deemed to be too unsympathetic a victim for the "test case" (Montgomery civil rights leaders eventually chose Rosa Parks as their candidate) that what would lead to the most influential bus boycott in history. Her status as a pregnant unmarried teen marked her as a "fallen woman." She decided to have her baby despite having been the victim of statutory rape by a much older man. Real reproductive choice was nonexistent in an era in which black women were routinely maimed or killed by illegal abortions and the Black Church considered abortion a mortal sin. Despite her "transgressions," Colvin would not have been overtly labeled a bitch or ho in the parlance of 1950s America. The mainstreaming of those terms coincided with the decline of the women's movement. So while the conventions of popular speech were not the same in "idyllic" 1950s Ozzie and Harriet America the sexual assault of black women by any man was still not considered a crime.

Like other historically obscure black women before her Colvin defied the class, race, age, and gender expectations of knowing her place. Unknown to youth of color, Colvin's radically humanist act makes their citizenship and relatively unfettered access to public space possible. Her obscurity makes their deification of King, and to a lesser extent, Rosa Parks, possible. The dominant culture dictates which histories are "culturally relevant." It legitimizes these histories by disassociating them from the larger context of structural oppression and inequity. In his book *Lies My Teacher Told Me* James Loewen criticizes exceptionalist depictions of American historical figures. In most history textbooks, "the past becomes a simpleminded morality play" driven by heroic trailblazers who confirm the essential greatness of the U.S.[34] If they cannot be crafted into morally unimpeachable individualists who pulled themselves up by their own bootstraps, black women do not fit into the traditional narrative of American exceptionalism. Then as now, there were high stakes for young black women living in a world where white supremacy *and* black patriarchy put their humanity in question. Then as now, social conventions driven by religious and cultural norms determined how "transgressive" black women were perceived.

In many respects, the sexist gender politics of the civil rights era continue to define political and economic priorities in African American communities. Charismatic black male leadership is still the privileged model of leadership. Racism is still the primary axis of black identity politics. There is still much public fixation on the cult of male religious leaders as sages and spokesmen. Black children continue to walk over the unmarked graves of their ancestors, oblivious to their sacrifice and struggle. In 1935, twenty years before the Montgomery bus boycott, Zora Neale Hurston wrote:

> I accept the challenge of responsibility. Life, as it is, does not frighten me, since I have made peace with the universe as I find it, and bow to its laws...It seems to me that organized creeds are collections of words around a wish...I know that nothing is destructible; things merely change forms. When the

> consciousness we know as life ceases; I know that I shall still be part and parcel of the world.[35]

Ashes to ashes, dust to dust. Hurston's acknowledgment of the moral importance of responsibility, and the possibility of *social* regeneration, rather than eternal reward, is critical to black humanist social thought. Grounded in struggle, Hurston's prescience aches in an age where celebrations of the first black president mask the reality of the new Jim Crow. Without a new humanist framework, true to the feminist legacy of Claudette Colvin's act, we will still be waiting for saviors and worshipping false idols.

Endnotes

1. Michelle Alexander, *The New Jim Crow: Mass Incarceration in the Age of Colorblindness* (New York: Free Press, 2010).
2. Gaylor, *Women Without Superstition*, p. 10.
3. Ibid., p. 11.
4. Carol Kolmarten, *The American Life of Ernestine L. Rose* (Syracuse: Syracuse University Press, 1999), 249-251.
5. In an 1869 speech Stanton famously declaimed, "If American women find it hard to bear the oppressions of their own Saxon fathers, the best orders of manhood, what may they now be called to endure when all the lower orders of foreigners crowding our shores legislate for them and their daughters. Think of Patrick and Sambo and Hans and Yung Tung who do not know the difference between a monarchy and a republic…making laws for Lucretia Mott or Ernestine Rose." Kolmarten, 250.
6. In her introduction to Stanton's work, Gaylor's book doesn't mention Stanton's racist imperialist views nor reference the racial conflicts that wrenched both the abolitionist and women's suffrage movements.
7. Alfreda Howard, Survey Interview, October 2010.
8. Jamila Bey, Survey Interview, November 2010.
9. Ibid.
10. Naima Cabelle, Survey Interview, November 2010.
11. In an informal survey I conducted 38% of the respondents described themselves as "spiritual" while only 18% described themselves as religious.
12. Cabelle, November 2010.
13. Michelle D. Mitchell, Gabrielle L. Hargrove, et al. "Coping Variables That Mediate the Relation Between Intimate Partner Violence and Mental Health Outcomes Among Low-Income, African American Women," Journal of Clinical Psychology, Vol. 62(12), 2006, pp. 1-18;" Prayer is Key Stress Reliever for Black Women," *Emerging Majorities Magazine*, December 2004.
14. Ibid., p. 3.
15. Hatcher, December 2010.

16. Kamau Rashid, Survey Interview, April 2010.
17. Shaun Brown, Survey Interview, June 2010.
18. Ibid.
19. Donald Wright, *The Only Prayer I'll Ever Pray: Let My People Go* (Indianapolis: Dog Ear Publishing, 2009), 60.
20. Jamila Bey, November, 2010.
21. Tanya McGumerait, Survey Interview, November 2010.
22. Ibid.
23. Elizabeth Ross, Survey Interview, November 2010.
24. Ibid.
25. Kamela Heyward-Rotimi, Survey Interview, November 2010.
26. Diane Griffin, November 2010.
27. Cabelle, November 2010.
28. National Assessment of Educational Progress 2005 Assessment Results (http://nationsreportcard.gov/science_2005/s0111.asp?printver=).
29. See the Education Trust "Statement on NAEP Science Results," *Education Trust*, March 24, 2006 (http://www.edtrust.org). According to the Ed Trust many African American and Latino students are taught by teachers who are not credentialed in science. "Low-income students in secondary schools overall are far more likely than their more affluent peers to be taught science by teachers who did not major or minor in the subject in college."
30. See for example the Advancement Project report on discipline. Large school districts have employed a "push-out" policy to remove problem students who drag down test scores.
31. Griffin, November 2010.
32. Richard Wright, *Black Boy (American Hunger): A Record of Childhood and Youth* (New York: Harper Collins, 1944), 114.
33. Phillip Hoose, *Claudette Colvin: Twice Toward Justice* (New York: Farrar, Strauss and Giroux), p. 32.
34. James Loewen, *Lies My Teacher Told Me: Everything your American History Textbook Got Wrong* (New York: New Press, 2007), p. 6.
35. Hurston, "Religion," p 181.

Index

CPSIA information can be obtained
at www.ICGtesting.com
Printed in the USA
LVOW04s0314071216
516151LV00008B/73/P